12
15
17

VULTURE

KATIE
FALLON

Vulture

THE
PRIVATE
LIFE
OF AN
UNLOVED
BIRD

FOREEDGE

ForeEdge

An imprint of University Press of New England

www.upne.com

© 2017 Katie Fallon

Manufactured in the United States of America

Designed by Eric M. Brooks

Typeset in Fresco by Passumpsic Publishing

Unless otherwise specified, all photos were taken by the author.

For permission to reproduce any of the material in
this book, contact Permissions, University Press of New
England, One Court Street, Suite 250, Lebanon NH 03766;
or visit www.upne.com

Library of Congress Cataloging-in-Publication Data

NAMES: Fallon, Katie, author.

TITLE: Vulture: the private life of an unloved bird / Katie Fallon.

DESCRIPTION: Lebanon, NH: ForeEdge, 2017. |
    Includes bibliographical references and index.

IDENTIFIERS: LCCN 2016038535 (print) | LCCN 2016054859
    (ebook) | ISBN 9781611689716 (cloth) | ISBN 9781512600308
    (epub, mobi & pdf)

SUBJECTS: LCSH: Turkey vulture—United States. | Avian
    Conservation Center of Appalachia. | Birds—Conservation—
    Appalachian Region—Anecdotes. | Wildlife rescue—
    Appalachian Region—Anecdotes.

CLASSIFICATION: LCC QL696.C53 F35 2017 (print) |
    LCC QL696.C53 (ebook) | DDC 598.9/2—dc23

LC record available at https://lccn.loc.gov/2016038535

5 4 3 2 1

CONTENTS

INTRODUCTION The Spokesbird
1

ONE Vulture Culture
17

TWO The Private Lives of Public Birds
33

THREE Rockshelter
52

FOUR Wings and Prayers
69

FIVE Rebirth
88

SIX Hill of the Sacred Eagles
105

SEVEN On the Move
122

EIGHT Virginia Is for Vultures
141

NINE Battlefield Ghosts
159

TEN Welcome Back, Buzzards
175

EPILOGUE Spokesbirds for the Spokesbirds
193

AFTERWORD *What You Can Do* 205
ACKNOWLEDGMENTS 211
BIBLIOGRAPHY 213
INDEX 223

Illustrations appear after page 104.

VULTURE

She unfurled her brown-black wings and stretched them wide to soak up the morning sun. It was spring; the snow had finally receded, although she hadn't seen it. She'd arrived just a few days earlier, and while frigid winds still rushed across the boreal marsh, the prairie crocuses had already bloomed. An ocean of rippling grass stretched from the base of the spruce she'd spent the night on to the small grove of quaking aspens near an abandoned two-story house. The glass of the house's windows had long ago shattered, but the roof was mostly intact. A sturdy foundation, hidden by the windswept grasses, held up the house's wooden frame. Generations of harsh Saskatchewan winters hadn't felled the silent structure, which, even though humans no longer inhabited it, was still a home—at least, a summer home.

She turned her red head and stony eyes skyward, perhaps watching the horizon for a black V. Although she hadn't seen her mate since late September (he'd spent the winter months on Venezuela's Caribbean coast, not far from Caracas, and she'd headed for the familiar grove of palms on the farm near the Colombian border), instinct told her to wait. He'd be back.

The Spokesbird

A turkey vulture is a perfect creature. It is neither prey nor predator. It exists outside the typical food chain, beyond the kill-or-be-killed law of nature, although without death it would starve. On six-foot wings it floats above our daily lives, waiting for the inevitable moment that will come to each of us, to every living thing. Then the vulture transforms these transformations—these deaths—into life. It wastes nothing. It does not kill. It is not a murderer, and it is not often murdered. The turkey vulture waits. Waits and wanders on its great wing sails.

Watching a soaring turkey vulture is like meditating. Gently rocking with the breeze, wings fixed in a shallow dihedral, a vulture's flight looks peaceful and elegant, almost contemplative. Although their movements are purposeful, the birds appear relaxed and unhurried, like long, slow breaths. In times of stress or struggle, gazing at a vulture overhead is a reminder to glide, to sail, to use the prevailing winds.

I have a thing for vultures, especially turkey vultures. In addition to their grace and elegance, I admire their thrift, their role as the gentle recyclers of the animal kingdom, and their unique beauty. When the sun hits a turkey vulture just right, its feathers look iridescent, a shimmering purplish black. In other light, the backs of its wings are a rich chocolate, nearly bronze, with soft golden edges. In flight, which appears almost effortless, a turkey vulture floats like a kite, mastering the winds. Although its wingspan rivals an eagle's, the turkey vulture lacks an eagle's bulk, brute strength, sharp talons, and killer instinct; the Cherokee call them "peace eagles," and their Latin name, *Cathartes aura*, means "breezy cleanser." Large, docile, and usually silent, the turkey vulture often goes unnoticed, although its distant black silhouette is omnipresent, floating on the horizon.

▼ The turkey vulture is the world's most widely distributed and abundant scavenging bird of prey, found from southern Canada to the tip of Argentina and nearly everywhere in between. Like humans, they've adapted to a variety of habitats, from the mountains to the prairies, the coastlines to the deserts, the forests to the canyons. In the United States we sometimes call them *buzzards* (although a buzzard is actually an Old World hawk); in Mexico they're often *aura cabecirroja* or simply *aura*; in parts of Uruguay, they're known as *jote cabeza colorada*; and in Ecuador, *gallinazo aura*.

Currently, six subspecies of turkey vulture are recognized by science. Around my home in West Virginia, the locals are the partially migratory *Cathartes aura septentrionalis*; in the western United States and western Canada, most are *C. a. meridionalis*, which are complete migrants, traveling as far as northern South America in the fall. *C. a. aura* turkey vultures live in the American southwest through Central America, *C. a. ruficollis* in central South America, *C. a. jota* in the interior of South America's southern cone, and *C. a. falklandica* on the Falkland Islands and coastal southern South America. Whereas *meridionalis* and *septentrionalis* appear physically similar, the turkey vulture subspecies near and in the tropics are slightly smaller and sleeker, with fewer warty protuberances on their faces. One subspecies, *ruficollis*, has a large white spot on the back of its featherless head.

This wide distribution makes turkey vultures visible to nearly everyone in the Western Hemisphere. It's an equal-opportunity bird that unites people—rich and poor, rural and urban—across continents, countries, languages, and cultures.

▼ When I hold a wild turkey vulture—its back against my chest, wings restrained by my embrace, clawed feet in one hand and hooked head in the other—my heart races along with the bird's as it struggles to free its great black wings, to flap, to leave me on the ground where I belong. It tries to swivel its head and nip my fingers, my face, whatever it can reach. I smell the warm, musky odor of its feathers, and perhaps the sharp smell of vomit, a turkey vulture's only true defense. It parts the bone-colored hook of its beak and pants, its sharp pink tongue visible inside. The bird is desperate, and when I look into its stone-colored eyes, something looks back at me. In a turkey vulture's eyes I can see a mind at work, a mind that's trying to figure things out, figure *me* out, and determine the best way to escape. Of course, the restrained bird won't escape, and not because of my skills as a vulture wrangler, but because most turkey vultures I've held have been injured. Some injured gravely, some dying. Some riddled with shotgun pellets, others weakened by toxic lead in their bloodstreams. Broken wings, broken legs, broken backs, wounds filled with maggots, head trauma. At our nonprofit, the Avian Conservation Center of Appalachia (ACCA), we care for all species of injured wild birds, and while we try our best with every patient, I admit that I try a little harder with the turkey vultures.

The ACCA treats more than 200 wild birds every year, including iconic bald eagles, charismatic peregrine falcons, always-dramatic loons, tiny chickadees and wrens, and everything in between. My husband Jesse and I, along with our fellow bird-brained friends Todd and Erin Katzner, decided to found the organization because of a need for an avian conservation center in our region. The ACCA is located near Morgantown, West Virginia, fewer than ten miles from the Mason-Dixon line and the Pennsylvania border, and fewer than thirty miles from the western edge of Maryland. We regularly receive injured birds from all three states; most come to us via members of the public, although we work with state and federal agencies to receive birds, too. Our cadre of the best volunteers anywhere assists with advanced surgeries, conducts educational programs, writes grants, administers medications, constructs enclosures, prepares diets, scrapes bird excrement, sweeps floors, and more.

Jesse, a veterinarian, specializes in avian medicine. Every patient admitted to the ACCA gets an immediate, comprehensive examination, including radiographs and ultrasonography when necessary. Birds are rehydrated and treated with appropriate medications, which might include antibiotics, antifungals, pain medicine, or chelation therapy for lead toxicity. An added convenience is that the animal hospital where Jesse practices is open twenty-four hours a day, seven days a week, so injured birds can be dropped off soon after they're found. In addition to rehabilitation, the ACCA is dedicated to outreach and research. Wildlife biologist Todd Katzner oversees graduate students working on avian-related projects, and his own important research focuses on a variety of raptor species, especially golden eagles. Erin Katzner and I both have previous experience in environmental education and bird training; Erin is one of the few people to hold the prestigious title of Certified Professional Bird Trainer—Knowledge Assessed, given by the International Avian Trainers Certification Board. She's worked with birds of many species at several zoos and wildlife centers.

While many birds hold special places in my heart, turkey vultures affect me the most. One of my first experiences with a wild turkey vulture had come several years before we'd founded the ACCA. I'd stood, transfixed, just outside the door of an enclosure at a small wildlife center where I'd been volunteering. Late-summer sunshine beamed through poplar and oak branches to dapple the ground around me. A big brown-black bird stood on the dirt floor of the narrow enclosure, all the way in the back, as far away from me as possible. We watched each other, my wide blue eyes searching the bird's beady stone-colored ones. It was love at first sight. Well, perhaps love mixed with pity, and certainly unrequited. The vulture stood almost directly under a shoulder-high T-shaped perch made of a four-by-four driven into the clay with a rope-wrapped two-by-four attached sloppily across its top. Another perch of similar construction stood at the opposite end of the narrow pen. As I moved to unlatch the door to get a closer look at the bird, it hunched down, peered up at the perch, and unfurled its great black wings. It flapped them weakly but didn't make it and crashed awkwardly back to the ground.

I unlatched the door and the turkey vulture began to run back and forth along the far wall of the enclosure. Each time it met the mesh dividers between its pen and the ones on either side, it would lift a flat, chicken-like foot and push against the mesh, almost as if testing the barrier's integrity. I backed out of the enclosure and re-latched the door, and although the bird stopped the frantic back-and-forth movement, it never took its small eyes off me. It parted its hooked beak and appeared to pant in the afternoon heat. What a magnificent, intelligent, tragic creature, I'd thought, and promptly fell in love. (And then I rearranged the perches so the poor bird could get off the ground.)

I'm not sure why many of us have a negative impression of turkey vultures; perhaps it's their naked heads, or perhaps we find their diet of the dead and desiccated unappealing. They lack the proud scream of a red-tailed hawk, and they certainly don't sing a sweet song like a wood thrush or meadowlark; because they posses a uniquely modified syrinx (the organ birds use to produce sound) turkey vultures tend to only grunt and hiss. Instead of defending themselves with talons or teeth, they vomit in the general direction of a threat, certainly not the most charming attribute. Above all, I think we dislike turkey vultures because they remind us of our own mortality, and that life will continue after we die—and that, as with all animals, something will be waiting to consume our bodies.

▼ In North America, turkey vultures and black vultures are plentiful and perhaps increasing in population; however, other vultures in other parts of the world are not so fortunate. According to raptor expert Dr. Keith Bildstein, Sarkis Acopian Director of Conservation Science at Pennsylvania's Hawk Mountain Sanctuary, on a global scale vultures are more likely to be threatened than other types of raptors; in fact, turkey and black vultures are two of only a few examples of successful vultures in the world today. BirdLife International lists fifteen of the planet's twenty-three vulture species (or 65 percent) as species of conservation concern; five of these are critically endangered, and several others may be "uplisted" soon. In southeast Asia, the white-rumped vulture, Indian vulture, and slender-billed vulture suffered catastrophic population declines, starting in the mid-1990s; by 2013, at least 97 percent of the individuals in these species had died. The news is only slightly better for vultures in Africa, where seven of the continent's eleven species are vulnerable, threatened, or endangered. In North America, the California condor is critically endangered; as of this writing, fewer than 500 exist in captivity and the wild.

Turkey vultures counter this trend, but despite their abundance and visibility, until recently few researchers had studied them. Biologists at Hawk Mountain began studying turkey vulture migration patterns in 2002, and in the process learned a great deal about their natural history. This information could help us understand and conserve other species of vultures worldwide; the turkey vulture could become a "spokesbird" for vultures everywhere.

While it isn't fully understood why turkey vulture numbers in North America seem to be increasing, several theories are plausible. "One suspect," Keith Bildstein told me, "is an increasing density of roadways. These birds are obviously feeding on roadkill. Another is an increased deer population; our birds are certainly using gut piles during hunting season. There's a trade-off there—and a trade-off with the roads, too." Like other avian scavengers, turkey vultures can suffer from lead toxicity after inadvertently ingesting spent ammunition in offal. Collisions with vehicles are also frequent because turkey vultures can be somewhat slow to take off when feeding on a carcass.

Biologists and birders also have noticed that in addition to an increase in total numbers, turkey vultures and American black vultures seem to be pushing farther north than previously documented. Climate change could be, at least in part, the cause of this range expansion, as could an increase in large cities, which create urban "heat islands," allowing vultures (and carrion) to stay warm in colder temperatures. "Also," Keith added, "something that kind of gets lost historically, is that back in the day turkey and black vulture populations were substantially held in check in the southeastern United States." In the early part of the twentieth century, it's estimated that Texas ranchers killed more than 100,000 black and turkey vultures. They blamed the birds for spreading disease, while in fact the opposite is true; a turkey vulture's strong stomach acid and gut flora can neutralize dangerous pathogens sometimes found in carrion, such as anthrax, botulism toxin, cholera, and salmonella. Both black and turkey vultures were eventually granted protection under the federal Migratory Bird Treaty Act, making it a crime to intentionally shoot, trap, poison, or harass them. When we stopped killing so many vultures in the Southeast, Keith told me, healthy populations started expanding northward.

In the United States we often take our plentiful vultures for granted, and the birds go unnoticed and unappreciated. Turkey vultures have an undeserved reputation as dirty, sneaky sorts. Many people find them ugly, disgusting, or worse, and they have even been accused of killing calves and lambs, although no documented accounts of this exist. It's likely that they are attracted to livestock giving birth—both turkey vultures and black vultures have been known to eat nutrient-rich placentas. The scientific literature on turkey vultures goes to great lengths to document any instances of them taking live prey; these instances are very few and far between, and most involve "unnatural situations," such as birds caught in traps or birds in captivity. The only animals ever documented to be killed by turkey vultures include a ruffed grouse chick, small fish, turtle hatchlings, and nestling or sickly birds. If it's available (and it usually is) turkey vultures prefer carrion, and they play an important role in the health of an ecosystem. As scavengers they decontaminate the landscape, removing dead animals that might otherwise contribute to the spread of disease. Unlike some mammalian scavengers, vultures do not carry rabies or distemper; they are perfectly adapted to cleanse, purify, and renew.

Even though they are peaceable, harmless, and helpful, turkey vultures are still persecuted by humans; each year the ACCA admits several with human-inflicted injuries. I remember one of our vulture patients, emaciated and suffering, that was euthanized on arrival because of a rifle shot that nearly severed its left wing. Another's wings and torso were peppered with shotgun pellets, the small projectiles lodging in muscle and bone. While perhaps unintentional, another had been caught in a leg-hold trap meant for a small mammal. Even turkey vultures admitted for vehicle-related injuries sometimes have old, healed-over wounds concealing shotgun pellets under the skin.

In addition to intentional injuries caused by human activity, vultures sometimes find themselves unwanted by their human neighbors. Especially in the South, and especially in the winter, large flocks of turkey and black vultures will often roost together—usually in large pine trees but sometimes on the warm roofs of houses. Perhaps because of their geographic location or other favorable habitat features, vultures often congregate in quaint, classy, brick-and-ivy Virginia towns, such as Leesburg, where some of the non-vulture residents don't welcome them. Occasionally, the USDA's Animal and Plant Health Inspection Service (APHIS) is called in to disperse the roosts; often this involves fireworks and noisemakers, but sometimes it involves shooting several vultures, despite the role they play in the health of an ecosystem, and despite protection by federal law. In many parts of the world, environmental health as well as public health suffers because of a lack of vultures, while here, sadly, we sometimes overlook their importance or seek to remove them from our presence.

▼ I fell in love again as soon as the volunteer lifted the bird from the cardboard box. The turkey vulture nipped weakly at her fingers, but its wings and legs drooped. Emaciated, exhausted, and certainly in pain, the injured creature seemed to give itself over to our prodding. Jesse wound his hair into a loose bun, swung the bright light over the treatment table, and switched it on as the volunteer arranged the vulture on its side on the table. I watched, chewing on my lower lip, hoping that we'd be able to save this bird, that one day it would fly free again.

But that hope soon faded. Jesse took the vulture's hooked head in his hand and leaned closer. "Poor guy's got a sunken eye," he said. "It looks like it's an older injury." Jesse continued the examination, running his hands along each of the bird's wings, its torso, and its legs. He listened to its heart and lungs, looked into its mouth, and then whisked it into the lead-lined room to take radiographs. When Jesse emerged a few minutes later, hugging the vulture against his torso, he shook his head. "Old, already-healed fractures in the shoulder joint, bruising along the inside of the humerus, and soft-tissue injuries to its leg. All on the left side. That's also the side with the sunken eye. I wonder if he got creamed by a car because he couldn't see it. We can fix the leg, but there's not much we can do for the shoulder." Jesse paused and looked at me; it was a familiar look, the one that came moments before he recommended euthanasia.

I swallowed. "Maybe he'll be a good candidate for education? He seems calm."

Jesse shrugged. "He could be calm because he's dying."

The vulture's head, pale due to dehydration, hung weakly. It seemed to have given up. I swallowed again. "I think we should give this guy a chance."

Jesse looked at me and nodded. "Well, OK. Let's try to put him back together."

The vulture received a large syringe of subcutaneous fluids and an injection of pain medication. His injured leg and shoulder were bound with pink elastic wrap covered in purple hearts. "All vultures love pink," someone snickered. Ten minutes later, the bird was standing on a special rubber mat in a clean enclosure. We fed him small amounts at first to give his gastrointestinal tract a chance to get moving again; I cut a mouse into tiny pieces and placed the pile on the mat in front of the vulture. I'd barely moved my hand away before the bird lunged for the mouse bits, gulping the entire pile in seconds. And then he turned his good eye toward me. I smiled. He shifted slightly on his big chicken-like feet and lowered his head to the mat again, delicately nipping at the spot where the mouse bits had been just in case he'd missed a morsel.

Even after closely observing a turkey vulture, it's difficult to know how to classify them taxonomically. They share some characteristics of hawks and eagles—hooked beak, diet of meat, excellent eyesight—but while traditionally grouped with birds of prey, turkey vultures lack the true talons of other raptors. Scientists, too, have struggled to categorize them. Genetic studies in the mid-1990s suggested that New World vultures—California and Andean condors, and black, king, yellow-headed, and turkey vultures—shared a common ancestor with storks, not hawks or eagles, and in 1998 the American Ornithologists Union (AOU) moved the vultures' family

Cathartidae from the order Falconiformes (hawks, eagles, and falcons) to Ciconiiformes (storks). These genetic conclusions were challenged, however, and in 2007 the AOU moved Cathartidae back to Falconiformes, but with an asterisk to indicate "uncertainty as to exact placement." The AOU determined that the 1998 move to Ciconiiformes was "in error, although the true relationships and thus placement of the family are still not fully resolved." Then, in 2010, the AOU created a new order, Accipitriformes, and moved New World vultures there, along with hawks and eagles. (The order Falconiformes now contains only falcons and caracaras.) While the debate about the origins of New World vultures continues, Old World vultures *do* share an ancestor with hawks and eagles. And now many folks lump all vultures—New and Old World—with raptors again, often making the distinction between "predatory raptors" and "scavenging raptors."

New World and Old World vultures are an excellent example of convergent evolution, which *ScienceDaily* defines as "the process whereby organisms not closely related (not monophyletic), independently evolve similar traits as a result of having to adapt to similar environments or ecological niches." Most Old and New World vulture species have featherless heads and long necks; this allows the birds to plunge their faces into rotting carcasses without getting bits stuck to their feathers. Both Old and New World vultures share similar foot structure, as well—flat and chicken-like, better adapted to walking and running than to grasping. Both groups eat primarily carrion, though some species will attack weak or dying animals.

Despite the many similarities between vulture species worldwide, there is also diversity. Although most of the world's vultures find food strictly by eyesight—soaring high over the landscape, searching the ground for dead animals—three species in the New World's *Cathartes* genus (the turkey vulture and the greater and lesser yellow-headed vultures) also use a keen sense of smell to help them locate food, their wide, perforated nostrils positioned prominently above their beaks. Several Old World species have evolved to eat specialized diets; Africa's palm nut vulture, for example, often lives near water and primarily eats oil palm fruit. The bearded vulture, found in many locales in Europe, Asia, and Africa, subsists on a diet of bones; it also intentionally rubs soil rich in iron oxide on its feathers. Also known as the lammergeier or sometimes the ossifrage, the bearded vulture was once blamed for killing livestock, although this is untrue. Bearded vultures will fly high into the sky while carrying bones in their beaks, and then drop the bones onto rocks below; once broken, the bird eats the nutrient-rich bone marrow within. A related species, the almost all-white Egyptian vulture, uses rocks to break its food, too; the Egyptian vulture, however, carries smallish rocks and smashes them against large eggs to break their shells, and the bird then eats the contents.

In the New World, the *Cathartes* vultures are similar, but other species are quite variable. The king vulture, found in Central and South America, sports a bulbous and brilliant orange, red, and yellow face with tinges of purple and blue. Another bulbous-faced species, the Andean condor, is the largest flying land bird. American black vultures are one of the most social vulture species, but in general vultures worldwide are often gregarious and intelligent, and they tend to reproduce slowly (only one or two chicks a year). They mature slowly, too, and live relatively long lives; turkey vultures in the wild may live fifteen years, while in captivity they can live into their thirties.

I stared into our new patient's good eye and imagined us spending the next thirty years together. The future was still uncertain, of course; as the bird's health improved, its personality could change or perhaps return to its "true" temperament. Now, the vulture seemed complacent and satisfied, not aggressive or terrified. True, the pain meds could have mellowed its mood, and its spunk was dampened by physical weakness. Permanent captivity would be a cruel fate for any fearful, aggressive, or stressed animal; we would have to wait. I backed away from the enclosure and allowed my new friend to rest.

▼ What follows is a personal examination of the lives of North American turkey vultures; this book tracks the stages of a vulture's life, beginning in early spring and progressing through summer, autumn, and winter. We will end where we began, with the cycle starting over again in early spring. Through the process of researching this book, I learned a great deal about these amazing birds. I also learned that science still has a lot to discover about turkey vultures—indeed, about vultures in general. However, biologists are uncovering more and more information every day; it's an exciting time to be a vulture lover. My hope is that readers of this book will come away with a new understanding, a new appreciation, of this extraordinary bird—a bird we share with almost everyone else across the Americas.

She tilted her wings slightly and allowed the thermal
to lift her higher. She could smell it, the faint odor
wafting up through the pines, but when she cocked
her head and scanned the earth beneath her, she
couldn't see it. Elk? No, smaller—deer. The wind
whistled through her flight feathers, the warm air
buoying her, and the scent grew fainter. She circled
back, lower. Between the groves of aspen and spruce,
patches of bluegrass, bulrush, and wild rice billowed.
A bull moose stood knee-deep in a bog and drank
deeply. She could see the muscles moving beneath
his thick hide. When her wide shadow slid over the
moose, he raised his brown head, twin strings of drool
streaming from his lips. The moose twitched his ears
and lowered his head again.

   Out of the corner of her eye, she saw movement
—not beneath her, but behind her. She was being
followed.

   She rocked slightly to the left; the bird behind
did the same thing. For the moment, she abandoned
her search for food and let the thermal lift her again.
The one behind her caught the same thermal, floated
to the same height. Suddenly, she turned sharply,
and without flapping, zoomed toward the ground.

Her pursuer followed. She flapped twice, long, slow wing beats, and cruised parallel to the earth; the second bird followed close behind. Her flight slowed, and she dropped her legs, lighting gracefully on the peak of the abandoned house's pitched roof. A moment later, he landed beside her.

She roused, shook, and ran her hooked beak along one of her flight feathers, smoothing the edges. He spread his wings, turning so the morning sun hit his back. His feathers shimmered, iridescent in the bright light, the browns and blacks gleaming with an oily sheen that made him appear almost purple. The sun lit up his bone-colored beak tip and blood-red face. She fanned her tail feathers, reached her head around to her back, and ran her beak over the preen gland. She delicately combed each tail feather and then began to work on her chest. When she was finished she roused again, loosing a small cloud of feather dust. He turned his head toward her and blinked his steel-gray eyes.

They stood on the roof, in silence, while the sun warmed their backs and coaxed the wild strawberries to bloom.

Vulture Culture

Being a fan of vultures is sort of like being a fan of an obscure rock band; on most days, you feel as if you're the only one to recognize their greatness. You mention them to your friends, who typically roll their eyes and laugh but sometimes make disgusted faces, or go as far as to say *yuck*. So, mostly you keep your affection to yourself while you count down the days until the next concert, the next festival, where you won't feel weird or unusual for loving what you love—that which seems unlovable to most people. On those days of celebration, you are giddy and filled with childlike honesty and anticipation. I felt this giddiness on the days and weeks leading up to one of the largest turkey vulture festivals in the United States: Hinckley, Ohio's Buzzard Sunday.

The line for pancakes and sausage stretched almost to Hinckley Elementary School's front door, and we'd arrived early; in an hour or so, it would be snaking through the parking lot. Jesse and I were glad to be inside, out of the cold March rain. I'd only been to Ohio a handful of times, and each time had been the same: rainy and chilly with fog on the highways, which smoothed flatter and flatter as we left West Virginia behind. If I'd been asked to describe Ohio in three words, I'd have answered *rain, flat,* and *corn.* It didn't help that I came from a blue-and-white-bleeding Penn State family, raised on a hatred of all things Buckeye. But Ohio was well on its way to redeeming itself in my eyes; the hallways of this elementary school were hung with children's painting and drawings, each piece of art depicting the most noble of all birds and star of this weekend's festival: the turkey vulture.

For more than fifty years the town of Hinckley has held a "Return of the Buzzards" celebration on (or just after) March 15. The festival is held at the school and at Hinckley Reservation, a public nature preserve managed by Cleveland Metroparks. The reservation includes a lake, trails, picnic areas, and playgrounds, but on Buzzard Sunday the crowds gather at the Buzzard Roost, a large open field surrounded by trees near the intersection of State Road and West Drive. When the festival's designated Buzzard Spotter sees the first turkey vulture floating across the field to the roost site, spring has officially arrived in northern Ohio.

The turkey vultures in this region are members of the eastern subspecies *Cathartes aura septentrionalis.* They breed throughout Ohio and the entire central and southeastern United States, even north into Canada and New England, but in the autumn most vacate the region and head south. According to Keith

Bildstein, for *septentrionalis* "south" might mean anywhere from the New Jersey shore to central Florida. Keith has placed satellite transmitters on turkey vultures in nearby Pennsylvania; he told me that "about half of them don't do what some of us call 'migration.' They either stay in Pennsylvania or they go to coastal areas in south Jersey, which are significantly warmer during the winter." In addition to the coast, many eastern turkey vultures spend the winter in communal roosts in central and southern Virginia, while others, according to Keith, "go to Disney World."

Wherever northern Ohio's vultures spend the winter, their arrival in Hinckley in mid-March is well documented. Hinckley Township traces the "legend of the annual return of the buzzards" back more than a century, to the region's early residents, the Wyandot Native Americans. The first non-Native people to visit the area that would become Hinckley, William Coggswell and Gibson Gates, wrote that in 1810 they observed "vultures of the air" near the site of a Wyandot gallows. The vultures' presence was also noted after the "Hinckley Hunt" of 1818. According to Ohio History Central, the town's settlers —concerned for their families, crops, and livestock—killed "seventeen wolves, twenty-one bears, three hundred deer, and countless numbers of smaller animals," and when the vultures returned in the spring, they feasted on the remains and have been returning to the site ever since. Modern Buzzard Sunday celebrations began in 1957 after a reporter wrote a story about a Metroparks ranger who claimed that the buzzards returned on the same day every year, and had for the previous twenty-three years. After the article, curiosity grew, and folks interested in the vultures' return flocked to the Hinckley Reservation. The following year, 1958, the town was prepared, and the festival grew into the event it is today.

The mood in the elementary school's hallway was jovial;

behind us in line, a man with a round belly wore a floppy plush turkey vulture hat. Women sported vulture earrings and pendants. Many folks wore shirts from Buzzard Sundays past, featuring the festival's logo—a circle with a cartoon buzzard inside, wings spread and beak parted, a few drops of drool (vomit?) leaking from its mouth. Its eyebrows are sloped down in what we've learned to interpret as "mean." While the bird depicted isn't a turkey vulture—its long, featherless neck meets its body at a fluffy collar of feathers, like those of an African white-backed vulture—it was the only vulture logo I'd ever seen; accordingly, I purchased several shirts.

After being served generous helpings of pancakes and sausage, we headed for the cafeteria, where Boy Scouts and 4-Hers seated guests at long tables. Even at this early hour most of the tables were full. We sat across from an elderly man and woman and made small talk; they were local and came every year for the breakfast, but they had never been to the festival at the Buzzard Roost. I tried discreetly to push my sausage links onto Jesse's plate; despite my love for carrion-eating vultures and other carnivorous birds, I've been a vegetarian since the early 1990s. I didn't want the local couple to think I was dissing their sausage, and I was glad when Jesse stabbed it with his fork and rescued me from pancake-and-sausage-breakfast social ruin. As soon as our plates were empty, a swirl of Boy Scouts appeared to clear them away. We refilled our coffee cups, and since it was still raining outside, we headed to the school's gymnasium, where a craft fair had just opened.

I gasped as I walked through the gym's doors. Before me lay a glorious sight. Dozens of vendors displayed vulture-themed jewelry, paintings, magnets, clothing, stickers, mugs, signs, and cards. One booth offered buzzard face paintings. Another, temporary buzzard tattoos. There were stuffed vultures, vulture lawn decorations, and vulture Christmas ornaments. I quickly bought hand-painted buzzard wine glasses and several magnets. I felt a bit like the vulture in the festival's logo—drooling over the unique arts and crafts.

Jesse and I paused before a table displaying vulture-themed infant clothes. We'd recently found out that we were going to have a baby, but it was still early. We hadn't told many people the news, and we definitely hadn't bought anything for the baby yet; it seemed somehow like bad luck. I'd never been pregnant before, and getting pregnant had taken longer than I'd anticipated. I didn't want to do anything to jinx it. Although I didn't feel old, I'd been made to check the "advanced maternal age" box on the medical form. Despite this, I couldn't imagine having a child in my younger years—or rather, I could imagine it, but it wouldn't have been a good idea. Then, when it finally seemed appropriate, I found myself staring back at nearly two decades of fertility, while the time left ahead seemed short; in fact, almost spent.

I picked up a pink onesie emblazoned with a cartoon buzzard. Although it was still too early to determine the sex of our baby, Jesse and I had snuck into the radiology room at the animal hospital where he worked as a veterinarian and ultrasounded my belly. Typically used to find tumors or pregnancies in dogs and cats, the machine lacked the sensitivity of the ultrasonography used at our doctor's office; however, we could watch our baby's tiny heart pulsate and see the delicate features of the face, arms, and legs. We couldn't see anything definitive, but I had a feeling it was a boy. Jesse thought girl. I put the pink onesie back on the table and picked up a blue bib with a silhouette of a vulture on it.

"What do you think?" I asked Jesse, showing him the bib.

"A little early, isn't it?" He smiled nervously. "Blue?"

I shrugged and rummaged in my purse for my wallet. As I paid for the bib, I smiled. Our baby's first item of clothing featured a turkey vulture.

▼ Although to our modern sensibilities it may seem like a strange juxtaposition, several ancient cultures, including the Egyptians, linked vultures and motherhood. The predynastic Egyptian goddess Nekhbet, usually depicted as a griffon vulture with a *shen* (a symbol of eternity) in her talons, protected mothers and women during childbirth. Egyptians also considered vultures ideal mothers.

It's not completely clear why ancient Egyptians linked vultures with motherhood. In the article "The Goddess Mut and the Vulture," Egyptologist Herman te Velde explains some of the ways the vulture functions in Egyptian hieroglyphics and culture. "Nowadays," he writes, "we are far less fond of vultures than the ancient Egyptians." The word for *mother* (*mut*) was depicted with a vulture hieroglyph, as was the word for *womb*, and "eventually the vulture hieroglyph came to mean not only mother . . . but also goddess." While the progression from *mother* to *goddess* makes perfect sense to me, one possible reason that the Egyptians associated vultures with mothers is a bit peculiar. Horapollo, a fifth-century Egyptian priest, wrote that female vultures were so devoted to their offspring that they would "open [their] own thigh[s], and suffer [their] offspring to partake of the blood." Although vulture mothers do not self-mutilate in order to feed their chicks, many species do feed their young bloody bits of regurgitated dead animals; when the ancients observed this practice, instead of cringing in disgust, they praised the vulture for her devotion to her babies.

Ancient Egyptians further linked vultures and motherhood by believing that all vultures were female, and that the young were conceived by the wind. Herman te Velde quotes Horapollo's explanation of the process: "When the vulture hungers for conception, she opens her sexual organ to the north wind and is covered by it for five days. During this period she takes neither food nor drink, yearning for child-bearing. . . . When the vultures are impregnated by the wind their eggs are fertile. . . . And the race of vultures . . . is female only. Because of this the Egyptians place the vulture as a crown on all female figures, consequently the Egyptians use this as a sign for all goddesses." While my unborn baby was not conceived by the north wind, I too had yearned for childbearing. Perhaps the ancients watched the vultures and projected their desire to procreate onto the birds. If a species consisting of only females could bear children, certainly a human woman could, too. The story may have been comforting: *perhaps, if I hope and pray and hunger for a child, the very forces of nature will grant my wish.*

In addition to mothers and women in childbirth, Nekhbet protected the pharaohs. In Egyptian art, she is often shown with her wings stretched around the person she's guarding. Some of the most well-preserved Nekhbet artifacts come from the tomb of Tutankhamen, famously discovered in Egypt's Valley of the Kings by Howard Carter in 1922. Depictions of Nekhbet are literally all over Tut's tomb, from the walls and the coffins to jewelry and adornments. The griffon vulture floats discreetly above nearly every representation of the young king, including on "one of the greatest artistic treasures," writes Howard Carter in his important series, *The Tomb of Tut-Ankh-Amen*, "a painted wooden casket found in the Antechamber." The ends of the casket show the pharaoh in "lion form, trampling upon his alien foes. . . . In the war scenes we see the youthful but all-conquering monarch trampling under foot, with great gusto, his African and Asiatic enemies." In the upper corners of the painting, Nekhbet is shown in mid-flap, her wings in a downward dihedral.

In addition to protecting the king in battle, the vulture goddess kept him safe during hunts. On a small golden shrine, a seated Tutankhamen aims an arrow at a flock of ducks. His queen sits at his feet while his pet lion cub lurks by his side. Nekhbet flies above the king's shoulder, again clutching the *shen*, her wings spread above him protectively. In another depiction of a hunt, Tutankhamen rides in a chariot drawn by rearing horses; dying lions, impaled by his arrows, writhe before the chariot. Above the king's head are two painted vultures, watching over him.

Nekhbet also appears several times on Tutankhamen's coffins. The lid of the outermost coffin, writes Carter, features the king's "face and features wonderfully wrought in sheet-gold. The eyes were of aragonite and obsidian, the eyebrows and eyelids inlaid with lapis lazuli glass. . . . Upon the forehead of the recumbent figure of the young boy king were two emblems delicately worked in brilliant inlay—the Cobra and the Vulture—symbols of Upper and Lower Egypt." Only the heads of the vulture and cobra rise from the king's forehead, but they are depicted in great detail; the vulture's eye and eyebrow, as well as the curved end of her beak, feature prominently. But, continues Carter, "perhaps the most touching by its human simplicity was the tiny wreath of flowers around these symbols. . . . Among all that regal splendor, that royal magnificence—everywhere the glint of gold—there was nothing so beautiful as those few withered flowers, still retaining their tinge of colour." The flower wreath encircled both the vulture's head and the cobra's head; who placed the wreath there? Of course, we can never know. Perhaps the wreath symbolizes the unity of the two Egypts, or perhaps, like the *shen*, it symbolizes eternity; whatever the case, I agree with Carter; the wreath adds a touch of humanity, of love, among all the treasures.

In addition to appearing on the headdress of the king's effigy on the lid of the second coffin, two vultures are carved just below the effigy's folded arms. Their wings are outstretched as if embracing the king. The innermost (third) coffin also shows the two protective vultures. Carter writes, "The prominent feature of its ornamentation are the two goddesses, Nekhbet and Buto, in the form of vultures, superimposed over the arms and abdomen, in sumptuous cloisonné work—the inlay on these goddesses, like that of the collarette, is of semi-precious stones and coloured glass." Inside the coffins, Tutankhamen himself wore five golden vulture amulets around his neck; a breastplate called the "Collar of Nekhbet" (made of 256 segments); and perhaps the most exquisite item of all, a vulture necklace found close to the mummified body. Some researchers believe Tutankhamen may have actually worn this necklace in his lifetime. Carter describes the necklace: "Hanging over the upper part of the chest and secured around the neck by means of lapis lazuli and gold flexible straps, was a small pectoral ornament fashioned to represent a sated vulture. . . . This exquisite example of goldsmith's work, perhaps the finest of all found with the king, inlaid with green glass, lapis lazuli and carnelian, seems with little doubt, to be intended to symbolize the Southern goddess—Nekhbet of El Kab. . . . Around the neck of the bird goddess, in high relief, a tiny pectoral is represented in the form of the king's cartouche."

The vulture goddess is closely and intimately linked to this young king, so closely linked that she wore his name around her neck. Perhaps the hope was that she would protect him in death as she had in life.

▼ The sun came out just as Jesse and I arrived at the Buzzard Roost in Hinckley Reservation, where the vulture celebration was in full swing. Food trucks sold a variety of goodies, and a large tent sheltered official Buzzard Sunday shirts, water bottles, hats, and more. A large blue Buzzard Scoreboard stood at the edge of an open field. On the board, the Buzzard Spotter recorded the morning's vulture sightings. Another display allowed visitors to compare their own "wingspans" to a turkey vulture's, and a representative from a local wildlife center stood in front of a small crowd with a non-releasable turkey vulture perched contentedly on her arm. The bird's six-foot wings were outstretched, soaking up the morning sun. It occasionally cocked its head skyward, perhaps watching the groups of three of four turkey vultures that glided high above the field to the trees beyond. Whenever a vulture was spotted overhead, the crowd clapped and cheered, causing dogs to bark and children to squeal, pointing to the sky. Someone dressed as a turkey vulture moved through the crowd, posing for pictures.

As I sat on a wet wooden bench and watched the spectacle around me, it occurred to me that this festival ran counter to our culture's typical depiction of vultures. Not often are the birds celebrated, which is unfortunate given their peaceful nature and important role in healthy ecosystems. Vulture references are everywhere, but rarely are they flattering. "Ugh, the vultures are already circling," a self-righteous television character will sneer, referring to ambulance-chasing lawyers or the media descending on the scene of a crime. "Vulture capitalists" stalk Wall Street for bankrupt businesses. A "culture vulture" is a pretentious or insincere art aficionado. Whatever the case, when someone calls someone else a vulture, it's generally not meant as a compliment.

This trend of unfair vulture depictions continues even in cartoons; classic Warner Brothers shorts feature Beaky Buzzard, a stupid, timid bird who can't find anything for dinner. When his mother encourages him to leave the nest, he says, "Oh, no, no, no, nope, no, I don't wanna, nope, no, no." When he finally gets kicked out of the nest, he flaps along lazily, eyelids heavy, goofy smile on his beak. In another Beaky short, a sparrow says unkindly to him, "Beaky, what makes you so incredibly stupid?" In the Woody Woodpecker cartoon series, Buzz Buzzard is sometimes Woody's sneaky, greedy, overall-shady nemesis with a New Jersey accent. Buzz always seems to be dreaming up a new way to swindle Woody; in one episode he sneers, "I gotta find me a new dope I can con," and in another, "When you're good, you're mean."

Several animated Disney movies feature vultures, too. In their 1973 version of *Robin Hood*, two vultures (Trigger and Nutsy) guard the gallows with crossbows. One is stupid and the other cruel. *Fantasia* also briefly shows a vulture roosting on the gallows in the beginning of the "Night on Bald Mountain" sequence. A pair of sinister vultures follows Snow White's evil stepmother queen-in-disguise when they overhear her plan to give Snow White the poisoned apple. While the rest of the woodland creatures clean the house, help with the baking, and warn the dwarfs about the queen's scheme, the vultures silently wait around for someone to die, grinning devilishly at each other.

The closest thing to "heroic" cartoon vultures is the harmonious foursome in Disney's *The Jungle Book*, widely thought to caricature the Beatles. In the movie, Mowgli has been wandering in the jungle alone, feeling sorry for himself, and the vultures are roosting in a nearby tree. "What you want to do?" one vulture asks another. "I dunno. Watcha wanna do?" he answers. When they spy Mowgli below, they decide to have some fun with him, but when he starts crying, the vultures take pity. "Nobody wants me around," Mowgli whines. "We know how you feel," the vultures respond. "Nobody wants us around, either. We may look a bit shabby, but we've got hearts. And feelings, too." When Shere Khan the tiger attacks, the vultures distract him, allowing Mowgli to tie a flaming branch to his tail. For once, vultures help the good guy win.

But perhaps the most heroic of all vultures appears in a religious text, the Hindu *Ramayana*. The *Ramayana*, an ancient epic poem, tells the story of the Hindu god Rama and provides examples of how to be a good husband, wife, son, and ruler. In one of the stories, Ravana, the ten-headed king of Lanka, kidnaps Rama's wife, Sita. But brave Jatayu, who is the mystical king of the vultures, attempts to rescue Sita. He battles with Ravana and is mortally wounded when the evil king cuts off his wings. Rama finds Jatayu bleeding and lying on the ground, but just before he dies, Jatayu tells Rama where the kidnapper has taken his wife. Rama performs last rites for the vulture king, quite an honor for the heroic bird. Eventually, Rama kills Ravana and frees Sita—thanks in part to the vulture's sacrifice.

▼ While we don't treat our vultures with the same honor that Rama gives Jatayu, in Hinckley, Ohio, the local buzzards are greeted as sentinels of spring, bringing with them the promise of resurrected life, sunny days, picnics, and ball games to come. I shed my jacket and tied it around my waist, around my swelling belly, which also contained the promise of new life— perhaps my own contribution to spring. I patted my stomach and made my way into the large tent. One side was devoted to selling vulture-themed products, but in the other, three musicians were tuning up their instruments—a guitar, fiddle, and banjo. I hung around the edge of the tent and sifted through a stack of sweatshirts, waiting for them to start playing. Music has the unique ability to unite a crowd, giving its individual members a rhythm and melody to accompany thoughts, actions, and emotions.

Vultures can be linked to the development of human-made

music, too. In 2008, archaeologists in Germany's Hohle Fels cave unearthed the world's earliest musical instrument—a 40,000-year-old flute fashioned from a wing bone (the radius) of a griffon vulture. According to the description in *Nature*, the thirteen-inch-long flute "has five finger holes. The maker carved two deep, V-shaped notches into one end of the instrument, presumably to form the proximal end of the flute, into which the musician blew. The end of the flute corresponds to the proximal end of the radius." Researchers explain that the production of music is "an indication of fully modern behaviour and advanced symbolic communication." Without a healthy griffon vulture population in Paleolithic Germany, perhaps early humans would have failed to develop as a species; in fact, according to a report in *National Geographic*, some archaeologists believe that "music may have been one of the cultural accomplishments that gave the first European modern-human (*Homo sapiens*) settlers an advantage over their now extinct Neanderthal-human (*Homo neanderthalensis*) cousins. The ancient flutes are evidence for an early musical tradition that likely helped modern humans communicate and form tighter social bonds."

While reading reports about the vulture-bone flute, I discovered a link to a recording of someone playing a replica of the flute. The notes are clear and rich, not unlike the notes of a modern flute. I closed my eyes and listened again, and imagined a cave and a crackling fire, the flute's notes reverberating inside the walls. What tunes could these humans 40,000 years ago have played? And picture that curious person, the first one to imagine a future filled with song, perhaps picking through the carcass of a vulture, eyeing a long, thin radius and thinking, *what if . . .*

With the development of stronger social bonds came— eventually—the development of religion and agriculture. The world's oldest known temple, on a hill known as Göbekli Tepe near southern Turkey's border with Syria, was constructed some 11,600 years ago—earlier than Stonehenge, 6,000 years before the invention of writing, and 7,000 years before the construction of Egypt's Great Pyramid at Giza. Archaeologists believe hunters and gatherers built the temple at the end of the last Ice Age. There are two competing theories about how nomadic peoples of this time period transitioned to permanent, agricultural societies; one theory suggests that farming led to organized religion, and the other claims that organized religion led to farming. Some archaeologists believe that discoveries at Göbekli Tepe support the latter.

Göbekli Tepe's pillars feature carvings of stylized human figures as well as animals found in the region—boars, cranes, lions, foxes, gazelles, scorpions, snakes, and—of course—vultures. On one of the temple's pillars, a vulture is shown in profile. Its wing is outstretched, and it appears to be balancing a round object. Some scholars describe this object as a severed human head, since a headless body is carved lower on the stone. The vulture's head is bowed slightly as if it's examining the object, and it almost looks as if the bird is smiling.

Although the exact meaning of the animal carvings is unknown, according to *National Geographic*, anthropologists believe that such carvings "had to have been created by skilled artisans, evidence that hunter-gatherers were capable of a complex social structure." While some archaeologists interpret the carving of the vulture and the headless human as proof that this culture used vultures to dispose of their dead (and subsequently carrying their souls skyward), others don't believe enough evidence of this exists; few human bones were found near Göbekli Tepe. Animal bones, especially from deer and gazelle, were abundant; less common were the bones of birds, including vultures. Whatever the true meaning of the carvings, vultures clearly influenced the lives of Neolithic humans and helped spur them toward civilization.

Here in Hinckley, vultures were again helping humans strengthen their relationships. People of all ages had gathered in this small Ohio town; in addition to the folks watching the turkey vultures float above the field, families and strangers alike sat down to breakfast together, artisans displayed their wares, and people from near and far united to celebrate the return of spring. Boy Scouts, 4-hers, volunteer firefighters, wildlife rehabilitators, city officials, radio station employees, and others had all worked to produce this event, which certainly helped strengthen the community.

▼ Jesse and I stayed in Hinckley until midafternoon, then left the flatlands behind us and headed for the hills. While it still looked like winter outside our car windows, it wouldn't be long before vultures as well as other bird species (and other animals, of course) would begin nesting and raising their young. I felt a part of it this year, in a way that I hadn't before. I'd be bringing new life into the world, too. The newness, the freshness, the churning-up of the stagnant, the resurrection of the dead: vultures were birds of life, birds of rebirth. I watched the empty fields sweep by, still and silent, just weeks away from bursting into bloom.

The attic was warm and musty. Dust particles suspended in the sunbeams that streamed through the windows; the glass had shattered years earlier, leaving an opening wide enough for her and her mate to slip through, into the silent house. She hunkered down on the attic's wooden floorboards, two cream-colored, brown-speckled eggs between her feet. Each egg's dimension was about two by three inches, and she spread herself over them so they were completely covered by her body. Yesterday, her mate had incubated the eggs, and tomorrow, he'd take a turn again.

She turned her head toward the window, listening. A bay-breasted warbler's song floated through the attic's semidarkness. Inside, a broken wooden chair, dried and curled aspen leaves, dust and bits of grass in the corners. When the wind swept over the house, it would creak beneath her.

She turned her head down, eggward, and listened: the faintest scratch, a delicate, almost imperceptible tapping from within. She lifted the feathers of her chest and belly, adjusted her position slightly. She breathed, turned her head, listened. There, again. It wouldn't be long now.

The Private Lives
of Public Birds

The hayloft was dark and warm, and the humidity almost claustrophobic. Muted sunlight came through the loft's open windows, but an overcast sky and soft rain coated everything in musty dampness. A few bales lined the walls, and the floor was covered with a thick layer of loose hay. I stood on a vertical, rickety wooden ladder, my shoulders in the loft and legs below. Before me, two nestling turkey vultures toddled about on their oversized chicken feet. They hunched and lowered their heads, flipper-like wings drooping almost to the floor, and hissed at me—a low, reptilian sound, like air escaping from a bicycle tire. Both babies had already vomited. I couldn't tell what their last meal had been, but two baseball-sized piles of red and brown goo sat between the fluffy birds and me. The sharp, acrid smells of rot and stomach acid wafted from the piles, mingled with the humidity, and settled on my skin.

The hissing, vomiting, and posturing would be more than enough to drive a sane person down the ladder, but for me, the birds' reactions to my presence triggered something maternal, an almost *bless-their-little-hearts* response. These young vultures were vulnerable, proverbial babes in the woods. They couldn't fly away, had nowhere to run, and their parents were nowhere in sight. They had nothing but their sharp little beaks and stinky vomit to protect them. I imagined that they knew it, too, and that their hearts were racing inside their down-feathered chests. I descended the ladder slowly.

Despite their abundance, turkey vultures are secretive breeders. Until recently, we knew little about their private lives; that began to change when researchers at Hawk Mountain Sanctuary in eastern Pennsylvania took an interest in the ubiquitous birds. "We got into studying vultures for several reasons," Dr. Keith Bildstein, Hawk Mountain's director of conservation science, told me. "At that time—2002, 2003—there were very few people looking at vultures. Some hawk-watch sites didn't even count them. So, there wasn't much work being done on them. And they're intriguing. They're found in many different habitats, which meant that we could go out to many different places and see them. At Hawk Mountain we see them on most days, even during the two months that they're effectively out of here, December and January."

Located in the Appalachian Mountains north of Reading, Hawk Mountain Sanctuary is the world's oldest refuge for birds of prey. In the early part of the twentieth century, hunters hoping to claim the Pennsylvania Game Commission's bounties on raptors would gather on Hawk Mountain and shoot migrating broad-winged, red-shouldered, red-tailed, Cooper's, and sharp-shinned hawks by the thousands. In 1934, conservationist Rosalie Edge leased 500 acres on the mountain and stopped the shooting. By 1938, that property and more had been purchased and deeded by Edge to a newly formed nonprofit, the Hawk Mountain Sanctuary Association. Today, the sanctuary hosts thousands of guests annually and is open year-round, but it is busiest during the fall migration season, especially September and October. In addition to hawk-watching overlooks, the sanctuary boasts more than eight miles of hiking trails, presentations featuring live raptors, lectures on everything from birds to salamanders to wildflowers, and an educational center and bookstore. My high school ecology and conservation class took annual field trips to Hawk Mountain, and it remains one of my favorite places to visit.

In addition to being one of the world's preeminent experts on raptor migration, Keith Bildstein is a fan of turkey vultures. He's studied birds all over the world—in the Falkland Islands, Africa, the Middle East, Central and South America, and everywhere in between—and he literally wrote the book on raptor migration (titled, appropriately, *Migrating Raptors of the World*) as well as authoring or coauthoring more than 140 papers in ecology and conservation. His credentials are impressive and include several lifetime-achievement awards and editorships. But despite all this, he remains humble: "The more I learn about turkey vultures, the more I realize how much I don't know. I know more now than I did ten years ago, but I realize that it's far more complicated than anybody would've thought."

When I asked if I could talk with him about turkey vultures, Keith generously invited me to visit Hawk Mountain and stay in the scientist residence at the Acopian Center for Conservation Learning for a long weekend. Built in 2002, the Acopian

Center is a world-class biological field station and training facility. It includes housing for students, interns, and visiting scientists, as well as meeting rooms, one of the world's largest libraries of raptor literature, and a research center. Keith's office (easily the best office I've ever seen) sits at the back of the center's third floor; its floor-to-ceiling windows open onto a large deck with a panoramic view of the valley and Kittatinny Ridge beyond. The office's wooden shelves hold books, both scientific and popular, on birds of all species. Painting, drawings, and other art featuring kestrels, hawks, and—of course —vultures line the top shelves.

Keith and I sat at a round table in his office, and over cups of tea and coffee, he patiently talked me through maps, photographs, and scientific papers, and shared some of his vast knowledge of vultures. He wore jeans and a fleece vest, and despite his often-serious expression and intimidating credentials, he smiled easily, his gray mustache twitching. Keith's enthusiasm for the birds was infectious; in the days and weeks after my visit, I often found myself on my couch in the evening, clicking through turkey vulture migration maps on Hawk Mountain's website, imagining the day-to-day lives of the vultures in the study. While he hesitates to name a "favorite" raptor, after spending several days talking with Keith, I think it's safe to say that turkey vultures are it—well, turkey vultures, hooded vultures, and striated caracaras.

Although he admits that it's sometimes a challenge to get Hawk Mountain's interns excited about turkey vultures, one reason that the birds are important to study, Keith explained, is because of their numbers. "They're often in the sky when nothing else is in the sky except a couple of clouds," he said. "They're perfect for explaining how birds manage to fly long distances at a low cost. We can just point out, 'There's a turkey vulture. Look at your watch and see how many seconds it is before the bird flaps.' The cost of that kind of flight is basically nil. The question of costing flight is something that can be done in a wind tunnel, but on large birds it can be done by putting data loggers in their body cavities. They're a perfect study animal."

Also, despite being often overlooked, turkey vultures are abundant throughout the Americas. Conservative estimates say there are five million turkey vultures worldwide; Keith thinks the number is closer to ten million. "They are one of the very few examples of a successful vulture in today's world," he told me. "Fifty-seven percent of all the world's vultures—Old and New World combined—are globally threatened or endangered, some of them critically so. Understanding how a species works while it is still common provides us with important ammunition for protecting the species."

"'Ammunition'?" I interrupted, laughing.

"OK, I know," he smiled, "I sometimes use 'moving targets,' too, and people jump when I say that. But," he continued, "it's important scientific evidence that allows us to explain to people why vultures elsewhere are not doing quite as well. So they're really spokesbirds for endangered vultures. And vultures are disproportionately endangered compared with all other raptors. On a species-by-species basis, almost three times more likely to be threatened or in decline."

Through their recent research, Keith and Hawk Mountain biologists have made many important discoveries about turkey vultures. Since 2003, more than fifty "spokesbirds"—in Canada, Pennsylvania, Argentina, Arizona, and California—have been fitted with satellite transmitters to record their movements. The transmitters, contained in specially designed backpacks, allow researchers to pinpoint the birds' locations and movements as long as the bird lives. Although several birds died within a few months, other vultures have been transmitting data continuously since 2004, revealing a great deal of information about their private lives. In addition to answering some questions about migration, data about how birds behave during the breeding season was revealed or confirmed as well. They learned that in addition to exhibiting site fidelity (returning to the same area to nest each season), turkey vultures are monogamous. If one of the pair dies or disappears, the surviving bird will find a new mate, but otherwise both members of the pair return to each other after migration. During the non-breeding months, however, the pair separates, sometimes even spending the winters in different countries—separate vacations, so to speak.

Studies have also revealed information about breeding biology and behavior. Nesting in a barn's hayloft is not unusual; turkey vultures have also been documented nesting in abandoned houses, caves, burrows, fallen logs, and even abandoned vehicles. They don't build traditional nests, but will sometimes move leaves and sticks around or scratch a spot in the floor. Then, the female vulture lays two eggs; both parents take turns incubating the eggs for about five weeks, sometimes alternating days. On "off" days, a parent may spend the night at a local roost nearby instead of at the nest site. Once the babies hatch, the parents continue to take turns, brooding the chicks continuously for about a week. After that, the adults may leave the nest for longer periods of time, returning to feed the chicks by regurgitation several times a day. Finally, more than two months after hatching (and sometimes a few weeks longer), the young turkey vultures fledge from the nest. The parents often continue to feed them for a week or two, but by the time the vultures are about twelve weeks old, they're on their own.

In 2013, researchers from Saskatchewan studied the breeding behavior of several turkey vultures wearing Hawk Mountain wing tags and transmitters. Using infrared trail cameras, biologists were able to document what went on inside and around several nests. One important discovery involved the age when turkey vultures first reproduce. While it was previously thought that they began breeding as late as eleven years, researchers in this study observed wing-tagged vultures breeding at six and seven years of age. They also documented adult vultures other than the parents entering the nest site as well as roosting on top of the nest buildings. These observations, their published report contends, "raise the possibility of helpers at vulture nests." This fascinating behavior "warrants further investigation as to whether these birds contribute to parental care or whether they are just part of a social aggregation." Whatever the future studies prove, the idea that some adults spend time with the young of other turkey vultures adds a new dimension to the way we think about the intimate lives of these birds.

▼ Because the parents of the baby vultures I'd observed in the hayloft weren't wearing wing tags or transmitters, it would be impossible to tell if adult vultures entering and exiting the nest site were parents or "helpers." However, the young chicks in the hayloft were destined to become part of Hawk Mountain's turkey vulture research through collaboration with Todd Katzner's team of researchers and graduate students. Although these birds wouldn't be fitted with satellite transmitters, they would each be given a blue vinyl wing tag with a unique number, allowing people on the ground to read the number through binoculars and report the sighting. Traditional metal leg bands cannot be used with vultures because the birds cool themselves by urohydrosis—expelling both liquid and solid waste onto their legs and feet. This practice may also kill bacteria the vulture acquired by standing on a carcass. Turkey vulture excrement is an acidic mix of urates, urea, and feces; it corrodes metal leg bands, which can render them unreadable in addition to irritating the vulture's legs. I asked Keith if the wing tags impeded the birds' flight. "People ask me that all the time," he said. "The tags went through some rigorous testing on black and turkey vultures before they were used on California condors. They're perfect," he continued. "Light and floppy."

Since 2008, any vulture that fledged from this barn—part of Doug Knox's farm in Claysville, Pennsylvania—went out into the world wearing a blue vinyl tag. When Doug first noticed the vultures nesting on his property, he contacted someone who knew birds, who in turn contacted someone else, and eventually Todd, Jesse, and a team of assorted biologists and students traveled to the farm to tag, measure, and take blood samples from the young vultures there. Friendly and animated, the first time Doug met Jesse he laughed and asked Todd, "Who'd you bring with you, some long-haired hippie?" Doug and Jesse clicked instantly. On this day, they discussed fishing in Doug's farm pond and the health of his cats. He hoped we'd come back and spend an afternoon sometime. Doug had white hair, tufts of which stuck from under his camouflaged ball cap. He wore a white T-shirt and was an avid deer hunter.

The pastoral Pennsylvania countryside can be breathtaking. The landscape in the Claysville area is steep, sweeping, and rural, with dairy farms, cornfields, rolling hills, and, more recently, natural-gas wells. Doug's brown wooden barn stood halfway down a hill, at an edge where a field met the woods. Treetops rose above its gray metal roof on the barn's backside, and its front opened to the field filled with waist- and shoulder-high timothy mixed with jewelweed and Queen Anne's lace. We'd driven two pickup trucks through the tall, wet grass, and parked about fifty feet from the barn. Sticker bushes tugged at our pant legs as we jumped out.

Todd and Jesse waded through the damp grass to the barn, disappeared inside, and reemerged a few minutes later, each carrying one of the turkey vulture chicks. The heads of the down-covered birds, the color of soft charcoal and tipped with black beaks, would fade to red in about a year. Both birds' beaks were open, panting, sharp pink tongues extended. Their wide blue eyes rolled in their featherless heads above prominent nostrils; the eyes, too, would change as the birds aged, eventually becoming a stony brownish gray. On their wings the long flight feathers had only just begun to grow in, the sheathed quills extending an inch or two from the trailing edges. The fluffy, awkward vultures attempted to swivel their heads and bite feebly, but Todd and Jesse had done this before; they held the heads behind the commissures of the mouths, and secured the birds' feet in their other hands. In this position, the chicks weren't able to hurt themselves or anyone else.

I stood near Doug's pickup truck with Julie Mallon, one of Todd's graduate students. Several of Doug's neighbors had gathered, too, anxious to see the young birds. While Todd and Jesse waded through the grass with the baby vultures, Julie organized the equipment in the bed of the truck. A fishing-tackle box had been modified to contain everything the team would need to take blood samples from the young birds: gauze, needles, catheters, cotton balls, alcohol, and blood-collection tubes. Julie leaned over the box, extracted a butterfly needle, and brushed her shoulder-length brown hair out of her eyes. She focused intently, almost scowling, at the equipment.

Although her current research project investigates the flight behavior of black and turkey vultures, Julie is interested in other aspects of the birds as well. "One reason I like vultures so much," she told me, "is that they're perfectly adapted for what they do. They have to be so light—they weigh less than half of what an eagle does, but they have the same wingspan, almost. Seeing them in flight, eagles look clumsy compared to vultures. Vultures are much more slender and graceful." Julie's first experience with turkey vultures was caring for them at a wildlife rehabilitation center in New Jersey. She'd also spent a summer working at Hawk Mountain, where she assisted with an American kestrel research project. She observed and appreciated vultures during that summer, but she didn't realize she wanted to study them until she was close to completing her undergraduate degree. Part of her last year of college was spent in Ecuador, both on the southern coast and in the interior rain forest; her experiences with vultures there sealed the deal.

"Ecuador is overridden with vultures," she said. "First we were in the southern part of the country, along the coast. There were equal numbers of turkey and black vultures, feeding on marine life. We saw a pilot whale and three or four sea turtles that had washed up." Because a dry, unproductive forest bordered the coast, most of the vultures stayed near the shore. Part of Julie's class required students to conduct mini-research projects; she chose to investigate scavenging competition between the two local vulture species. She gathered fish entrails from a nearby market, dropped them on the beach, and retreated to watch what happened. She smiled at the memory, and mimed dropping the viscera. "It was gone in about ten minutes. From a distance they saw me drop the guts, and twenty-three birds came down. There was nothing left. Seeing the feeding frenzy was a really cool experience." Whereas the sea life and less-abundant creatures fascinated her classmates, to Julie, the vultures were the most interesting species. "The vultures were there all the time, and there were so many of them. They'd sit on houses and lampposts, just kind of hanging out. They'd hang out in the trees and wait. I identified with them a little bit," she said, smiling again, "because there was something going on that people were completely ignoring."

After spending several weeks on the coast of Ecuador, Julie lived in the rain forest for a month, where she continued observing the local vultures. On the initial trek into the deep forest, via trucks and boats, she saw both black and turkey vultures, but once she reached the interior of the rain forest, the turkey vultures gradually disappeared, and she began seeing greater yellow-headed vultures. She explained that "greater yellow-headeds are almost exactly the same as turkey vultures"; the only noticeable difference between the two species is the color of the exposed skin on their faces. From an observation tower, Julie watched king vultures soaring above the tree canopy (which, from above, resembled broccoli, she laughed). One day, her professor found a dead capybara and dragged it to shore and set up a motion-sensing trail camera. When she analyzed the images, Julie discovered three different vulture species—king, black, and greater yellow-headed— feeding on the same carcass.

Julie completed her bachelor's degree early—after only three and a half years—and decided to pursue a master's degree studying vultures. She approached Keith Bildstein for advice, and he secured a spot for her with Todd (another former Hawk Mountain intern) at West Virginia University. She expected one of her first research papers, detailing the way vultures use lift when flying low, to be published by the time she graduated from wvu. After her master's, Julie hoped to continue contributing to the body of scientific knowledge about the birds that fascinated her. "For something so common, you'd think there'd be more literature on them. You can just kind of sit and wait and they show up. When it's sunny out, and they catch the light, they have a halo. It's kind of angelic, the way the light catches their wing feathers." She paused, then added, "They're gorgeous creatures."

When Todd and Jesse reached the truck with the vulture

chicks, Todd quickly determined that the birds were approximately twenty-eight days old—too young to tag. The tags
would need to be secured by punching a hole through the vulture's patagium, the thin skin below the tendon on the wing.
Tagging a vulture too early could mean improper wing-tag
placement, hindering flight. Someone would have to return to
the farm in about a month to try again.

But the birds were in hand, so physical measurements as
well as blood samples would be taken from each. Todd gently
laid the first vulture chick on its back on the lowered tailgate
of the truck. Raindrops began to dapple the black corrugated
bed liner. He placed his right hand across the bird's chest and
torso, just below its head, and with his left he held the legs.
Todd leaned over the bird, smiling; his face, with its short,
dark-and-gray beard, was close to the vulture's own dark-and-
gray face. The bird panted, its eyes wide. Jesse re-twisted his
hair into a sloppy bun, leaned over the baby vulture as well,
and carefully extended its right wing, which he held against
the truck bed with his left hand. He worked a needle and syringe with his right, and in a few moments he'd filled a small
collection tube with the chick's blood. Julie handed him a cotton ball, and Jesse extracted the needle and held the cotton
over the spot to stop the bleeding.

A few minutes later, both chicks were back in the safety of
the loft, perhaps a bit dazed and tired. The whole experience
must feel like being abducted by aliens—torn from a warm bed,
restrained and prodded, and then returned, perhaps to remain
shaken from the experience (although there's no evidence to
suggest that turkey vultures have recurring abduction-scenario
nightmares). Maybe, by the time we returned in a month to tag
them, the baby vultures would have forgotten all about this
day's trauma.

▼ The sky was overcast again when Jesse and Julie returned to the farm to tag the young vultures. The birds were about eight weeks of age, and would be leaving the nest in another week or two. When Jesse ducked through the open barn door, he nearly stepped on one of the baby vultures; the bird wobbled unsteadily on the ground near the base of the ladder that led to the hayloft. It trailed a bloody wing. Jesse surmised that the bird had taken a misstep and fallen through the only opening in the loft's floor, and being still too young to fly, was stuck on the ground and very vulnerable. After tagging the uninjured baby and returning it to the loft, they boxed up the injured vulture and brought it back to the veterinary hospital. If the bird couldn't return to the farm immediately, we'd admit it to the Avian Conservation Center of Appalachia for rehabilitation.

The vulture panted under the clinic's bright fluorescent lights, its black pupils constricted. With one hand a volunteer held the vulture's head to prevent biting, and with the other held its feet. We placed a light cloth over its face to reduce stress; birds are very visual, and covering their eyes often calms them. Jesse began the routine examination by palpating the bird's chest and torso, searching with his fingertips for unusual bumps, protrusions, or wounds. He felt the bird's keel, the long bone that runs vertically up the center of a bird's chest. "Decent body condition," Jesse said softly. He continued palpating the bones of the torso, the coracoid and clavicle. "These feel fine." Jesse carefully stretched the vulture's right wing and slowly ran his fingers along the bones. "Nothing broken here. No wounds. Good extension. Nice feather condition. Almost all the way grown in." The trailing edge of the underside of the bird's wing—and the underside of all turkey vultures' wings—was a creamy silver. This was one reliable way to identify large soaring birds: turkey vultures had silver linings. Black vultures, by comparison, had white feathers on just the ends of the undersides of their wings, making them appear to have white "hands."

Jesse tucked the right wing under the volunteer's arm and extended the bird's left wing, the one with the bloody end. He repeated the same exam, but leaned close to the site of the injury and furrowed his brow. "Let's get some films of this," he said. He removed a lead-filled gown from its hook and disappeared into the radiography room, where he readied the computer. (Jesse still said *films* even though the clinic had been using a digital X-ray for some time.) Unfortunately for the young vulture, radiographs revealed two broken carpometacarpal bones, small but important bones near the end of its left wing roughly analogous to human hand bones. The injury required surgery.

Avian orthopedics (and orthopedics in general) had become something of a specialty for Jesse. In addition to fixing fractured bones, he performed all manner of surgeries on dogs and cats, including cruciate ligament tears, patellar luxations, femoral head and neck ostectomies, and more. He learned the basics of mammalian orthopedics as part of the general curriculum in veterinary school, but most of his training in avian orthopedics came from the Raptor Center at the University of Minnesota, where he spent several weeks as a veterinary extern. In the years since then, Jesse had operated on bald and golden eagles, peregrine falcons, and nearly every species of hawk and owl native to West Virginia. But turkey vultures were one of his favorite patients. "They're large enough, and the bones are robust enough, that they hold implants fairly well," he explained. "They also tend to eat well in captivity, and that helps with medicating. You can cut their food into pieces and hide their drugs in there. They seem to be intelligent, engaging, and are just neat to be around."

Before the surgery, the vulture received an opioid and a non-steroidal anti-inflammatory injection for pain and inflammation. A plastic cone was fitted over its head to induce anesthesia, and then, once the bird was asleep, an endotracheal tube was placed to prevent aspiration and provide positive-pressure ventilation. Jesse plucked the feathers from the surgery site, which was then sterilized and draped. In order to repair the fractures, he made small incisions in the skin and placed threaded surgical-steel pins through the larger broken carpometacarpal bone. These pins spanned the fracture and were stabilized by an acrylic bar on the outside of the body. This type of external skeletal fixation allows for minimal trauma at surgery, preserving blood supply to the fracture site while providing good stability. The entire surgery took fewer than twenty minutes.

I held the little vulture as it recovered from anesthesia, slowly blinking its eyes and getting its bearings. When the bird began to struggle against my restraint, I gently placed it inside a small cage we'd prepared. As soon as its feet hit the floor it scrambled and hissed, shrugging itself free. What could it have been thinking? Although some people deny that animals "think" at all, I believe they do. The chick had survived quite an ordeal so far: it hatched and lived a typical life in the loft for a few weeks, but then was snatched from the loft, prodded with needles and other instruments, and then returned to the loft. Several more weeks passed and then something—what?—made it fall out of the hayloft onto the floor of the barn below. I imagined the curious bird standing on the hay, head cocked, looking down the opening. Or maybe it simply got too close to the edge. Perhaps its sibling bumped into it, or perhaps a gust of wind through an open window precipitated the fall. Or it could have been something more nefarious: a marauding weasel or hungry raccoon.

Whatever the case, the young vulture was lucky the acci-dent happened a day or two before Jesse and Julie returned to the nest site; the bird was extremely vulnerable in the down-stairs of the barn, being unable to fly, and we weren't sure if its parents were still caring for it. From there, the bird's or-deal continued: it was scooped up again, hissing and vomiting, and forced into a large cardboard box. And then the surgery —a mask over its beak and nostrils, the feeling of growing drowsy, and then awakening slowly, out of sorts in an unfa-miliar setting filled with the smells of alcohol, dogs, and hints of perfume. Human scent, everywhere, all over its feathers. Again restrained, carried into another building, and placed in another box, this one plastic. The room was quiet and the smells more familiar: owl, hawk, and—what's that? Rodent? The door opens and a human hand places a small rat at its feet. The vulture bends its head, hunches its shoulders, and begins nibbling. It hooks a toenail on one side of the rat's al-ready-opened abdomen and another nail on the other side, and it makes a quick meal of the organ meat. Then it wipes its beak on the edge of a perch and waits.

The vulture would have to spend several weeks in the cage, small to restrict movement and give the bones time to heal. It was a feisty patient. We kept the door of the cage covered to minimize stress; whenever we lifted the cover to feed the vulture, it let out a frantic hiss and stomped its feet in a rapid staccato. The bird intimidated its volunteer caretakers, who were wary about sticking their hands in the cage to leave dead rodents and chicks. Often the vulture would jump straight up, bumping its head on the top of the cage and crashing against the door, perhaps sensing that its time to fledge from the nest was drawing near. Sometimes, when one of us would lift the cover, the bird would twitch its head and expel a lump of par-tially digested rat in our general direction. We wouldn't bother to remove the vomit because the bird would eat it again as soon as we lowered the cover.

After three weeks, Jesse anesthetized the vulture and removed the pins from the broken bones. Most birds with broken bones require the pins to remain in the bones longer; however, young animals heal much more quickly, and leaving the pins in too long could actually harm the vulture's growth. Around this time, too, the bird had lost nearly all of its fluffy white down feathers. Once the pins were out, we moved the vulture to a larger outdoor enclosure. While not large enough for true flight, the enclosure would force the vulture to use its wings to fly down from a perch to its food on the ground, and then fly back up the perch after eating. The size of the enclosure worked well to build the bird's flight muscles after several weeks of relative immobility.

The young vulture perched on a rope-wrapped two-by-four near the back of the enclosure, staring over its shoulder at me. I stared back. The distance was enough that the bird didn't vomit or crash around in fear, but I wouldn't claim that it enjoyed my presence. The sun hit the dark backs of its wings, making the feathers shimmer a deep, iridescent purple. A few more weeks of healing, and then this bird's fate would be determined: a full recovery and a life in the wild, or improper healing and a flightless life in captivity. We would both have to wait to find out.

She folded her wings over her back, stretched one leg behind her, then the other, and stepped off the branch into the air. She felt the column of warm air lift her as she fixed her wings and began to glide, leaving several roosting birds behind her in the aspen. With the sun on her back and the air beneath her, her body warmed quickly and her speed increased. Marshland, groves of trees, and small ponds passed in rapid succession. Soon, she reached the flat gray strip of land that looked like an unmoving river and smelled like hot tar. Her eyes scanned its gravel edges.

After only a few minutes she spiraled downward and landed on the stony surface; it was warm under her feet. She took two steps closer to the crumpled hare carcass. There was barely anything left, but she turned her head sideways and reached her beak into its crushed belly, finding the liver, heart, and lungs, which she tugged free and swallowed whole. She half-ran, half-hopped, unfurled her wings, and beat them hard, finally catching the air and rising again. Soon, she lifted above the trees, and although her nostrils detected other meals hidden in the tall grass, she headed for the little house.

The cluster of aspens came into view first. Her mate perched, wings spread, near the topmost branch. He turned his red head to watch her approach, but she swooped past him, into the attic's open window. She landed heavily on the wooden floor and hissed lowly. Two low hisses answered, one from a corner, near the broken chair, and the other from a cluster of dried leaves against the far wall. Both down-covered chicks toddled toward her, flipper-like wings drooping at their sides, gray heads extended and hooked mouths gaping. She extended her own head, contracted the muscles of her throat, and regurgitated the warm hare organs into the open mouths of her chicks. They hungrily swallowed the meat, and soon her throat emptied.

She turned her back to her sated chicks and slipped out the attic window. Her mate still sat, spread-winged in the aspen. She soared above him, the house becoming smaller as she rose into the sky.

Rockshelter

The definition of a good place to camp hasn't changed much in the past 16,000 years—not in western Pennsylvania, at least. Perched on a steep hill overlooking Cross Creek in Avella, the Meadowcroft Rockshelter—a small, natural amphitheater carved out of the sandstone, like a bowl on its side with southern exposure—has been attracting hunting parties, travelers, and vagrants since the Pleistocene, an "Ice Age" of glaciers, mastodons, and saber-toothed cats.

In 1955, Albert Miller reached into a groundhog hole in the rockshelter and came out with a flint knife and other artifacts from a bygone era. He waited for almost twenty years before contacting archaeologists about what he'd discovered on his property. When Dr. James Adovasio (then with the University of Pittsburgh, now with Mercyhurst Archaeological Institute) first visited the site in 1973, a fire pit along the rock wall contained beer cans, syringes, and other telltale signs of contemporary human use. A team of researchers began excavating, and beneath the existing campfire pit was another pit, and another, and another, and soon the team was digging further and further back into history, and then prehistory, and then—remarkably—into a layer that contained cultural material older than any other discovered in North America. Carbon-dating indicated that the basket fragments, stone tools, and bits of bone and wood in the lowest campfire pit were *16,000 years old*. Conventional wisdom placed humans in North America no earlier than 11,000 or 12,000 years ago. But here was evidence to the contrary. And the evidence revealed that the humans who visited this shelter weren't the oft-depicted spear-throwing mammoth killers but nomadic small-game hunters and gatherers.

The Meadowcroft Rockshelter is one of the oldest sites of continual use by humans in the Americas. Hunting parties, perhaps originating in the Ohio River valley, would follow Cross Creek, a tributary of the Ohio, and stop to camp in the rockshelter. Along the way, they'd collect abundant freshwater mussels, trout, and crayfish from the creek, which teemed with life. Hunters took deer, elk, rabbit, and squirrels, while others gathered hackberries, walnuts, and raspberries. In total, archaeologists uncovered more than 956,000 animal remains and 1.4 million plant remains from the rockshelter. While there isn't evidence that the site was used as a human burial ground, in one of the more recent historic stratum levels, a domestic dog appeared to have been buried intentionally.

Meadowcroft's researchers believe that the animals, habitat, and climate conditions in this region—just fifty miles south of glacial maximum, or the furthest reach of the glacier that covered most of Canada and the northern United States—looked much as they do now: diverse, temperate, and verdant. Of course, there are significant differences. Most of the megafauna—the eight-foot-long giant beaver, the tree-climbing American cheetah, the 2,500-pound short-faced bear, and many others—are long gone, although some absences are much more recent: the passenger pigeon, Carolina parakeet, Eastern cougar, and woodland bison.

Once a source of life for the bands of early Americans and the animals they hunted, today Cross Creek flows over a concrete dam and is plagued by pollution, including acidic mine drainage and raw sewage. But the forest surrounding the rockshelter still appears lush; Acadian flycatchers chirp from towering Eastern hemlocks, sugar maples shade the forest floor, and Virginia creeper drapes itself over sandstone boulders. Pawpaws grow along the parking lot at the base of a wooden staircase, which visitors climb to hear a docent recount the story of Meadowcroft and to lay their eyes on the excavated site. Many key features are highlighted by spotlights and markers, including a Pleistocene fireplace, shells, and bones, but about a third of the rockshelter remains unexcavated—an admirable bit of foresight on behalf of the archaeologists—in the hopes that technological advances will improve future excavations.

Holding on to the railing that runs along the edge of the shelter, staring at the site of an ancient fire pit, I'd wondered: what did folks talk about here? I pictured them huddled around a campfire, perhaps reclining on deerskins, leaning against the cool stone walls, maybe passing a basket of hackberries or hickory nuts, recounting the day's successes in whatever language people used 16,000 years ago. American lions, 600-pound relatives of today's 400-pound African lions, could have skulked just beyond the fire's light, while dire wolves howled at the same moon that will shine tonight.

Did the people share the same basic hopes, dreams, and worries that we have today—healthy children, enough food, a safe place to rest, long lives? They couldn't have been much different from the folks who passed by 10,000 years ago, 1,000 years ago, 50 years ago—indeed, they all stopped at the same place, all made fires, all ate around those fires, all slept on the same floor. I could almost hear their voices, their laughter, echoing inside the sandstone dome.

▼ The cave's muddy walls closed around me. The temperature dropped, and after only a few feet, the sunlight faded. Sounds from outside disappeared. My breath was loud in my ears as I crouched on the dirt floor, and I felt the cool, unforgiving stone against my shoulders. A momentary panic fluttered in my chest, the kind of panic that comes with sensory deprivation. I inhaled deeply and reminded myself that this damp, silent darkness was the only home the baby turkey vulture in my arms had ever known. While one day it would soar in the sunlight, a black V in a cerulean sky, for now it was cave-bound and helpless.

I inched my way to a hollow along the wall. There, a soft layer of brown oak leaves covered the floor. We'd surmised that this was the place where the adults had incubated their eggs and brooded their young. I extended my arms and gently set the vultureling on the bed of leaves. I crouched there a moment longer, breathing the cave air along with the bird, letting the silence and dampness settle onto my skin. "Good luck, buddy," I whispered, then turned and carefully wriggled out into the summer sunshine.

A few minutes before I'd returned the turkey vulture to the cave, the eight-week-old bird had been restrained on its back —blood drawn, measurements taken, wing tag affixed—not far from the area that normally held visitors to the Meadowcroft Rockshelter. The vulture cave was part of the same geologic formation, an opening in a sandstone jumble surrounded by a steep forest. Perhaps what made the location attractive to humans also made it attractive to vultures: southern exposure, a constant breeze, shelter from the elements, and a view of the valley below. No archaeological excavations had taken place in the cave where the vultures nested (yet), and I wondered if perhaps the birds had been raising their young there since ancient times, perhaps even earlier than the earliest humans. The idea that vultures and the first humans in North America could have been living literally side by side for thousands of years made my heart beat faster. What secrets could the vulture's nest cave hold beneath its cool floor? Perhaps the remains of turkey vultures, and below them, the remains of ancestral vultures, like the long-gone teratorns—victims, too, of the Pleistocene extinctions.

The world's largest flying bird ever—*Argentavis magnificens*—was a member of the extinct New World vulture family Teratornithidae, from the Greek for *monster birds*. The four species in this family were thought to resemble giant, modern-day vultures with larger bills, but unlike turkey vultures, who eat exclusively carrion, a teratorn's strong jaws would have allowed it to take live prey in addition to scavenging. *Argentavis* had a wingspan of twenty-five feet and weighed at least 160 pounds; it was roughly the size of a small Cessna airplane. While all *Argentavis* fossils come from Argentina, remains of the other three teratorn species were discovered in the United States. Fossils from more than one hundred *Teratornis merriami* individuals were found in the Rancho La Brea Tar Pits in California; Merriam's teratorn had a wingspan of "only" eleven or twelve feet and weighed about thirty pounds —slightly larger than the largest living flying land bird, the Andean condor. Researchers estimate that the last teratorns became extinct 10,000 years ago, along with 80 percent of the large animals living in North America.

I envy the early Americans who camped at Meadowcroft. Although the first people to cross the land bridge from Siberia may have already been familiar with wooly mammoths, steppe bison, and giant bears, imagine being the first person to cast your eyes on a saber-toothed cat, a creature found only in the Americas. Certainly, the shadow of a teratorn soaring overhead would have been unnerving, and could have led to the development of mythology and legends about enormous birds. Several Native American cultures pass down stories of thunderbirds—huge creatures responsible for storms and winds. In some of the stories, the thunderbirds are vengeful, powerful, and intelligent, and need to be appeased. In cultures of the Pacific Northwest, the thunderbird often appears at the tops of totem poles. Perhaps the sight of a teratorn was so dramatic and frightening that legends were born.

The History Channel series *MonsterQuest* explores the possibility that mythological or extinct animals are still with us; each episode is devoted to a different "hidden" animal, including the chupacabra, the Jersey devil, the Mothman, Bigfoot, and dozens of others. At least four episodes investigate unidentified flying creatures; one episode, "Birdzilla," focuses specifically on the possibility that teratorns still soar above the United States. After a discussion about the size and characteristics of *Argentavis*, the episode interviews eyewitnesses from Illinois, Texas, and Alaska who claim to have had terrifying encounters with giant birds. While the "Birdzilla" episode is entertaining (and the discussion of teratorn characteristics useful), the most fascinating point is discussed by Dr. Greg Bambenek, a psychiatrist. He believes that a fear of large birds is part of humans' genetic memory—part of our collective unconscious, left over from a time when large birds preyed upon our prehuman ancestors. If a fear of large birds can live in our genes, is it possible that birds could have affected the development of our species in other ways as well?

Concrete proof of ancient vulture-human Meadowcroft cohabitation could be difficult to come by, however. David Scofield, director of the Meadowcroft Rockshelter and Museum of Rural Life, has only observed turkey vultures nesting in the cave since 2008, although they could have been nesting there unnoticed previously. In the late 1700s, local resident Joseph Doddridge noted, "The buzzards, or vultures, grey and bald eagles, ravens, or as they were generally called corbies, were very numerous here in former times. It was no uncommon thing to see from fifty to one hundred of them perched on the trees over a single carcase of carrion." And Albert Miller himself—the Meadowcroft landowner who found artifacts in the groundhog hole—wrote that he observed turkey vultures in several areas of the property. However, among the animal remains unearthed so far from the rockshelter, which include the remains of many birds—passenger pigeons, hawks, turkeys, owls, and others—no vulture bones were found. But because a third of the rockshelter hasn't been excavated, it's certainly possible that evidence of other animals will be uncovered. "The absence of remains," Dave told me, "doesn't necessarily indicate vultures weren't here."

Earlier, Dave—tall and thin with a graying beard and dark hair, wearing jeans and a navy-blue polo shirt—stood in front of our small group at the base of the stairs that led to the rockshelter and explained the site's importance to archaeology and to our understanding of America's first humans. In addition to Jesse and me, our group consisted of Todd Katzner and fellow wildlife biologist Trish Miller and several of their graduate students, including Julie Mallon. Trish's two young daughters and her mother joined us as well.

As they did with the nest in Claysville, for the past several years biologists had been making the hour-and-a-half drive from Morgantown to the rockshelter to take samples and morphometric measurements from the nestling vultures in the cave. Through collaboration with researchers from Hawk Mountain Sanctuary, the birds are fitted with numbered tags so they can be identified in flight. Meadowcroft's young vulture was now also part of an ongoing study about turkey vultures as environmental sentinels by measuring the amounts of heavy metals, specifically lead, in their blood.

Lead is widely recognized as being toxic to humans and animals. According to the US Environmental Protection Agency, children and infants exposed to lead may experience learning difficulties, slowed growth, aggressive behavior, and attention disorders. Lead can cause a pregnant woman to miscarry or can affect the brain of her unborn child. In adults, lead can cause vomiting, seizures, headaches, and a wide array of other symptoms. Recognizing these dangers, the United States banned the use of lead-based paint in 1978. The Clean Water Act and the Safe Drinking Water Act regulate the discharge of lead into streams, rivers, and lakes. The Clean Air Act regulates lead as a toxic air pollutant. By 1995, lead had been phased out as a gasoline additive in the United States (although NASCAR continued to use leaded fuel until 2008). The use of lead ammunition to hunt waterfowl has been banned since 1991; however, for reasons that seem feeble at best, lead ammunition is still legal in most states for hunting other game species.

According to the Pennsylvania Game Commission, each year about one million hunters take to the woods and fields to stalk the state's abundant white-tailed deer. In 2014, hunters in Pennsylvania killed more than 300,000 deer; in neighboring West Virginia, hunters killed more than 100,000. Most of those deer are field-dressed—the intestines, stomachs, lungs, livers, and other organs are removed before transporting the deer out of the field. Typically, these remains are left in "gut piles," which provide easy meals for eagles, vultures, crows, ravens, and other carrion eaters (such as the critically endangered California condor in the western United States). Unfortunately, a gut pile can also be a death sentence.

When a lead bullet hits the body of a deer, it can shatter into more than a hundred pieces, some so tiny that they're virtually undetectable by a bird (or a human) eating the meat or viscera. A lead fragment as small as a grain of rice can be fatal to a bald eagle. Lead poisoning is the greatest obstacle standing in the way of the California condor's recovery; every year condors are found—dead and alive—with toxic levels of lead in their systems. At the Avian Conservation Center of Appalachia, lead toxicity is the cause of death in most of the bald eagles we treat. We've also treated other bird species for lead poisoning: red-tailed hawks, red-shouldered hawks, American crows, ravens, and turkey vultures. While turkey vultures can usually handle a greater amount of lead than a bald eagle, lead poisoning can still impair a vulture's ability to fly, feed, and thrive. But because turkey vultures *can* survive with some lead in their systems, they can be used to help us figure out how much lead is present in our environment, leaching into our soil and groundwater, washing into our streams and rivers, and, perhaps, eventually making its way into our bodies and affecting our health.

Jesse, Todd, and several other biologists collaborated with Shannon Behmke, one of Todd's graduate students, on a study to determine how much lead vultures had been exposed to over time. The team procured more than a hundred black and turkey vulture carcasses and took liver and femur samples from each—a long, stinky, and labor-intensive process. Whereas the birds' livers would reveal if they had been ex-

posed to lead shortly before their deaths, their femurs would
tell the tale of long-term lead exposure. The team discovered
that while only some of the vultures had evidence of lead in
their livers, analysis of the birds' femurs showed that 100 percent of vultures in the study had been chronically exposed to
lead. Further analysis determined that the sources of lead included coal-fired power plant emissions, zinc smelting plant
emissions, and rifle ammunition. Although only a fraction of
humans in the eastern United States are at risk for lead exposure from rifle ammunition, we are all breathing the same
air as the vultures, which means that everything and everyone who breathes—all of us—are exposed to lead from power
plant emissions.

In an effort to reduce lead in the environment, several organizations, including the American Bird Conservancy, the Association of Avian Veterinarians, and the hunting group Project
Gutpile, have petitioned the Environmental Protection Agency
to ban the use of lead ammunition, but so far their efforts have
fallen short. Even though alternatives exist—such as copper
and steel—outcry from pro-gun groups, especially the National Rifle Association, has been shrill and predictable. Instead of acknowledging the legitimate threat to public health
as well as to the health of our most recognizable bird—the
bald eagle, our national emblem, itself only recently removed
from the endangered species list—the NRA has characterized
lead opponents as liberal gun-grabbers. Banning lead ammunition is a slippery slope, they cry; next thing you know, it'll be
your hunting rifles.

I am the product of a hunting culture. I grew up in northeastern Pennsylvania, perhaps the white-tailed deer capital of
the world, and I would never suggest that anyone stop hunting deer. In fact, I encourage it; there are too many deer, and
they have few surviving natural predators other than humans.

While I don't plan to kill deer myself, I support those who do choose to hunt them. I believe that most hunters and gun enthusiasts—including my father, father-in-law, and many of my friends—would be mortified if they knew that a bald eagle had died from ingesting lead from one of their gut piles. But how to spread the word about lead ammunition without drawing the ire of the NRA? Perhaps their leadership should witness, firsthand, what an eagle suffering from lead toxicity looks like.

Often, a bald eagle with lead poisoning cannot stand. Imagine the huge bird: once powerful, dark-brown wings that measure six feet from tip to tip, matted with green feces from where the eagle had fallen down in its own excrement. Imagine its long, yellow, claw-tipped talons balled into useless fists, its white-feathered head drooping down to its chest, its fierce eyes unable to focus. The eagle trembles and convulses, off balance. Its breathing is labored. It cannot feed itself. Despite an intravenous catheter, despite tube feeding, despite chelation therapy, despite around-the-clock care, the eagle will usually die, crumpled on the feces-soaked newspaper that lines its cage. Nothing deserves to die like that—especially not a bald eagle, and especially not if it's preventable. Choosing copper or steel over lead bullets will save the lives of our most majestic birds—not to mention the lives of other carrion eaters—as well as protecting our own health. The choice is simple.

▼ The young vulture's long, hooked beak gaped. With my right hand, I held the bird's head between my thumb and forefinger, just behind the commissures of its mouth, so it could not turn and bite Julie, who prepared to insert a sharp, tiny needle into a thin vein along the underside of one of the vulture's long wings. The bird was restrained on its back; with my left hand I gently extended the wing so Julie could work. She leaned close to the vulture and squinted her eyes, her light-brown hair falling in front of her face despite her wide red-and-yellow headband. Jesse held on to the bird's feet and kept a hand on its torso, his own long hair tucked under a blue bandanna. He nodded encouragement to Julie; this would be her second time taking a blood sample from a young vulture. The bird's chest rose and fell rapidly.

I focused on the vulture and wondered, anthropomorphically, what this experience must be like for it: strange, unfeathered, two-legged creatures tore it from its nest, held it down on its back, and prodded it with sharp objects. We were doing this to help other vultures, to learn more about them, about our environment, but the bird couldn't understand any of that, of course. Its steel-blue eyes seemed to fix on a point above our heads. The gray flesh of its face and neck was warm and soft, and reminded me of fine, butterskin leather. While most of the bird's long, black feathers had grown in already, its body was still covered with quite a bit of fluffy white down, giving it a patchy, Dalmatian-like appearance. If everything continued to go well, the vulture would soon lose the rest of the down, and would probably fledge from the nest in another week or so.

Unfortunately, things did *not* go well for this vulture's sibling. When we first entered the nest cave, we discovered the chick's lifeless carcass lying facedown on the leaf-littered floor. It hadn't been dead long; the chick looked about the same age as its living brother or sister. The body seemed undisturbed, as if it had died on its feet and fallen forward. Despite the fact that turkey vultures survive on carrion, it hasn't been documented that they eat the dead of their own species. We wondered: what could have killed the baby vulture? A raccoon or other predator would have taken the body, or at least torn it apart in the process of eating it. Jesse commented that he wouldn't be surprised if it had died of lead toxicity. But instead of taking the carcass with us to test it, we left it in the cave, where it would become part of history, perhaps part of a future archaeological excavation. In retrospect, Jesse wished we'd taken a sample from the dead chick, because laboratory results later revealed that the surviving chick had very high—perhaps lethal—levels of lead in its blood.

I thought about the vulture mother returning to her nest in the evening with a gullet full of partially digested food; I imagined her gingerly stepping around her dead chick, reaching her neck toward the living one, regurgitating carefully into its beak. While we might find swallowing a mouthful of already-eaten carrion revolting, to the chick, it means life, and the only way it can survive until it's old enough to leave the nest. Sadly, for one of the chicks, it also meant death: the life-sustaining food, carried back for it by devoted parents, may have been poisoned, containing tiny flecks of undetected metal. The parents killed their baby by feeding it. While I know, rationally, that the adult vultures would never, could never realize why one of their chicks died, I quietly grieved for them, and for the living chick, unable to escape its dead sibling, spending each long day and night in the quiet, cool darkness with the corpse.

Julie finished collecting the blood sample and backed away from the vulture, allowing Trish to move in to measure the bird's tarsus and upper beak. Trish's young daughters inched forward to watch their mother work, leaning over the vulture to see better. The older girl took pictures with a cell phone while Trish's mother kept a hand on the younger one's shoulder. It struck me, suddenly, that perhaps the historically male-dominated field of wildlife biology was evolving. Here were several generations of women watching, learning, and collecting data on turkey vultures, certainly not a glamorous or "girly" species to study.

I wondered if women had been members of the nomadic hunting and gathering groups that had camped here 16,000 years ago; they must have been. But for some reason, I realized I'd been picturing early rockshelter visitors as entirely comprised of men: sharpening spear points, gutting deer, lounging bare-chested in front of a crackling fire. Certainly these images came from somewhere—a patriarchal, sometimes misogynistic culture that reinforces "traditional" gender roles, perhaps—and I was ashamed of myself for excluding women from my imagined prehistoric scenes. Suddenly my mind filled with other possibilities: visions of long-haired women skinning squirrels with stone knives; kneeling on the banks of the creek catching crayfish; sitting cross-legged, shoulder blades against the sandstone walls, nursing mewing infants; stalking the worn paths after deer, toddlers strapped to their backs. Prehistory expanded.

▼ The young turkey vulture panted; it didn't know it, but soon the ordeal would be over and I would return it to the safety of the cave. But first we had one more task to complete. A stack of bright-blue vinyl cattle ear tags sat next to the vulture on the bench. One side of each tag displayed a large black number; the other side included contact information with instructions to call if the bird or tag was recovered.

A student held the vulture's head while another held its chicken-like legs. Todd extended the vulture's right wing while Julie sprayed alcohol on an area of thin skin on the wing's underside. Jesse fitted a tag over the wing—#255—and prepared what looked like a large hole puncher. He leaned his face close to the vulture's wing and lined up the hole puncher; a few centimeters in either direction would mean a severed tendon and a flightless future for the young bird. When he and Todd were satisfied with the alignment, Jesse squeezed the handle. Todd grinned nervously as the bird squirmed. I held my breath and cringed. Jesse slid the puncher away and the tag remained. He ran his fingers along the edge of the wing, flexing it gently at the joints before nodding and standing up. The vulture was ready to return to the cave.

I gathered the vulture in my arms and lifted it against my chest. The bird's eyes seemed glazed over, his mouth open, tongue extended. I turned and began carefully stepping along the steep, rocky path while using both arms and hands to hold the vulture. I learned, quickly, that hiking and balancing without the use of one's arms is difficult. A few feet from the cave, the large bird began to kick and buck. It struggled its head loose and bit me, hard, on the biceps—twice, leaving two parallel red marks that would turn purple by the next day. Vulture kisses, I called them.

The walk to the cave seemed to take a long time. Greenbrier tangled around my ankles, and whenever I loosened my grip, even slightly, the vulture struggled. I paused for a moment to readjust my hands again, and leaned my back against a cool rock wall covered in Virginia creeper. I hugged the warm bird tightly against me and felt its heavy breathing. I caught my own breath and made my way to the mouth of the cave, really no more than a crack in the side of the mountain. I leaned forward and peered inside. A cool breeze from within lifted my hair. And then the vulture and I slipped into the cave, into the damp, timeless darkness of sandstone, where senses fail and prehistory is a whisper away.

She perched on a branch of balsam poplar above the
house, watching one of her chicks wobble unsteadily
on the thin sill of the attic's paneless window. He
rocked forward and back, wings partially unfurled,
half-flapping them to maintain his balance. Most
of the chick's feathers had grown in, although some
fluffy down still clung to his neck and shoulders.
The sunlight shone on his sleek gray face, slate-blue
eyes, and black hooked beak—quite a contrast to
her own red face, stony eyes, and white-tipped beak.
Her feathers gleamed iridescently in the sun; his were
a softer, velvety black.

   As the chick swayed unsteadily on the sill, he
cocked his head skyward when a blue jay flew through
the yard, calling. He listened to the rustling of the
wind in the aspen leaves, and he smelled the air, the
various scents of a late Saskatchewan summer filling
his nostrils—the marshy damp, something blooming,
faint mammalian rot. The sun was warm on his face
and his chest. She watched from the tree as he parted
his beak and panted in the summer heat.

   He wouldn't be able to spread his wings all the
way without bumping them against the sides of the
window, but as he turned sideways and stepped slowly

along the sill, he extended them both and flapped
hard, revealing more downy patches underneath and
nearly tumbling out into the world. Perhaps realizing
this, he hopped back inside the attic, into the safe
darkness. He thudded on the wooden floorboards,
and his brother hissed.

She looked away from the empty window, over
the tops of the aspens, poplars, and spruces, and
began to preen.

Wings and Prayers

People were jumping off the bridge. I didn't know it at first glance, but they were wearing harnesses attached to ropes, perhaps learning how to rappel. More than 400 feet below, the blue-green Colorado cut through red sandstone, the steep, sheer cliffs rising sharply from the edges of the river. I rested my elbows on the steel railing; to my right was the Navajo Reservation, from where we'd just come, and to my left—west —Arizona, and eventually the North Rim of the Grand Canyon. But between here and there lay our first destination: the 294,000-acre Vermilion Cliffs National Monument.

While backpackers and canyoneers know this region for the Paria Canyon Wilderness and Buckskin Gulch's spectacular slot canyons, bird enthusiasts know it for a different reason —as a release site of captive-bred California condors, one of the world's most endangered species and cousin of the turkey vulture. According to the Arizona Game and Fish Department, the Vermilion Cliffs were chosen as a release site because the remote habitat there matched what the condors needed: rugged cliffs with steep ledges and caves. The area surrounding the cliffs is classified as both "Great Basin Conifer Woodland," dominated by juniper trees and pinyon pines, and "Great Basin Desertscrub," featuring sweet-smelling sagebrush and rabbitbrush. Nature writer and activist Edward Abbey called this region "the slickrock desert. The red dust and the burnt cliffs and the lonely sky—all that which lies beyond the end of the roads."

Jesse and I made this trip west in the hopes that we'd glimpse some of the iconic birds, and we'd stopped here, at Navajo Bridge, which spans Marble Canyon, because we'd heard rumors that condors sometimes actually perch on the bridge itself, and then we'd watched a video on YouTube that proved it. We'd flown into Phoenix the previous evening, rented a car, and set out for the Vermilion Cliffs first thing in the morning. After briefly stopping for lunch in Flagstaff, we continued heading north, watching the landscape fade from desert to pine forest to scrub to sandstone cliffs. It was late afternoon when we pulled into the Visitors Center at Navajo Bridge; we hoped to visit the release site and find somewhere to camp before nightfall. We'd have to hurry. We watched another young man push himself off the bridge and into the air, and we scurried back to our rented compact, heading for the sun.

▼ My favorite nature writer has always been Edward Abbey. I can't remember the first time I read *Desert Solitaire*, but I must have been young, probably in high school. I found him inspiring, and his work prompted me to visit the American South-west whenever I got a chance, despite his warning in that book's introduction: "Do not jump into your automobile next June and rush out to the Canyon country hoping to see some of which I have attempted to evoke in these pages. In the first place you can't see *anything* from a car . . . walk, better yet crawl, on hands and knees, over the sandstone and through the thornbush and cactus."

I would have preferred walking, but in true American tourist fashion, we had places to see and limited time to get to them. House Rock Valley Road was unpaved and lonely, and our car kicked up quite a bit of dust as we headed for the condor view-ing area, about two miles from the turn into House Rock Val-ley. We skidded into the viewing area's empty parking lot and tumbled out into the windswept desert scrub. I tried unsuc-cessfully to tie my hair in a knot and finally gave up, allowing the warm wind to tangle it into knots of its own design. Across a vast, burnt, and sharp-looking field, red sandstone cliffs rose into an impossibly blue sky. The cliffs seemed fake, like an il-lusion, or like a movie set depicting the western desert. They were too huge, too angular, too orange, red, and salmon, the contrast with the sky too stark. Different strata were easily dis-cernable, like the layers of a cake. It was obvious why Abbey loved and defended this land.

The viewing area consisted of a shade shelter, a restroom, and informational signs, including one that compared the wingspan of a California condor with a golden eagle and red-tailed hawk; my "wingspan," only slightly larger than the golden eagle, fell several feet short of a condor's. I raised my binoculars and scanned the cliff's top edge for signs of life and regretted not having a spotting scope. Jesse did the same. Tears caused by the wind ran down my cheeks as I squinted and scanned.

"I think I see whitewash," Jesse ventured.

I panned to where he was looking. "Are those—those black things above the whitewash—are those condors?" I adjusted my binoculars' focus. "I think they are," I said, and switched from binoculars to camera. After snapping a few pictures, I viewed them on the back of the camera and was able to magnify closer and closer. The black blobs were definitely California condors, sitting on the cliffs. I counted three. Then I noticed two more on lower ledges. Jesse and I giggled like children. Locating, viewing, and photographing one of the world's rarest bird species seemed too easy—yet there they sat, perched like black gargoyles on the red crags.

Although we were too far to see the details of their plumage, California condors have dusty-black feathers. From beneath, the leading edges of the undersides of their wings are bright white, making it appear that the birds have thickly applied deodorant to their "armpits." Their wings are broad and tipped with long primary flight feathers, which extend like fingers from the ends of their wings. A California condor is North America's largest flying land bird, and its outstretched wings measure more than nine feet from tip to tip. They top the scales at twenty pounds, almost twice the mass of a golden eagle, a bird that the California condor interacts with—often unpleasantly—throughout its current range. The naked skin of a juvenile condor's head is a dull gray, but by age six or seven, a condor's face and neck become reddish orange and the hooked tip of its beak white. When a condor is excited, air sacs in its face and neck fill and create a puffy appearance, making the bird look swollen, almost as if it's suffering from the mumps. A ruff of spiky black feathers around the red-orange face completes an adult California condor's punk-rock appearance.

By the time Abbey published *Desert Solitaire* in 1968, there were few California condors soaring over the American West in search of carrion. The vulture Abbey often mentions and admires is our old friend the turkey vulture. He calls the turkey vulture the "master of soaring flight" who is "never in a hurry to get anywhere or do anything, an indolent and contemplative bird." But while turkey vultures may look unhurried, in reality they're probably searching for their next meal using their excellent eyesight and sense of smell. Despite being related to turkey vultures, biologists don't believe that California condors can find carrion by its odor. "The Condor," write Noel and Helen Snyder in their comprehensive book, *Introduction to the California Condor*, "is rarely the first scavenger to discover a carcass, and the species relies mainly on observing the activities of other scavengers such as Common Ravens (*Corvus corax*) and Turkey Vultures (*Cathartes aura*) to find food." Unfortunately for industrious ravens and turkey vultures, "once on the ground at or near a carcass, California Condors rarely hesitate in displacing smaller species." But for the past hundred or so years, until very recently, Arizona and Utah's turkey vultures, ravens, and eagles had carcasses mostly to themselves.

The story of the decline and subsequent recovery of the California condor is well known and has been thoroughly documented in books, news features, published reports, and websites. Many nonprofit, governmental, scientific, private, and zoological organizations make up the California Condor Recovery Program; they collaborate to breed, release, monitor, manage, and study these huge vultures, and include the Peregrine Fund, San Diego Wild Animal Park, the Los Angeles Zoo, the Ventana Wildlife Society, the National Park Service, the Oregon Zoo, the Bureau of Land Management, Arizona Game and Fish Department, the US Fish and Wildlife Service, and several others.

In 1987, the California condor was officially extinct in the wild when the last of twenty-two individuals was captured.

An intensive captive-breeding program was launched, and in 1992 the first group of captive-raised condors was released in Southern California. Unfortunately, the birds were recaptured in 1994 because of their penchant for hanging around humans and human-made structures. The program released another group in 1996, and established a second release site at the Vermilion Cliffs in the same year. In 1997 and 2002, respectively, two more release sites were added, at Big Sur in California and Baja California, Mexico. Today, almost three decades since the last surviving members of the species were captured, more than 400 California condors are alive, more than half of which live in the wild in Arizona, Utah, California, and Baja. Collectively, the California Condor Recovery Program partners spend more than $5 million annually on these efforts.

Six condors were released at the Vermilion Cliffs in late 1996, near the location where we viewed the birds; according to the Arizona Game and Fish Department, the release marked the first time California condors were flying free in the state in almost one hundred years. In 2013, seventy-six condors lived in the wild in Arizona (which meant that Jesse and I observed, at the same time, about 6.5 percent of the wild condors in that state). The birds are intensely managed and constantly monitored by biologists. Each bird wears a wing tag, not unlike the tags we placed on young turkey vultures, as well as a satellite transmitter. In between his work with golden eagles and turkey vultures, a rigorous academic schedule, and trips to Asia to study other birds of prey, Todd Katzner traveled to California in 2014 to assist with placing transmitters of his company's own design on several California condors. (I admit that the pictures of Todd up close and personal with the large birds made me very jealous!) In addition to tracking movements, data from the transmitters will be used to understand how the condors' flight behavior responds to weather and topography.

Todd described the condors as "big, exciting, and dramatic" —and while he isn't sure if there are enough wild condors yet to play a role ecologically, when I asked if the expensive and labor-intensive recovery efforts were worth it, he replied, "Absolutely."

The California condor capture and captive-breeding programs were criticized by some as futile efforts; it was a species with "one wing in the grave," a Pleistocene relic that should have disappeared with the mastodons and saber-toothed cats. But if that were true, why *didn't* California condors go extinct 10,000 years ago, along with most of the continent's large land animals? The answer could lie underwater. Like turkey vultures, California condors are obligate scavengers; no accounts of the huge birds taking live prey exist. As obligate scavengers, they cannot "create" their meals—they must wait for something appropriate to die. At the end of the Pleistocene, inland condors (along with other species of large avian scavengers) found themselves in a tight spot. The terrestrial megafauna they relied on—bison, horse, mammoth—were disappearing. However, the Pacific Ocean off the North American coast harbored an array of marine mammals—especially seals, sea lions, and large whales, including the blue whale, which is the largest animal ever to have lived. The authors of "Dietary Controls on Extinction versus Survival among Avian Megafauna in the Late Pleistocene," a paper published in the journal *Geology*, write, "The late Pleistocene extinction decimated terrestrial megafaunal communities in North America, but did not affect marine mammal populations. In coastal regions, marine megafauna may have provided a buffer that allowed some large predators or scavengers, such as California condors . . . to survive into the Holocene." Isotopic evidence from the fossils of Pleistocene-era California condors near the Pacific coast revealed that the birds fed on the marine carcasses as well as

Pleistocene land mammals. It made sense; a dead thirty-five-ton California gray whale washed up on a lonely beach, for example, would provide an opportunity for scores of scavengers, condors included.

In addition to California condor remains, the paper's authors analyzed the remains of the extinct Merriam's teratorn (*Teratornis merriami*) and the extinct Western black vulture (*Coragyps occidentalis*). The Merriam's teratorn, a giant with a twelve-foot wingspan who likely took live prey in addition to scavenging, was a common species discovered in the La Brea Tar Pits in Los Angeles. The Western black vulture was a larger version of today's black vulture; some scientists believe that it may be the same species or perhaps a subspecies. The researchers also analyzed the remains of bald and golden eagles, two species that survived the Pleistocene to thrive in the Holocene.

The study revealed that the scavengers who relied solely on terrestrial megafauna (the teratorn and Western black vulture) followed them into oblivion, while scavengers with a more varied diet of both terrestrial and marine megafauna—bald and golden eagles and California condors—escaped extinction. However, in regions of North America where California condors did not have access to marine mammals, the birds disappeared. Once ranging across the entire West and Southwest, and all the way east to Florida and even north to New York, the California condor's range shrank and shrank until, by the 1980s, it was restricted only to the California coastline, and its wild population had dwindled to just twenty-two birds. Those birds were captured, and the rest, as they say, is history.

Interestingly, the Snyders point out that "many more scavengers were able to survive the end of the Pleistocene in the Old World, especially in Africa, which did not experience the massive mammalian die-offs seen in the New World. The large grazing mammals that still occur in Africa today represent a basically intact Pleistocene fauna, and not surprisingly, there are now more than twice as many vulture species remaining in the Old World as in the New World." Had more of North America's megafauna survived, we might have had a richer vulture culture here today.

▼ After seeing the five California condors on the cliffs, Jesse and I continued on the deserted road toward what we hoped was somewhere to spend the night. Eventually, we found Stateline Campground, a cluster of rustic campsites on the Utah-Arizona border. Only one other site was occupied; we were delighted to have the place almost to ourselves. We pitched our small tent on the rocky red dust amid clusters of sweet-smelling sage. We tried to position it half in Utah and half in Arizona, but I'm not sure if we were successful. A blue-gray gnatcatcher serenaded us from a nearby juniper as we toasted Edward Abbey and watched a supernatural moon rise over the crimson cliffs. Whenever I visit the desert—"the center of the world, God's navel, Abbey's country, the red wasteland"—I wonder why I've always lived in the eastern United States. "There is *something* about the desert," writes Abbey. "There is something there which the mountains, no matter how grand and beautiful, lack; which the sea, no matter how shining and vast and old, does not have." I know what he means. I grew up in Pennsylvania, moved to West Virginia, then down to southern Virginia, and now back to West Virginia again. Our winters are harsh. Mold counts are high. Summers are humid. Here in the desert, I can breathe.

The next day we were up before dawn, which came crisp, cool, and windy. We drank bad instant coffee and burned the rest of our firewood, blinking groggily in the rising sun. We loaded our gear in the rental car and headed to the nearby Wire Pass trailhead. From there, we'd hike a few miles into Buckskin Gulch, reportedly the longest slot canyon in the world. Then we'd hike out and drive back south to Sedona (no condors there, but we had plans to meet family) and then the following day we'd travel north again to Grand Canyon National Park's South Rim to search for more condors.

Jesse and I hadn't been hiking on Wire Pass for long when a sandstone wall loomed before us. The trail headed straight into a crack in the cliff. Inside, the walls were orange, salmon, red, and pink, and they undulated in rocky waves, rising around us on both sides as we entered the canyon. Claustrophobia set in almost at once, and the sense that the walls could cave in and bury us was overwhelming. But as my feet pushed through the fine sand of the trail, and as I brushed my fingertips along the cool stone walls, I began to settle. It was breathtaking, like nothing I'd seen before. The path twisted through the rippling walls, red mud pooling in some spots, a tumble of rocks partially blocking our way in others. We climbed and scrambled a bit, but mostly we strolled, breathing in the smell of damp sandstone. Sunlight beamed through the narrow crack in the ceiling, high, high above us, illuminating certain walls and leaving others in shadow.

Water did this: water, sometimes violent and gushing, sometimes trickling and dripping, cut through this rock and left a canyon. Warnings posted at the trailhead and in the guidebooks instructed hikers and backpackers to check the weather before entering the slot canyon; flash floods were common. Of course, we hadn't checked the weather, and even though the sky above us seemed clear, a rainstorm miles away could cause a problem here. Jesse and I made light of the situation by taking thirty-second videos of each other pretending to run away from a flash flood. What would it sound like? Thunder, we imagined, distantly booming and then louder as the wall of water approached, carrying with it uprooted junipers, boulders, and unfortunate deer and bighorn sheep. Above us, white-throated swifts swirled and chittered, pausing to cling briefly to the canyon walls before swooping into the air again. We hadn't seen any other bird life since entering the slot canyon. I wondered: did California condors once nest here? Perhaps the walls were too narrow, too tight a space for a bulky condor to negotiate. We know they nested in the nearby Grand Canyon, which is not far away as the condor flies.

Our chances of seeing California condors at Grand Canyon National Park were quite good. As of this writing, five active condor nests were located in caves in the park and the Vermilion Cliffs, but during the Pleistocene there were many more. Analysis of fossilized condor remains from nest caves in the Grand Canyon revealed that until about 10,000 years ago, condors nesting there ate horse, bison, mammoth, and other large, now-extinct mammals; when the canyon's megafauna disappeared, so did the condors. In his 1987 study "Age and Diet of Fossil California Condors in Grand Canyon, Arizona," Steven Emslie warns, "Since condors could not survive in the canyon at the close of the Pleistocene, and when modern flora and faunal communities were gradually established by 8,500 [years before present], it is unlikely that it could survive there today unless supplemental food supplies are provided on a regular basis." While some food *is* supplied to the condors living in the Grand Canyon today, the birds living there during the Pleistocene did not have access to the same "human subsidies" that modern condors (and other vulture species) do. Today's condors may not have mammoths, but they do have dead cattle, sheep, and other livestock from the region's ranches and farms, in addition to mule deer and other unfortunate animals killed by "mechanized tourists," as Edward Abbey would call them, traveling the superhighways in their "metallic shells."

But, as is the case with turkey vultures, relying on human subsidies comes with a price—an often-deadly price. A 2012 study published in the *Journal of Wildlife Diseases*, "Patterns of Mortality in Free-Ranging California Condors (*Gymnogyps californianus*)," reports that "a total of 135 deaths occurred from October 1992 (the first post-release death) through December 2009, from a maximum population-at-risk of 352 birds, for a cumulative crude mortality rate of 38%." Of those 135 birds, "a definitive cause of death was determined for 76 of the 98 submitted cases." While a few birds died of "natural" causes (predation by coyotes, mountain lions, and a golden eagle; brush fires; and one rattlesnake bite), fifty-three of those seventy-six condors (70 percent) died because of anthropogenic—human—causes, some of which were the direct result of taking advantage of human subsidies.

A surprising number of condors died after eating inappropriate items, including bottle caps, broken glass, metal nuts and washers, rubber bits, Styrofoam, a Latex glove, and a rubber flip-flop. One condor, a six-year-old bird from the Arizona population, died after swallowing "8 pennies, 2 penny fragments, one dime, and one quarter"—forty-five cents. Parent birds bringing trash to their nests and feeding it to their babies "was the most important cause of death in this age class." Although "the reason(s) for this aberrant behavior remain open for speculation," authors of the study write that "one plausible hypothesis is that it reflects misdirected attempts to provide bone or mollusk shell fragments as a calcium source for nestlings." Other birds in the study were electrocuted after colliding with or attempting to land on power lines, and still others were killed intentionally by humans; at least three died of gunshot wounds and one died after being shot with an arrow.

After analyzing the range of natural and human-caused mortality for California condors, the study reached a significant conclusion: "The most important mortality factor for the combined free-ranging populations was lead toxicosis. . . . The evidence that the principal source of exposure was lead ammunition is overwhelming and includes the recovery of lead shotgun pellets and bullet fragments from the upper GI tract, . . . tissue lead isotopic signatures that match lead ammunition and not other sources of lead, . . . confirmed exposures from a pig carcass containing spent ammunition, . . . exposures coinciding with the hunting season and foraging activities in popular hunting areas, . . . the high prevalence of bullet fragments in hunter-killed carcasses and gut piles from field-dressed kills," as well as several other reasons. Lead ammunition is, so to speak, the smoking gun—and one of the world's most critically endangered birds may not be able to recover unless hunters switch to alternative ammunition, such as copper or steel. Although turkey vultures also suffer from lead toxicity, California condors, like bald eagles, are much less tolerant of the metal. Current literature suggests that thirty-three to sixty-five micrograms of lead can be fatal to a condor, which is "approximately 0.3–0.6% of the mass of a 9,700-mg rifle bullet. . . . When a rifle bullet fragments into a lead snowstorm, there may be more than 200 fragments of this size produced that remain within the carcass or viscera left in the field," according to a 2010 report published in the *Auk*.

Unfortunately for the condors, gun industry-supported groups have done their best to convince the public that an opposition to lead ammunition is an opposition to hunting; in reality, nothing could be further from the truth. Condors *need* carcasses that have been killed by large predators. And since saber-toothed cats, dire wolves, and American lions are gone, the dominant remaining predators are humans. Condors need human hunters to help them survive and thrive in this new era. This is supported by the 2010 paper "Status of the California

Condor (*Gymnogyps californianus*) and Efforts to Achieve Its Recovery," which states that "condor recovery cannot be achieved unless exposure to lead from ingesting ammunition fragments while feeding on carcasses and gut piles is eliminated," and the authors declare, in no uncertain terms, that "a reduction in hunting, depredation permits, or other types of shooting would not promote condor recovery." The authors admit that although "such actions might effectively reduce lead in the environment, . . . they would also result in a significant reduction in the condors' food supply. Humans are the dominant predators in most of the condor's range, and carcasses and gut piles resulting from hunting and other types of shooting are important food sources for condors." To further emphasize the point, the article states, "It is essential that humans continue to harvest deer, pigs, and other wildlife throughout the condor range —but using nonlead rather than lead ammunition." Sadly, this message is lost or ignored by some hunting groups. And California condors are paying the price with their lives.

I ran my hand along a cool sandstone wall again and wondered about the trend of mistrusting science that seems so prevalent these days. I'm not a religious person (although I certainly appreciate spirituality); I place my faith in evidence, hard facts, the peer-review process, and the scientific method. I've read the studies, most of which are readily available on the Internet, that prove California condors are poisoned by spent ammunition remaining in carcasses or offal left on the landscape. The case is closed. Or it should be. Perhaps Upton Sinclair's famous quote—"It is difficult to get a man to understand something, when his salary depends upon his not understanding it"—is applicable here, as it has been in the case of climate change. When particular industries see potential (and permanent) losses in earnings, they fight back with all the tools in their arsenal, hard facts and science notwithstanding. To an extent, I can understand their desire to protect their bottom lines. But what about us, the regular people, the consuming public? How have industries and their allies managed to convince us to believe *them* over scientific evidence? "Paranoia is a very effective educational tool," Keith Bildstein told me when we'd talked about this conundrum. "They teach people that this is the first incremental step to not only taking away your bullets but to taking away your guns. That's a tough nut to crack."

▼ I walked up to the black railing and wrapped both hands around its warm surface. Edward Abbey would be rolling in his grave. The area had been paved almost to the edge of this overlook. There were railings and stairs. I'd been to Grand Canyon National Park once before, back in 1999, and things had changed since then. Not the canyon itself, of course—I recognized the oft-photographed red, tan, and green sweeps and crags, the humbling vistas, and awe-inspiring sandstone. But now there were new parking lots, a large visitor center, and vending machines. Everything was very nice, of course, but some of the wildness and danger had been lost. Children shuffled around me, shouting and pointing, cameras clicked, and a couple nearby conversed in a language I didn't immediately recognize—not German but something vaguely similar. A sign along the railing warned people against throwing coins into the canyon because of the danger it posed to California condors. I thought of the condor that died after ingesting forty-five cents; I'd assumed the bird had collected coins that had fallen through a hole in someone's pocket or had been inadvertently dropped, but perhaps they had been intentionally tossed into the canyon—for good luck, I suppose, although it was decidedly unlucky for one poor bird.

We headed for Grand Canyon Village; we'd heard it was one

of the best places to view condors in the park, and we planned to listen to a ranger presentation on condors there later in the afternoon. In the meantime, we decided to leisurely hike Bright Angel Trail, a dusty path that we'd traversed years before when we'd backpacked all the way to the bottom of the canyon, camped one night, and hiked back out. I hadn't remembered it being quite so steep—perhaps my twenty-two-year-old self was more fit than my thirty-something self. Hikers coming all the way up from the bottom were easily discernable (by their sweat, dust, blood, and limping) from the day hikers near the rim. It felt strange to be part of this other, "softer" group—we had no packs, walking sticks, or water, just our binoculars and cameras. We stomped confidently down the dusty switchbacks.

An hour or so passed, and while we didn't see a condor, we met several friendly squirrels on the trail and were afforded great views of a black-throated gray warbler and canyon wren before we scrambled back up the steep trail to the Village. The condor presentation would begin soon, and we didn't want to be late. We sat cross-legged on the ground where a crowd of thirty or forty people had gathered. A ranger, complete with a wide-brimmed hat and neatly pressed uniform, smiled at newcomers and prepared to begin her lecture. We were a diverse crowd of children, adults, elderly couples, serious hikers, and those who appeared less serious; I was heartened to see so many tourists assembled to hear a talk about a vulture species.

As the ranger began her presentation, I adjusted my blue bandanna and listened to a discussion of the condor's natural history and the efforts to save the bird from extinction. As the presentation went on, I became aware of a man a few feet in front of me and to the left. Unlike most of the others, he was standing, and he kept shuffling his cowboy-booted feet. While everyone else seemed to be listening, smiling, nodding, and laughing at appropriate times, this man had his arms crossed in front of his chest and seemed to grow increasingly uncomfortable. Perhaps it was his jeans—they were tight, bordering on obscene, and when he turned to look over his shoulder, I noticed a large golden belt buckle glinting in the sun. His flannel shirt was neatly tucked into his waistband, and a camouflage ball cap was pulled tightly over his gray hair. He scowled. I soon realized I'd been paying more attention to the anxious man than the presentation. I considered asking him to sit down like everyone else, or at least move to the back so as not to obstruct anyone's view.

I shouldn't have been surprised when he interrupted the presentation. The ranger had been talking about condors dying from ingesting spent lead ammunition.

"You don't know it's from ammunition," he said suddenly, almost shouting. "They could get lead from somewhere else."

The ranger clearly expected this kind of response. "No, sir," she smiled, and added calmly, "They've done isotopic studies on the lead that proves the condors are eating spent ammunition—"

"They eat lead paint, too."

"Lead in ammunition has a different isotopic fingerprint from paint, and besides—"

"You just want to ban hunting," the man interrupted again.

Other audience members, clearly uncomfortable, murmured and frowned at the man. "Let her talk," someone called from the other side of the group.

Without losing her composure, the ranger kept smiling. "I encourage you to read the scientific studies. The lead comes from ammunition. Now, condors are captured regularly and monitored for lead toxicity, and they're brought into captivity and treated if necessary . . ."

The ranger continued talking and smiling, not to the man

but to the audience as a whole, and the man kept grumbling under his breath, something like, "You can do your studies and your studies and your studies," and then he abruptly turned and stalked away. The audience breathed a collective sigh of relief.

"Do you think he was a plant?" Jesse whispered. I nodded, then shrugged. The man had looked—and acted—like a stereotype. I wished he hadn't. I also wished the ranger had seized the opportunity to talk about the importance of hunters to the California condor's recovery. Perhaps it's wishful thinking at best or naïveté at worst, but condors need allies, and they need hunters—and this man could have been both. Instead, he chose to behave like a rude, ignorant bully. And that's the impression of him that folks in the audience took home. I kind of felt sorry for him, and I considered following him from the crowd to try to find out why he didn't believe the science, to tell him how our nation's largest, most dramatic, most iconic birds suffer and die from lead poisoning, and to plead with him to switch to copper or steel ammunition. I wanted to tell him how the condors *needed* human hunters, and how easy it would be for him to do his part to help save this critically endangered species from the finality of extinction.

Naïveté indeed. "If I had been as capable of trust as I am susceptible to fear," wrote Edward Abbey, "I might have learned something new or some truth so very old we have all forgotten it. . . . We are obliged, therefore, to spread the news, painful and bitter though it may be for some to hear, that all living things on earth are kindred." I gazed out at the impossibly large chasm behind the ranger, and hoped that a condor would come soaring up from its depths, manifesting from the canyon like a dream or a distant memory, like a mammoth or saber-toothed cat, back to walk among us once again.

*She circled higher and higher, sunward, letting the
warm air lift her above the southern boreal forest's
canopy. One of her chicks followed at some distance,
riding the same wind but still far below her. She
hadn't seen her other chick for a few days, and her
mate had begun to spend more and more time at the
aspen roost. As the days shortened, she began to feel
it—time to leave, soon. The sun already seemed to
slink lower on the horizon. Purple asters had begun to
bloom, the tiny flowers quivering in the warm breeze.
She tilted her wings and began heading for the roost;
a quick glance back told her that the younger chick
still followed.*

Rebirth

Macy stood at the edge of the highway, her dark hair whipping around her face. She squinted against the wind and the bright sun. The young turkey vulture felt the wind, too, and struggled, but Macy hugged the bird tightly against her body, its great wings held down by her arms. The bird swiveled its gray head from side to side.

Finally, after weeks in the outdoor enclosure and several conditioning sessions on a creance (think kite string), the vulture from the Claysville hayloft was ready to be released. Its fractured carpometacarpal bones had healed completely, and through exercise and physical therapy, the bird had regained full function of the injured wing. We contacted Doug Knox, but he hadn't seen the vultures around his farm for several weeks, so we decided to release the bird near a huge sycamore that also served as a vulture roost; I'd counted as many as thirty turkey vultures in the tree at one time, as well as several black vultures. The tree stood about a hundred feet from the highway, on the border of a cow pasture.

Macy, one of the Avian Conservation Center of Appalachia's most dedicated volunteers (and future avian veterinarian), had taken a particular liking to this vulture. She'd assisted with physiotherapy and creance exercise, so it seemed appropriate for her to release the bird. We stood outside our car and waited for the wind to die down. Although the highway had four lanes, it connected Morgantown, West Virginia, with Uniontown, Pennsylvania, and was lightly used; a busier road would be a dangerous place to release any bird. We nodded to Macy, and she took a deep breath and gently tossed the bird skyward. This was the vulture's first free flight. It flapped hesitantly, its blue Hawk Mountain wing tag #284 obvious in the bright sunshine. The bird tottered a bit in the wind like an awkward kite, then straightened out, fixed its wings, and caught the breeze. We hoped it would head for the sycamore, but of course the vulture bypassed the tree and kept going, finally landing on the ground in the pasture several hundred yards beyond the tree. When we returned to check on the bird a few hours later, we couldn't find it; a few black vultures were hanging around near the sycamore, and several turkey vultures floated overhead, but our young bird wasn't among them. We hoped for the best, for a wild life free on the wing: keep calm and carrion, friend.

The ACCA admits turkey vultures suffering from a variety of injuries, most the result of interactions with humans. The mystery of the Claysville vulture's fall is unique; the causes of other injuries are more obvious: hit by vehicle, gunshot, caught in trap, lead toxicity. The "mysterious" injuries typically involve young vultures. In addition to the Claysville bird, we treated another pre-fledgling vulture during the same season, this one pulled from a creek in Lost River State Park. The bird's black feathers had mostly grown in, but its head and neck were still covered in fluffy white down. The poor vulture could barely breathe; it came in limp and gasping for air. After rehydrating with subcutaneous fluids and B vitamins, we placed it in an oxygen tent in one of the animal hospital's surgery suites. The bird immediately began breathing more easily, although its black chest still rose and fell more rapidly than normal. Through the clear plastic walls of the oxygen tent, the vulture watched us with calm, steel-blue eyes. We dimmed the lights and left for the evening; at some point in the wee hours of the morning, a veterinary technician peeked in to check on the patient and discovered that the young vulture had passed away.

In the morning Jesse performed a postmortem exam, cutting into the dead bird's chest and abdomen. The smell was nauseating; the vulture's lungs were filled with thick, cheese-like pus, its air sacs rotten with infection. Was this the result of spending time in chilly water? How had it ended up in the creek? Could it be that both of the bird's parents had disappeared and the bird left the nest out of desperation and hunger? Or perhaps at some point it had regurgitated out of fear and inhaled the vomit into its trachea, where it putrefied throughout its respiratory system. Whatever the case, from the state of the vulture's organs it appeared that nothing we could have done would have saved its life—a sad end for a bird that could have lived for twenty or more years.

Around the same time that we admitted the Claysville bird, we'd admitted still another turkey vulture, this one an adult with soft-tissue injuries. Having both vultures at the ACCA at the same time allowed us to observe their different behavioral patterns, physical characteristics, and "personalities." Whereas the young Claysville vulture had sort of a spastic, frantic attitude, vomiting and explosively leaping when we got too close, the older vulture seemed less afraid. It still hissed lowly when someone drew near, but it didn't vomit and behaved less aggressively in general. While I loved both vultures, of course, something about the older one touched my heart —the look in its eye, the careful way it ate its food, the sly, around-the-shoulder way it looked at me. Perhaps with age comes wisdom, or maybe the young vulture's early session of sampling and measuring had firmly cemented a wariness of humans. The baby was a very wild bird.

Other turkey vultures we treat vary from docile—never hissing, stomping, or vomiting, moving timidly around their enclosures, soundless and calm—to terrified and defensive, sometimes lunging at us with open beaks, hissing menacingly. But without exception, all seem curious, intelligent, and infused with a strong will to live despite the odds—unlike, for example, a sharp-shinned hawk, a bird that seems to wait for any excuse to die, even anesthesia, a wing wrap, a cage, and so on. Turkey vultures look *at* you, *into* you—they meet your gaze. Folks who rescue or work with the species notice this, too; nearly everyone who has transported, rehabilitated, or trained a turkey vulture comes away with a new appreciation for these unsung birds.

▼ She wasn't sure, she said, her voice breaking, if she'd just bumped the bird with her car, or if she'd run it over. *Please let me know how he does*, she requested, and wrote down two phone numbers and an e-mail address. The sun was about to set, and the turkey vulture had been eating something in the road; she hadn't been able to slow down in time for it to fly away. She covered her mouth with her hand, bent her head, and turned and hurried out of the clinic.

The injured vulture couldn't stand. Its pale legs dangled uselessly as Jesse cradled the bird and carried it back to an exam table. It also seemed to have trouble flapping its wings. But the vulture's stone-colored eyes were bright in its red head; warty gray bumps rose around its wide nostrils and hooked beak. The bird swiveled its head from side to side, hissing, blinking under the animal hospital's bright fluorescents. As Jesse began to palpate the vulture's wings and torso, it vomited its last meal, a stringy, red-brown blob, some of which landed on the screen of Jesse's smartphone. Normally, vulture vomit would be met with disgust and a touch of anger, but not tonight. We knew that this bird would likely be dead within the hour. We would allow it this last defense.

Jesse took the vulture into the X-ray room and emerged a few minutes later, shaking his head and frowning. As expected, the bird's back was broken. Although he couldn't tell for sure, Jesse suspected that the spinal cord had been severed, and there was nothing he could do—nothing anyone could do—to repair the damage. He squeezed several of the vulture's toes with a hemostat to check for deep pain, but the bird didn't flinch. The vulture would never stand again, would never feel a warm column of air under its great wings, would never incubate an egg or feed a chick.

Jesse slipped a cone-shaped plastic mask over the bird's head; the vulture struggled and nipped at the mask. "I'm sorry, buddy," he said softly, and dialed up the isoflurane. The vulture's impeccably feathered chest rose and fell, and in a moment, it relaxed, grew limp. Jesse gently arranged the sleeping bird on the surgery table, smoothing its feathers and straightening its neck. He drew a syringe of pink euthanasia solution and extended one of the huge wings. Jesse lowered his head, found a vein, and a moment later, the vulture's breath stilled; its spirit was gone.

Gone, but the vulture's work on this mortal plane was not quite finished. Jesse pushed the stethoscope's bell into the vulture's chest, turned, and dialed off the iso. He removed the mask from the bird's face. In his poem "Hurt Hawks," Robinson Jeffers writes that he'd "sooner, except the penalties, kill a man than a hawk." I feel the same way about most birds. The decision to euthanize always hurts my heart, although often it's the kindest choice. The dead vulture had become a feather duster, relaxed and diminished. Jesse turned his attention to the bird's tail; he spread the feathers, examined them, and then, using large pair of dog nail clippers, he cut each feather close to the bird's body. Jesse removed all the tail feathers and most of the long flight feathers. When he finished, he carefully arranged them, in order, and fixed the ends of the shafts to a long strip of surgical tape. He again smoothed the feathers, running his fingers down their soft, silken edges.

While it always feels mercenary and a little creepy to "harvest" feathers from a still-warm, deceased bird, the feathers give another bird a chance to have its life back—a chance to return to the skies. Despites our best efforts, injured birds that require weeks or months of rehabilitation often break or damage their long tail or flight feathers. Because these feathers can take months to regrow, broken feathers can mean a longer stay in our rehabilitation center. And when new feathers finally do grow back, a bird may immediately re-break them on the sides, door, or perches of its enclosure. While birds in our care are typically fitted with tail guards—custom-made envelopes fashioned from X-ray film, carefully taped over a bird's tail feathers—it's nearly impossible to keep one on a turkey vulture. Vultures usually have their tail guards off in a matter of seconds.

An alternative to waiting until a bird molts and grows new feathers is a surgical procedure called *imping*. A live bird with broken feathers is placed under anesthesia, and its broken feathers are clipped off close to its body. Then, the shafts of the dead bird's plucked feathers are glued into the shafts of the live bird. Bamboo splints can be used to help stabilize the shafts. When the glue dries and all the broken feathers are replaced, the bird wakes up with new, intact feathers. We usually wait a day or two, and then we fly the bird on a creance to evaluate feather placement before releasing it back to the wild. In addition to giving injured birds their freedom weeks or months sooner, the imping process also returns a dead bird's feathers to the sky, at least until the living bird molts normally and sheds them—a kind of rebirth for both birds.

▼ We'd received a call about an injured vulture when I was seven months pregnant. On the phone, I'd tried to convince the finder to shoo the bird into a box, but he was afraid to get too close. Two other volunteers and I made the two-hour drive to Clay County, West Virginia, to rescue the downed bird. When we arrived at the finder's house—all of us young women and one of us obviously pregnant—his surprise (and perhaps embarrassment) was obvious. I'd stuffed a pair of heavy leather gloves under my arm and followed the elderly gentleman through his yard, which bordered West Virginia's Elk River. The other volunteers carried a large cardboard box and a bath towel. Despite being aided by a cane, the man stepped along quickly as he complained about the difficulty he'd had finding someone to help the injured vulture.

"The officer I talked to said he was too busy to come, but when I asked if I could shoot the bird and put it out of its misery, he told me they'd fine me five hundred dollars. I've been watching the poor thing suffer for three days."

"Next time," I said, smiling, "tell them you found an eagle."

"Sure," the man laughed, "we're just old folks and don't know the difference."

A red-eyed vireo called from an ancient sycamore along the bank, and an Eastern wood-pewee sang his plaintive song from across the river. Sweat trickled down my neck despite the late spring breeze. A small pack of dogs—a Lab mix, a boxer, a husky puppy, and a few others—trotted along beside us. The dogs had been first to find the vulture three days earlier but had kept their distance. Now, they slowed and sniffed the air.

"He was right around here," the man said, pointing with his cane into a tangle of thick jewelweed and saplings.

I scanned the dense green for movement. And then I heard flies buzzing.

"I see him," one of the volunteers said from behind me. "I think he's in a trap."

I frowned, we both stooped forward, parting the brush with our hands, and in a moment I saw the bird, too. It was lying down, half on its side, half on its keel, a cloud of flies swarming around its body. The vulture turned its head toward us, hooked beak open and gaping, tongue dry. Its face, normally scarlet, appeared pale, a sign of dehydration and low blood pressure. The vulture's stony eyes seemed desperate. I pulled the heavy gloves over my hands and forearms. When I leaned closer, the bird struggled briefly, attempting to stand and flap its huge brown-black wings.

I expected a wrestling match, but the turkey vulture was so weak I had no trouble reaching down and scooping it up; with a hand on each side of its body, I held down its wings and lifted it off the ground. The rusted, heavy trap dangled from its left foot, and I could see that the trap's jaws had almost severed the vulture's middle toe. The foot was swollen to twice its normal size. A volunteer grabbed the trap and began to work on prying it open; after several unsuccessful attempts, we lowered the bird and trap back to the ground, and she stepped on the trap, releasing the jaws. The suffering vulture was finally free.

I lifted the bird again and prepared to put it into the cardboard box. For a moment, I held the vulture against my body, and I could feel its labored breathing. Could my unborn daughter feel it, too? I imagined them hearing each other's hearts beating, and both quickening.

▼ While I don't have a scientific study to support my claim, anecdotally I know that turkey vultures are smart birds. In captivity, individuals of intelligent bird species will sometimes self-mutilate—parrots and crows pluck or chew their feathers, or scream incessantly, for example. An adult female turkey vulture in our care exhibited this behavior as well. (The only accurate way to determine the sex of a turkey vulture is through DNA blood testing—when we sent a blood sample to a laboratory to test for lead, we had them run a DNA test as well.)

The female vulture had been found down in a field, lethargic and unable to fly. Radiographs revealed shotgun pellets sprinkled throughout her body, lodged in muscle and soft tissue. Surprisingly, none of the pellets had broken any bones, and we'd anticipated that she'd make a full recovery once the wounds healed. We administered a course of antibiotics and pain medication as well as treating the wounds topically. Things progressed well for a few days; the vulture hung near the back of a small enclosure, head often bowed, but she had an excellent appetite and would hiss lowly at us when we approached with food. One day, I entered the ACCA to find blood splattered on the floor in front of the vulture's enclosure. The white plastic inner walls were also sprinkled with blood drops, although the bird cowered in the back corner as usual. I brought her a dead mouse and was able to convince her to turn around, which allowed me to see a fresh puncture wound on her chest; rich, red blood seeped down the vulture's black breast feathers.

Immediately I assumed she'd injured herself somehow in the cage; however, our ICU enclosures were top-of-the-line, hard-plastic banks of cages that lacked sharp edges. I looked for something else to blame. In the enclosure next to the vulture, a large first-year red-tailed hawk perched calmly in the center of the cage, watching me with blue-green eyes that hadn't yet darkened. Had the hawk somehow reached through the bars of its door and sunken its talons into the vulture's chest? Opportunistic hunters, red-tails will attempt to catch prey as varied as squirrels, snakes, crayfish, pigeons, and almost anything else they can get their talons on. But a turkey vulture? It didn't seem right. And the more I thought about it, I didn't believe that the red-tail could bend its legs and talons in such a way that it could grab the vulture, even if it had wanted to. I squatted in front of the vulture again. The bird swallowed her mouse whole and stared at me, perhaps waiting for another treat. That's when I noticed it—bright-red blood on the end of her beak. Since she'd swallowed the mouse, I knew the blood wasn't from her recent meal. And volunteers had last fed her almost twenty-four hours earlier. The blood was hers.

I pulled on a pair of heavy leather gloves, awkwardly scooped her out of the cage, and carried her down the hill to the veterinary clinic. An exam revealed one deep puncture wound and several smaller wounds. We treated her, started another course of antibiotics and pain meds, and moved her to a larger, outdoor enclosure. We hoped the change of scenery would help her psychologically. We also gave her toys to provide enrichment—a phonebook, a miniature rubber tire attached to a rope, pine boughs, and eventually an entire cut pine tree. We stuffed dead mice into a Kong dog toy as well as rubber "holey" balls; we thought she'd have to work to figure them out, but she'd removed the mice in seconds. We weren't sure if this vulture would end up to be releasable or not—but if not, we couldn't commit her to a life in captivity if she continued to self-mutilate. We would have to wait for her to heal, both physically and mentally.

▼ Some of the saddest cases involve vultures suffering from lead toxicity. One of our patients, a young bird still gray in the face, suffered from severe lead poisoning in addition to a badly broken wing. We suspected a collision with a vehicle caused the wing injury, and then the bird likely wandered on the ground, flightless, until it found a deer carcass or gut pile. It would have wolfed down the meal, not realizing it had ingested tiny pieces of lead. Soon, it would stagger and have difficulty breathing. Unable to fly, flee, or even walk, the vulture was completely vulnerable. Somehow, it made it to an open shed behind a house; the shed's owner called us, and a volunteer shuttled the bird to the ACCA.

While turkey vultures seem to be more tolerant of lead than condors or eagles, even relatively low levels of lead exposure can cause clinical signs. "Mild" symptoms in turkey vultures can include lethargy, weakness, and loss of appetite. Because these signs can mimic head trauma, we test the blood of every vulture we admit for lead toxicity. It was heartbreaking to watch the young vulture, to see how quiet and lethargic it was, how it wouldn't eat—not even rat hearts and livers, not day-old chicks. I held the bird while Jesse gave calcium EDTA shots in its chest. I sat cross-legged on the floor next to its cage and worried, while the bird's head drooped lower and lower. After a day or two it could no longer stand; I gently lifted its body, slid a carpet square underneath it, and propped the bird up with a rolled bath towel. I feared that this vulture's baby-gray face would never blaze red, that it would never see its first spring. Despite our efforts, the vulture died one evening a few days after admission, its body and head still pillowed by the soft towel.

▼ A small crowd had gathered on the overlook at Cooper's Rock State Forest. Children, dogs, folks with binoculars, and a news crew pressed against the rocky outcrop's wooden railing. Far below, the Cheat River wound between the mountains. My two-week-old daughter slept in her basket next to me, a gauzy blanket pulled up to her chin despite the early September heat. Although conventional wisdom suggests that newborns stay at home for the first month or two of life, it seemed important for her to be here. On this day—the little-known celebration of International Vulture Awareness Day—we would be releasing the turkey vulture that we'd rescued from the trap.

After several months and two surgeries, the bird had made a full recovery, but at first we'd thought the vulture would die. In addition to the injuries to its foot, the bird had open sores on its chest from where it had lain on the ground for days. The sores had been filled with maggots. We'd anesthetized the bird, flushed the sores, and then painstakingly plucked out the stubborn larvae with hemostats and tweezers. I had never seen so many maggots in one place before; there may have been thousands. I can still smell the sour, rotten odor and see their writhing white bodies. We drowned them and washed them into the drain. The maggots were also part of the circle of life, turning decaying flesh into food, and in this case probably prevented further infection. The vulture survived.

And now, the bird stomped its foot and hissed lowly from inside the large pet carrier. It also wore a blue tag on its right wing, emblazoned with #254. Soon a few speeches would be made, the carrier opened, and then—fingers crossed—the turkey vulture would soar from the overlook and return to its wild life.

I crouched down next to my daughter. Her eyelids, violet and delicate, were closed over her bright-blue eyes. A thin coating of auburn hair covered her head. Her round cheeks hadn't filled out yet; she still had the dark, ruddy look of someone just born. Fragile and tiny yet unafraid, blissful, and trusting. Despite the hum of conversation from the crowd, she kept sleeping. She slept when women bent over her and smiled, she slept when dogs pushed their noses against her feet, and she kept sleeping when the newspaper's photographer snapped a few pictures of her. I pulled down the blanket a bit to reveal the message printed across the chest of her onesie: "I ♥ Vultures."

I began to sweat in the hazy afternoon heat; the gentlest of breezes moved across the overlook, and three or four turkey vultures floated just beyond the outcrop, buoyed by thermals rising from the deep valley. Jesse swung open the carrier's door and we held our breath.

From inside, the vulture hissed and stomped but did not emerge. Jesse reached in and pulled the reluctant bird from the carrier. He counted to three then tossed the vulture skyward. The crowd gasped, the vulture dipped, hung in the air a moment, then unfurled its great wings. A few flaps and we were left behind. It became a shallow V, cruising south along the river, and then disappeared. Made new again, the vulture will in turn create life from death: resurrections, new beginnings. The crowd cheered. The baby stirred.

▼ Not all of the vultures we admit end up dying or being released. Occasionally, one may demonstrate a temperament or "personality" appropriate for permanent captivity. While I wish all injured birds could fly free again, seeing a turkey vulture up close invites people to appreciate them. A non-releasable turkey vulture could become a spokesbird for the spokesbirds—an ambassador for its species, which is in turn an ambassador for vultures worldwide. A vulture I'd fallen in love with—the sad, sunken-eyed bird with the bum shoulder and injured leg—would never return to the wild. But before any permanent decisions could be made about this bird's fate, the injuries would need to heal. A DNA test revealed that this vulture was male; I began to call him "Lew," in honor of Beat poet Lew Welch, who penned "Song of the Turkey Buzzard," and also for Lewis County, where he'd been hit by a vehicle.

The bird spent about a month in a small indoor enclosure; for the first two weeks, his shoulder and injured leg were bandaged. We left the leg wrapped for an additional two weeks after the wing wrap was removed. The bird seemed calm, almost shy, turning his back to me when I'd approach, hunching his brown-black shoulders and peeking around his body at me. He had a ravenous appetite; after his initial coyness, if the vulture noticed meat in my hand, he'd turn slowly and take a cautious step or two in my direction. I'd leave the food near the door, and as soon as I'd pull my hand away, the bird would stretch his long neck to the pile and rapidly snap down his meal. Because of his leg injury we'd been cutting his food into bite-sized pieces; vultures use their toenails to hold carcasses in place, allowing them to tear chunks with their sharp beaks. Jesse didn't want him to strain his injured leg, so each day the volunteers minced mice, a rat, chicks, or quail, often leaving them in a small bowl just inside the enclosure's door.

We also changed the vulture's water daily. While most raptors can get their required moisture from the blood and organs of the animals they eat, turkey vultures drink and seem to enjoy bathing, and the same held true for this bird. Once his bandages were removed, he watched as we approached with a dish of fresh, cool water, and his whole body actually trembled. The vulture shuffled over to the dish, roused his feathers, and lowered his chest into the water. He splashed his chest up and down while shaking his wings, perhaps attempting to get more of his feathers wet. Except for his red, naked head—which flushed deep red with excitement—the bathing vulture looked a lot like a duck.

When the vulture was well enough to be moved outside, I scooped him up and carried him into the sunshine. The new enclosure wasn't huge, but it afforded the bird ample space to spread and flap his wings, move around on the ground, bathe comfortably, and spend time in (or out) of the rain or sun. His wing still drooped from the injured shoulder—irreparably damaged, according to Jesse—but the vulture seemed able to use it enough to maneuver around the enclosure. I arranged several rocks, a turf-wrapped six-by-six, and a large angled branch to create "stairs" to allow the bird to reach the highest perch. But for the first week or so, he walked back and forth across the six-by-six and appeared content there, near the ground. I never saw him attempt to use the stairs or to fly up to the high perch. Perhaps his shoulder injury was worse than we'd thought, and even a life as an education ambassador would be too stressful for the unflighted bird. Then one morning I approached the enclosure to find him perched quietly in the center of the highest perch. When he saw me he stomped his foot and hissed lowly, then cocked his head to look at my hand—perhaps wondering if it concealed a mouse or chick for him.

Satisfied that the vulture's permanent injuries would allow him to reach all of the perches and weren't causing him pain, I began to think seriously about his future. His calm personality hadn't changed since admission, and he hadn't shown any signs of aggression, self-mutilation, or excessive stress. Keeping a non-releasable bird to use for educational purposes required an additional federal permit, and I began the necessary paperwork; it would take me a while to complete, and if something changed with the bird before I submitted the forms, I would reconsider. In the meantime, I began to spend time with him, sitting cross-legged in the corner of the enclosure, just allowing him to do his thing, while becoming accustomed to my presence. I wanted him to know I wasn't dangerous.

Whenever I entered the enclosure I made sure to bring a few dead mice in my pockets, so not only would he know I wasn't a threat, but he'd associate me with food as well. I'd enter the enclosure, lay a mouse on the six-by-six, and sit down on the floor with my back against the wall. The vulture would peer at the mouse for a few moments, then cautiously make his way toward it, snap it in his beak, and drag it to the back of the enclosure. He'd deftly arrange the mouse belly-up, hook a toenail on the skin of its abdomen, and slice it open with his beak. He'd pull off the head and swallow it. Then, using his sharp bill like a lobster fork, he'd reach in and remove all of the organs before finally gulping down the remaining skin. Satisfied for a moment, the vulture would smack his beak a few times and "feak," or rub the sides of his mouth and face along a perch to clean off any remaining entrails. He was a remarkably clean and efficient eater—a gourmand, an epicure. Once one mouse had been devoured, the bird would look back toward the six-by-six, then to me, in search of another. Perhaps a partnership—even a friendship—was in our future.

The September sun warmed her back and outstretched wings. High clouds flew overhead in the clear blue sky. She heard a rustle below and cocked her head toward the ground. A doe leaped from between the trees, froze, swiveled her ears. A moment later she leaped again and disappeared, just as a buck emerged from the brush nearby. He sniffed the air and followed, purposefully. High in a tree above the deer, she lifted her head and gazed back across the tops of the trees, stretched each leg behind her one at a time, then roused, loosing a small cloud of her own. A quick preen, and she stepped off the branch, pumping her wings twice, three times, before catching the warm column of air. She fixed her gaze on the horizon and didn't look back.

Lew the turkey vulture peeks out from his shelter box at the ACCA.

Adult turkey vultures have mostly featherless red heads and bone-white beak tips.

A turkey vulture chick is removed from its nest in Pennsylvania for biological sampling and wing tagging.

Turkey vulture chicks toddle around their nest in a Pennsylvania hayloft.

Turkey vultures may sit with their wings spread to thermoregulate or to dry their feathers.

A turkey vulture stretches before taking flight at Boyce Thompson Arboretum State Park near Superior, Arizona.

Vultures roost together at dusk near Asheville, North Carolina.

Turkey vultures crowd a sycamore tree in southwest Pennsylvania.

Social black vultures rest and preen together in Myakka River State Park near Sarasota, Florida.

Black vultures make use of human subsidies at Myakka River State Park near Sarasota, Florida.

Turkey vultures roost in a pine tree near Jacksonville, Florida.

A turkey vulture cruises above Boyce Thompson Arboretum State Park near Superior, Arizona.

Turkey vultures kettle over Gila Bend High School, Gila Bend, Arizona.

Maverick the black vulture cannot return to the wild because of injuries sustained after being hit by a car.

A curious black vulture wanders close to a parking lot in Myakka River State Park near Sarasota, Florida.

From below, turkey vultures in flight appear to have "silver linings."

A turkey vulture near Jacksonville, Florida, finds a meal.

The official Buzzard Scoreboard at the Buzzard Roost in Hinckley, Ohio.

Katie Fallon sits in the opening of a cave that holds a turkey vulture nest near the Meadowcroft Rockshelter in Avella, Pennsylvania.
Photo: Jesse Fallon

A sign at the Vermilion Cliffs National Monument in Arizona compares the wingspans of the California condor, golden eagle, and red-tailed hawk.

Jesse Fallon checks wing-tag placement before returning this turkey vulture chick to its nest.

An ACCA volunteer prepares to release a rehabilitated turkey vulture near Morgantown, West Virginia.

A rehabilitated turkey vulture wearing a transmitter prepares to return to the wild.

Katie Fallon feeds Lew the turkey vulture. Photo: Jesse Fallon.

Hill of the Sacred Eagles

There were no eagles at Thirukalukundram's Eagle Temple. The famous pair of large white birds vanished years ago and hasn't returned. They were not, in fact, eagles, but Egyptian vultures, *Neophron percnopterus*, scavengers that soar on five-and-a-half-foot wings above dry landscapes from southern Europe to central Africa. Their featherless yellow heads, punctuated by a long beak with a sharp black tip, are enscarved by ruffs of pointy white feathers, contributing to the vulture's chicken-like appearance when not in flight. In fact, the Egyptian vulture is sometimes called the "pharaoh's chicken," and until the mid-1990s they were common throughout India, including the coastal region of Tamil Nadu that Jesse and I were currently visiting, halfway between Chennai and Pondicherry. The vultures once nested here, on the rocky peaks above the town of Thirukalukundram, and each day at noon they would swoop down to be fed by the temple's priests.

According to a local legend, several *rishis*, or Hindu sages, demanded to be reincarnated as gods. This request angered Shiva, who instead turned them into eagles; they could only be freed from this form by devoutly worshipping him. The Egyptian vultures that visited the temple daily were believed to be the eagles of the legend, coming down to pay homage to Shiva. When the town's beloved vultures disappeared, the priests believed it was a bad omen.

After lighting five clay *diya* candles before a Ganesh *murti* —a black granite statue of the many-armed, elephant-headed deity housed in a nook behind a locked gate—I left my hiking boots in the care of a round woman in a blue sari and began climbing the 565 stone stairs to Vedagiriswarar (as the Eagle Temple is officially known). The late-morning sun baked the slabs beneath my bare feet; I cuffed my jeans and aimed for patches of shade along the stone walls that bordered the wide staircase. In the center of each stair's riser, a yellow swath of paint with nine red dots ran along the nosing. Gnarled trees and shrubs shouldered up to the walls, crows croaking from the leafy branches. After only a few steps my legs began to ache; I tried sidestepping, but then I took a hint from an orange-saried woman and zigzagged my way up the stairs.

Soon I reached a landing, complete with a bench under the shade of a square cement roof held aloft by white pillars. A crumpled form slouched on the ground against a wall; the elderly man wore a pale-pink shirt and a short white dhoti, a wraparound cloth skirt, tied at the waist. When I drew near, he reached one of his wrinkled hands toward me and with the other, he gestured toward his bare, kindling-thin legs, which extended uselessly in front of him. I passed him a ten-rupee note and continued up the stairs, trying to wrest my eyes from his skeletal appendages. Although "wild" polio had been declared eradicated in India in 2014, from 50,000 to 150,000 people contracted the crippling disease annually until the mid-1990s. As I climbed I felt guilty. I should have given him more. A dozen steps later, I stopped to catch my breath and lifted my eyes to the hazy blue sky. Not surprisingly, no Egyptian vultures circled overhead. Neither did any Indian vultures, slender-billed vultures, or red-headed vultures. The white-rumped vulture—*Gyps bengalensis*, also known as the Oriental white-backed vulture, once the most abundant large bird of prey on the planet—was also conspicuously absent from the skies above Thirukalukundram. The International Union for the Conservation of Nature (IUCN) has included each of these vultures on its Red List of Threatened Species; the Indian (*Gyps indicus*), slender-billed (*Gyps tenuirostris*), red-headed (*Sarcogyps calvus*), and white-rumped are "critically endangered," and the Egyptian vulture is simply "endangered."

In the mid-1990s, naturalists in India began to notice an abundance of vulture carcasses along roadsides, hanging from trees, and below roosting sites. Three to five times heavier than a turkey vulture, the white-rumped vulture can weigh more than fifteen pounds and sports a six- to seven-foot wingspan. It plunges its strong silver beak and long, almost serpentine neck into the carcasses of domestic livestock, especially cows. Indians rely on their vultures to clear the landscape of dead cattle; because the majority of Hindus do not eat cows, which are regarded as sacred, when the animals die their hides are taken but the rest is left. The Bombay Natural History Society claims that a flock of vultures could "reduce an adult cow carcass to bare bones within an hour." But fewer and fewer vultures showed up at cattle dump sites, creating a public health crisis. By the early 2000s, most of India's vultures had disappeared; white-rumped vultures suffered a 99 percent population decline. While the Egyptian vulture's population collapse does not appear as drastic as the white-rump's, the IUCN estimates that "the species has undergone a catastrophic decline (>35% per year) since 1999 in India," and now "just a few thousand pairs" remain.

In 2004, researchers, including the late veterinary pathologist Dr. Lindsay Oaks, discovered the primary (and perhaps the only) cause of India's vulture decline: a widely used veterinary non-steroidal anti-inflammatory drug called diclofenac. This effective drug is used to treat a variety of bovine ailments, from pain and swelling to fever. Unfortunately, when a vulture consumes a dead animal that had recently been treated with a standard veterinary dose of diclofenac, the vulture suffers kidney failure and dies within a few days. The governments of India, Pakistan, and Nepal acted quickly, banning the manufacture of the drug in 2006; however, it still remains on many veterinarians' shelves. While diclofenac has not yet been established as the smoking-gun cause of the decline in red-headed or Egyptian vultures (as it has been in white-rumped, Indian, and slender-billed vultures), researchers believe that "the geographic extent and rate of declines are very similar" to the declines in India's other vulture species; there is, therefore, "a real and alarming possibility that diclofenac is affecting populations of these species and other scavenging raptors across the Indian subcontinent." Four captive-breeding facilities, as well as "vulture restaurants" that supply wild birds with clean carcasses, have been working to slow and reverse the vulture decline. The first cohort of white-rumped, slender-billed, and Indian captive-bred vultures are slated for release soon; only time will tell if these efforts will be successful.

The sudden loss of India's most ubiquitous birds has had a dramatic effect on the day-to-day lives of its human residents. An absence of large scavenging raptors can be linked to an increase in human and animal diseases as well as the contamination of water and soil. Without the vultures to dispose of dead livestock, feral dogs descend on the carcasses, increasing the risk of rabies. The majority of the world's rabies cases come from India (more than 20,000 human cases per year) and more than 95 percent of those are caused by dog bites. Researchers from the UK's University of Bath and India's Institute of Economic Growth estimate that the absence of the large birds has resulted in 38.5 million *more* dog bites, causing an additional 47,300 deaths from rabies, which cost the Indian economy $34 billion.

While North America doesn't share India's problems with rabies and feral dogs, a dramatic decline in our largest common scavenging raptor—the turkey vulture, of course—could also cause public health problems. Turkey vultures remove and neutralize dangerous pathogens such as anthrax and botulism toxin, and they clean up carcasses before they foul the water, air, and soil. Recognizing the importance of common, taken-for-granted species such as the turkey vulture will allow us to understand how to help the species recover in the case of an unforeseen catastrophe. Although it's difficult to imagine an unknown force suddenly killing all of our turkey vultures, it would have been equally improbable—or even more so—to imagine India's white-rumped vulture, once the world's most abundant scavenging bird of prey, facing extinction.

▼ Vultures in other parts of the Old World are facing population declines, as well, especially in Africa. A 2015 study of eight of Africa's vulture species determined that "at least six appear to qualify" for IUCN listing as critically endangered, including the African white-backed vulture (*Gyps africanus*), which is a close relative of India's white-rumped vulture. Other imperiled African vultures species include the Rüppell's vulture (*Gyps rueppellii*), Cape vulture (*Gyps coprotheres*), hooded vulture (*Neocrosyrtes monachus*), lappet-faced vulture (*Torgos tracheliotos*), and white-headed vulture (*Trigonoceps occipitalis*).

Like most other Old World vultures, Africa's vultures are probably more closely related to eagles than to New World vultures, which seem to require their own taxonomic category. Like India's white-rumped, the African white-backed can weigh almost sixteen pounds and has a seven-foot wingspan. While the white-backed is considerably heftier, the hooded vulture is comparable in size to the turkey vulture. According to Keith Bildstein, who has several vulture research projects under way in Africa, "If there is an Old World equivalent to the turkey vulture, it's the hooded vulture." Smallish with a pale-pink face and "hood" of fawn-colored fuzz, hooded vultures appear big-eyed and (in my opinion, at least) adorable. Although it is listed as an endangered species, the hooded vulture is locally common in some parts of Africa. "The place to see hooded vultures," says Keith, "is the Gambia. There's no *Gyps* vulture in the coastal area, so they're the only vultures in town. And they're in every town, in high numbers." Like the turkey vulture, the hooded vulture often lives near people and makes use of "human subsidies," especially garbage dumps and slaughterhouses.

At the carcasses of large, dead mammals, however, hooded vultures often have to wait their turn; they lack the beak strength of larger vultures and may have trouble tearing through tough hides. "The first animals on a carcass," Keith told me, "are the most efficient scavengers of all. You'll get a lot of *Gyps* vultures coming in"—white-backed, Rüppell's, Cape vultures —"and also the lappet-faced." But near some of Africa's big parks, the vultures' efficiency is also their downfall. "A critical threat right now in Africa is the increasing use of carbofuran." When Keith explained the potency of this chemical, which he called a "broad-spectrum vertebracide," his voice quieted and his smile faded. "It's being used by herdsmen. They lace carcasses with it and then they purposely place these highly toxic carcasses out on the landscape to protect their livestock. The idea is that they'll kill lions, hyenas, jackals, and feral dogs." Unfortunately, the poisoned carcasses also kill vultures— sometimes dozens or hundreds at a time.

Poachers have begun to use a similar tactic as the herdsmen; however, the poachers specifically try to kill vultures. An article in the *Wildlife Professional* described a 2013 incident in which "600 vultures died near a poisoned elephant carcass near Namibia's Bwabwata National Park. . . . Elephant poachers were behind the poisonings that directly targeted vultures. Poachers poison the scavenging birds as they tend to congregate in the skies above a carcass, which signals to game rangers that something's amiss." Researchers from the Peregrine Fund report that between 2011 and 2015, "there have been at least 10 poisoning incidents that have, collectively, killed at least 1,500 vultures in six southern African countries." Current poaching trends in Africa are troubling; the International Conservation Caucus Foundation (ICCF) notes a steep increase in poaching since the early 2000s, especially of rhinoceros and elephant. Ivory continues to be a lucrative commodity, despite a 1989 international ban on its sale. Poverty in African communities complicates the illegal ivory trade; according to the ICCF, "tusks of a single adult elephant can be worth more than ten times the average annual income in many African communities." Demand for rhinoceros horn also continues, especially in Asia, where it's believed to have medicinal properties. The ICCF notes that powder made from crushed rhino horn costs more than $30,000 per pound, "making it more valuable than gold and cocaine."

Further complicating the trade in African wildlife products is that illegal poaching runs counter to Africa's legitimate ecotourism industry. Without the continent's megafauna—not just elephants and rhinoceros but lions, giraffes, zebras, and more—tourists from abroad will be less likely to spend money and time visiting Africa's national parks. Poaching also makes travel to Africa more expensive because of security costs; the terrorist groups that are funded by illegal ivory and rhino-horn sales often outgun and outnumber the guards hired to protect the parks and tourists. Africa's vultures find themselves caught in the middle by simply doing what they do—because their presence in the air above carcasses also allows rangers to locate illegally killed mammals, they are slaughtered by the poachers for being "snitches."

In addition to being poisoned intentionally by poachers and accidentally by herdsmen, vultures in southern Africa are also being killed for their brains (yes, their brains). Traditional South African medicine, known as *muti*, uses vulture brains to help practitioners see the future, such as how to determine which lottery numbers to choose or which horse to bet on. Keith explained that vulture brains are believed to help the user "be better at guessing whether your team is going to win." This practice reportedly spiked during the 2010 World Cup, held in South Africa. Additionally, according to the *Wildlife Professional*, "Crushed vulture brains and skulls are believed to cure migraines as well as provide clairvoyance powers and increase intelligence." Pulverized vulture brains can be smoked in a cigarette or burned and the fumes inhaled. Some claim that smoking the brains allows the user to dream of the winning numbers, or to simply "know" how to bet—much like the way vultures seem to suddenly appear in the sky over a carcass as if they magically know where to look—as if they saw into the future and predicted where a large animal would die. Because most of Africa's vulture species are slow to reproduce, individuals that are killed cannot be replaced quickly. "These birds are long-lived—at least four, five, six years until reaching maturity," Keith explained. "So what we're seeing in Africa right now is a loss of an important component in the big parks." Like turkey vultures in the New World and white-rumped vultures in India, Africa's scavenging raptors play a crucial—and necessary—role in decontaminating the environment. Their losses will result in a decline in the health of entire ecosystems unless these trends are reversed.

▼ I took a deep breath and began climbing Vedagiriswarar again. The temple itself, a red-and-white-striped base crowned with a flat-topped stone pyramid displaying three-dimensional deities, loomed high above the staircase on a rocky outcrop. Beyond the temple rose dry, stone hills. According to the IUCN, Egyptian vultures preferred to nest "on ledges or in caves on low cliffs, crags and rocky outcrops"; the habitat here seemed ideal. There would be no shortage of domestic livestock to eat, either; agricultural fields and rice paddies surround Thirukalu-kundram, and untethered cattle, goats, and water buffalo wandered everywhere.

In addition to the public health concerns caused by the decline of vultures at carcass dump sites, there is spiritual significance to the conspicuous absence of the "eagles" at Thirukalukun-dram. According to some reports, the white birds disappeared in 1994; others state they were last sighted in 2000. A 2002 article in the *Hindu*, India's oldest English-language newspaper, titled "Eagles Enhance the Sanctity," claims that Thiruka-lukundram "is one of the most celebrated places of religious importance in Tamil Nadu." According to the article, "The two sacred eagles appearing over the temple to worship the Lord every day are a major attraction" for "pilgrims and tourists from all parts of India and abroad." The eagles, the article continues, "come down to a rock where sweet rice is offered as food. To watch these eagles taking the food is a rare experience." After eating the rice (certainly not a typical food source for vultures) the birds "take off, circle around the tower again and fly off. This has been going on for centuries now." The town's name —Thirukalukundram—reflects this; translated to English, the name means "hill of the sacred eagles."

While Egyptian vultures do live long lives, no individual bird survives for centuries. However, the phenomenon is mentioned in the *Illustrated Guide to the South Indian Railway*, published in 1926. The guide states:

> The following interesting daily event takes place at Tirukalukundram temple, picturesquely perched on top of a hill . . . the feeding of the white vultures (Pharaoh's chickens) euphemistically called "Eagles" by pious Indians. For hundreds of years, so the tradition runs, a pair of these birds have thus been fed by the priest in charge of the temple. The fact is mentioned in the District Records, and Dutch and other records dating back nearly two centuries contain authentic accounts of the daily ceremony. At 11 o'clock every morning in the presence of pilgrims and worshippers to the famous shrine, the priest emerges and places a sumptuous and unctuous meal on a rocky eminence adjoining the temple with a brief religious ceremony. He sits there and waits patiently until the two birds, first merely white specks in the far distance, gradually approach in the wheeling flight particular to them and finally settle on the rock and dispose of the meal so ceremoniously provided. These birds are not uncommon, but the notable point is that there are never

more than two. How this continuity is kept up, how one pair succeeds another, is a matter for conjecture.

A matter for conjecture indeed. Perhaps the birds that visited the temple were all successive generations of the same family; perhaps the fledglings observed their parents and learned the unusual behavior. Or perhaps a visit to the temple for a quick, albeit atypical, meal was easier than foraging. The temple could be the halfway point between the vultures' roost in the hills and the agricultural fields where they searched for carcasses. Whatever the reason, the Egyptian vulture phenomenon at Thirukalukundram had been going on for a long, long time—until the birds disappeared.

Other Indian communities have suffered culturally and spiritually because of vulture declines as well. The Parsis, a Zoroastrian religious community, use the vultures in their funerary practices. When a Parsi dies, his or her body is placed on the Towers of Silence; before the vulture crisis, the large birds would quickly and efficiently consume the body. Members of this religion believe that a body burned, buried, or drowned desecrates the air, earth, or water. They offer their dead to the sky as a final act of charity. But without the once-abundant vultures to consume the dead, the Parsis are forced to find other ways to handle deceased members of the community, which can be upsetting.

In addition to the Parsis, cultures elsewhere in Asia utilize vultures to dispose of the dead. In the Himalayas of Tibet and other parts of China and Mongolia, certain Buddhists practice "sky burials"; after a ritual dismembering, a dead body is placed on a mountainside for the vultures to devour. This practice is practical as well as spiritual; in these high mountains, the soil is rocky and thin, and there are no trees to burn to allow for cremation. Although curious onlookers are strongly discouraged, quite a number of pictures and videos (some quite graphic) are floating around the Internet, and the BBC produced an episode of their *Human Planet* series called "Mountains—Life in Thin Air" that features the practice. In the episode, the narrator explains that a sky burial is "a sacred act, an offering that will sustain the life of another being." In Tibet, those beings are vultures, of course, mostly huge Eurasian griffons (*Gyps fulvus*) and bearded vultures (*Gypaetus barbatus*) that seem to wait on the rocks near the ceremonial site. A funeral procession of brightly dressed lamas climbs the mountain, singing, twisting hand drums, and ringing bells. After family members and mourners pay their respects and depart the ritual site, an undertaker using an ax dismembers the body so that the vultures can more readily consume it. Hundreds of birds may feast on the offering, the deceased's final act of charity. The practice of sky burials has continued since at least the eighth century, but new evidence suggests the Nepalese may have been engaging in a form of the ritual 300 years earlier than that. Archaeologists have recovered human bones from cliff-side caves in Nepal that show evidence of postmortem defleshing. Perhaps these bodies were prepared in similar fashion to the Tibetan bodies in the *Human Planet* episode.

Although the practices sound gruesome, I believe the Parsis and Tibetan Buddhists have it right. Being embalmed and locked away in a hermetically sealed casket seems like a waste; what better way for your spirit to be reborn than to fuel the wings of a high-flying vulture? If my body can be useful, can be reused, especially by vultures, then I am all for it. And I am not alone. In his poem "Vulture," Robinson Jeffers writes, "To be eaten by that beak / and become part of him, to share those wings and those eyes—/ What a sublime end of one's body, what an enskyment; what a life / after death." Lew Welch, a poet of the Beat Generation who disappeared and probably committed suicide in 1971, wrote in "Song of the Turkey Buzzard," "On a marked rock, following his orders, / place my meat. [. . .] With proper ceremony disembowel what I / no longer need, that it might more quickly / rot and tempt / my new form." Perhaps my favorite being-eaten-by-a-vulture sentiment comes from Edward Abbey. In *Desert Solitaire* he writes about being lost in the desert without water. He instructs such a person to "comfort yourself with the reflection that within a few hours . . . your human flesh will be working its way through the gizzard of a buzzard, your essence transfigured into the fierce greedy eyes and unimaginable consciousness of a turkey vulture. Whereupon you, too, will soar on motionless wings high over the ruck and rack of human suffering. For most of us a promotion in grade, for some the realization of an ideal." Although it may be illegal in the United States to feed dead humans to vultures, to me it sounds like the perfect way to return a body to the ecosystem—or perhaps to heaven.

▼ As I approached the hill's summit, I reached another landing. A skinny, tan dog with pointed ears and a sharp muzzle lounged across the top stair, in the shade provided by another concrete roof supported by white pillars. The dog watched me approach, calmly sniffing the air before resting his chin on his paws. In the center of the landing, a wrinkled woman in a turquoise sari sat behind a laid-out blanket on which she displayed small green bananas and bottles of water for sale. Two more tan dogs sprawled in the dusty shade nearby; one's face and flank were crisscrossed with gray scars. He slept deeply, eyes squeezed shut, front paw occasionally twitching. What do dogs in India dream about? Cattle carcasses and not a vulture in sight?

I turned the corner and continued up the last set of stairs, which ended at the open door of Vedagiriswarar Temple. Just past the threshold, a gaunt elderly man sat on a folding chair, collecting the five-rupee (about eight cents, US) admission fee. My eyes adjusted to the low light as I stepped past him into the temple's cool, stony darkness. *Diya* candles flickered on trays before deities, and plumes of incense curled toward the high ceiling. Two *murtis* flanked a short, brass-colored staircase that led to Shiva's inner sanctuary.

I sat cross-legged in front of another black Ganesh idol; the cool marble floor soothed my aching leg muscles after the long climb up the stone stairs. Worshippers of all ages trickled in and out of the temple and the inner sanctuary: young men in jeans and polo shirts, grizzled women with gray hair dressed in ragged saris, girls with long black braids clutching infants, bald Gandhi lookalikes wearing ankle-length dhotis and carrying walking sticks. Most entered the temple, blinked against the darkness, and made their way to one of the idols. They paused before Ganesh, touched their palms together, and murmured prayers before climbing the brass stairs. I peered past them into the small sanctuary. A priest, wearing only a short white dhoti, attended to the handful of worshippers. The priest's forehead was covered in a wide swath of white. Some worshippers sat on the floor of the sanctuary, and some stood along its walls. Several repeated the mantra *Om namah shivaya*, "I bow to Shiva," in unison.

I longed to rise and enter the sanctuary, but out of respect for a religion that wasn't my own, I didn't. Instead, I bid farewell to Ganesh, stood, and continued through the temple. I passed a man sitting cross-legged in a tan dhoti, a newspaper spread on the marble floor before him. He glanced at me briefly and resumed reading, resting his chin in his palm. I followed the narrow hallway as it wound out of the temple, onto a concrete platform that looked out over all of Thirukalukundram and the surrounding pastures, rice paddies, and

hills. I could see another well-known local site, Sangu Theer-tham, a 1,000-square-yard tank filled with water with a temple in its center. From my vantage point, I had a clear view of
the tank's greenish water and concrete sides. The temple reportedly housed a collection of more than 1,000 conch shells,
which, according to another legend, "emerge" from this freshwater source once every twelve years. Other tall temples rose
above the town, too; I counted at least six.

Through my camera's zoom lens I watched the bustling
streets far below me. Open-fronted stalls that lined the main
roads sold coffee; chai; bananas; sandals; bottles of Pepsi,
Coke, Fanta, and Aquafina; beaded necklaces; *diya* candles;
tires; cell phones; and more. Hero Honda motorcycles zipped
between rumbling, open-air buses filled with worshippers; untethered goats and gaunt cows with painted horns rummaged
in trash cans; and a handful of rhesus macaques lounged on
the roof of a shop that sold miniature Ganesh, Shiva, Vishnu,
and Parvati *murtis*. Subcompact cars sounded their horns and
did their best to avoid wandering goats, dogs, and children.
Thin men in dhotis and women in magenta, peach, teal, orange, and lime-green saris began to throng below, near the en-
trance to Vedagiriswarar's stone staircase.

Beyond the busy town, a few mountains jagged on the horizon. In other directions, fertile green fields, several heavily
flooded, added a measure of calmness to the landscape. I sat
cross-legged on a concrete ledge, breathed deeply, and tried to
take everything in. I had no doubt this was indeed a holy place;
I felt life all around me, through me, in me. I felt at peace. I
looked up; a few clouds wisped in the pale-blue sky, but it was
empty of birds, and in spite of my serenity I was reminded of
the absence of the sacred vultures and considered the intersection of the biological and the divine. I accepted as truth that
diclofenac had killed these birds, the same way it killed most

HILL OF THE SACRED EAGLES

other vultures—sacred or not—throughout India. But what if I was wrong: can a pharmaceutical company destroy even *holy* creatures? Had science finally killed God? The priests may have been correct in their belief that the vultures' disappearance presaged troubled times to come; in recent years India has had its share of tragedy, notably the 2004 tsunami and the 2008 Mumbai attacks. Or, perhaps instead of a bad omen, the vultures' departure showed that the *rishis* had finally proven their sincerity to Shiva, and after centuries of devout worship they had achieved salvation.

A young man wearing a linen button-down shirt and jeans stepped onto the observation deck, shaking me from my thoughts. His long-haired wife followed, clutching an infant against her yellow sari. "What country?" the man asked me, smiling.

I smiled back and answered, "USA."

He smiled, bobbled his head slightly, and then turned to take a photograph of his wife and son with Thirukalukundram in the background.

As I began my descent down the stone staircase, I glanced up at the dry hills beyond the temple and imagined what the Egyptian vultures would have looked like on their approach: two angels, floating on eagle's wings, coming to worship with the people.

The familiar landscape spread beneath her in all
directions: a windswept prairie pocked with small
ponds, gentle grassy hills, groves of maples beginning
to blush with fall color. Her wings were strong, body
swollen with fat. She hadn't eaten in days, and she
wouldn't eat for many more. She cruised, buoyed by
air, ever southward.

   Human settlements crowded below her, and she
saw them but did not stop until the winds quieted and
the earth darkened. She smelled the acrid plumes of
exhaust as she careened above the streaming vehicles
on Interstate 80, then 70. She didn't know the names,
but she looked down at Wichita, Oklahoma City,
then Dallas, then Waco, Austin, and San Antonio.
She floated high over human trials and traumas,
accidents and death and high school football, steady
in her journey.

On the Move

I was being left behind. I pressed my belly against the wooden railing and leaned out over limestone boulders, hickory trees, and the town of Gap Mills, West Virginia, wedged far below me in the valley. I lowered my binoculars to the railing and sighed. The osprey was gone, headed south, disappeared into the Appalachian fog, now not even a black spot on the horizon. She had been our second osprey of the day. Also tallied were three sharp-shinned hawks and two Cooper's hawks. The broad-wings made their move last week; red-tails would be next week. Today the sky belonged to ospreys and accipiters.

A handful of late September hawk-watchers had gathered at

Hanging Rock Raptor Observatory in southeastern West Virginia to glimpse migrating birds of prey. A former fire tower, the observatory sat on one of the tallest peaks in view; it's a simple one-room square structure, surrounded on all four sides by a deck with a railing. The valley below me to the west was a patchwork of green farm fields and tracts of forest. Tiny cars slid along the valley's only visible road. To the east the view was similar, but fewer houses clustered in the valley. Cows dotted a far-below field. I raised my binoculars; no, they were round bales of hay. Beyond the field, the forested mountains of the Alleghenies rolled to the horizon, and beyond them, the Blue Ridge.

When we lived in Blacksburg, Virginia, I taught a class at the local YMCA called "Hawk Watching for Beginners." After several slide presentations and lectures on identifying raptors in flight, we traveled to Hanging Rock to test our skills in the field. Blacksburg was only about thirty miles from Hanging Rock, but those were thirty dirt-road miles, up a mountain, down a mountain, up and down and then up again. The woods were thick along the West Virginia–Virginia border, pocked by occasional hunting cabins and silver trailers hung with Confederate flags.

The crowd on the fire tower gasped as a sharp-shinned hawk suddenly dropped from the sky like a winged bullet, aiming for a plastic great horned owl on a post next to the tower. The owl had been placed here for just this reason—hawks will try to "scare away" an owl, and this way folks on the tower get to see a stooping hawk up close. The sharpie veered at the last moment, perhaps realizing its folly, and resumed its determined southerly flight along the ridge.

Worldwide, migrating raptors tend to follow one of five "flyways"—sort of superhighways for birds. These roads in the sky include the Western European–West African Flyway, the

Eurasian-East African Flyway, the East-Asian Continental Flyway, the East-Asian Oceanic Flyway, and the Trans-American
Flyway. The Trans-American consists of several smaller flyways, including the Atlantic, Central, Mississippi, and Pacific
Flyways. The Appalachian Flyway, usually considered part of
the Atlantic Flyway, includes both southern West Virginia's
Hanging Rock Raptor Observatory and Pennsylvania's Hawk
Mountain Sanctuary. Raptors traversing the Appalachian Flyway make use of the strong winds—updrafts and thermals—
coming up the mountainsides out of the hollows and valleys.
I liked to imagine that the birds and the mountains depended
on each other symbiotically; the mountains propel the birds
to greener wintering grounds, and the hawks cull the ridges,
keeping rodent and pest populations from overrunning the
mountains. And the vultures, of course, clean up everyone's
messes.

I, too, have followed the Appalachians all my life. I was
born in the shadows of eastern Pennsylvania's Endless Mountains and learned to drive my father's Ford pickup on the
windy roads of Larksville and Plymouth Mountains. I watched
smoke rise from forever-burning coal-mine fires, took detours
to avoid the region's many sinkholes and subsidences, grew
up hearing stories of the Knox Mine disaster and the Molly
Maguires, and knew that the Susquehanna River was too pol-
luted from mine drainage and mercury to eat its fish. From my
central Pennsylvania college campus I could see the wooded
peaks of Mount Nittany and Tussey Mountain. After college I
kept following the mountains south into West Virginia, and a
few years later, I followed them further to Blacksburg, somewhere between the Alleghenies and the Blue Ridge. But, like
a migrating bird, I eventually headed back north to West Virginia, where we've made our home. Many of the birds that
travel along this ridge likely soared over eastern Pennsylva-

nia only a few days earlier, above the Kittatinny Ridge of Hawk Mountain Sanctuary. Hawk Mountain's groundbreaking work on turkey vulture migration (and raptor migration in general) has illuminated this mysterious and dangerous part of a bird's annual life cycle.

I lifted my binoculars again and spotted the dark silhouette of a turkey vulture, a member of the eastern subspecies *septentrionalis*, swaying above the valley. I watched as the vulture swept closer and closer to the tower, rocking on its brown-black sails. The skin of its head was gray, not the red of an adult bird—this turkey vulture was making its first trip south, traveling away from home on its own for the first time. Was it afraid of what lay beyond the next ridge and the ridge after that? How would it know when to stop moving? The vulture came closer still, straight at the tower, straight toward me, wings fixed, and I could see its pale legs tucked beneath its body. I didn't need my binoculars; I lowered them and stared at the bird. The vulture bent its black finger-wings gently and dipped its tail a bit, and it soared higher suddenly, barely missing the roof of the tower. The crowd gasped, then laughed when someone quipped, "It must've smelled something dead —who hasn't showered?"

One of the native Cherokee creation stories tells that a mythological vulture formed the Southern Appalachian Mountains. When the earth was covered by water and soft, unsculpted land, the animals all lived in the sky (perhaps in a place that Christian religions call *heaven*). It grew too crowded for all of them to coexist comfortably, so Grandfather Buzzard swooped down to see what was beneath them. It took the old bird a long time to reach the earth, and when he finally approached its surface, he began to grow tired. At first he soared, and his wings created plains, deserts, and flatlands, but as his energy waned and he began to sink closer to the soft ground, he was forced to flap slowly and deeply; where his wings brushed the earth, a valley was created, and when they flapped skyward again, they made a mountain. Turkey vultures now live everywhere Grandfather Buzzard flew, but the mountainous land he created became Cherokee country. I smiled and turned to watch the young turkey vulture as it left me behind, gliding south above the ridge.

▼ The world's leading expert on turkey vulture and raptor migration, Keith Bildstein, leaned back in his chair across the table from me. "The turkey vulture has an enormous geographic range, and individuals encounter incredibly different habitats throughout that range. It's a bird that's migratory in some populations, non-migratory in others, living in forested habitats in some populations, living in savannas in others, living in the desert, and also living on islands. And they do well." He took a sip from his mug. We were sitting in the common area of the Visiting Scientist Residence at Pennsylvania's Hawk Mountain Sanctuary's Acopian Center for Conservation Learning, discussing some of Hawk Mountain's recent discoveries about turkey vulture migration, some of which were surprising and warranted more research. Bookshelves along the wall held field guides, scientific volumes, and popular nonfiction books about birds of all species. The tile floor was impeccably clean, and a cathedral ceiling with exposed wooden beams soared overhead.

I took a sip from my own cup of tea. In an effort to learn more about turkey vulture migration, between 2003 and 2014 Hawk Mountain placed more than fifty transmitters on individuals of four of the six subspecies: *meridionalis*, *ruficollis*, *septentrionalis*, and *aura*, and they had plans to study the remaining two subspecies, *jota* and *falklandica*, as well. Data garnered from these birds has been fascinating. But before delving into the specific migration patterns of the different subspecies, I tried to develop an understanding of raptor migration in general. Keith's important book, *Migrating Raptors of the World: Their Ecology and Conservation*, is indispensable for anyone hoping to grasp this subject. My copy is dog-eared and highlighted, and my pink sticky notes litter the pages.

Migrating Raptors defines *migration* as "directed movements from one location to another, recurring seasonally and alternating in direction." Many animals (and even plants) participate in migrations of one kind or another—whales, butterflies, wildebeests, some reptiles, algae, and a host of others. The book pinpoints the primary reasons that raptors migrate: "Migration evolves in sedentary populations of raptors when habitats change so that they are no longer capable of supporting overwintering populations or when populations increase to the point that recently fledged young are forced to disperse into areas that provide inadequate year-round habitats." This makes sense, of course: if an animal's "home" fails to provide food and shelter year-round, the animal must move, at least temporarily, to a new "home." Or if the neighborhood becomes too crowded to support all of its residents, some of the kids move out, but they may come back temporarily when conditions in their new home make survival difficult. Then they leave again. And come back. And the cycle repeats. However, migratory patterns are not as fixed as we might think. Keith writes, "Due to both behavioral flexibility and rapid evolutionary change, shifts in migratory tendencies can appear and disappear in raptors within decades." Turkey vultures are clearly an adaptable species, so it makes sense that their migration patterns are adaptable, as well.

Turkey vultures emerged more than a million years ago in the early Pleistocene, and their range was probably restricted to the tropics. At first, this region would have provided everything the species needed: adequate food, shelter, and safe places to breed and raise young. As their population became successful and grew, young birds began to range farther and farther, and eventually, new populations formed. "Turkey vultures," Keith explained to me, "are at heart a tropical species. Their densest populations and the greatest diversity in *Cathartes* are in the tropics. That's where they came from, and that's where they've been most of the time. Getting out of the cold weather is important for them." So, in only about a million years (a relatively short time, geologically) turkey vultures have evolved into several different populations with distinct migratory patterns, including complete migrants (populations of birds that completely vacate a region to "shuttle seasonally between breeding and non-breeding areas"), partial migrants (when "fewer than 90 percent of all individuals migrate"), leapfrog migrants ("in which migratory individuals breed at higher latitudes than sedentary individuals and overwinter at lower latitudes"), reciprocal migrants (resident populations that move in response to pressure from arriving migrant birds), and sedentary populations—a diverse and adaptable bird, indeed.

The champion travelers of the turkey vulture species are western North America's *C. a. meridionalis*. These super-flocking complete migrants may travel more than 8,000 kilometers (approximately 5,000 miles) between the northern reaches of their range in south-central Canada and the southern reaches in northern Venezuela and Colombia. According to *Migrating Raptors*, they may use the sun, the stars, and the earth's magnetic field to guide them. Data from solar-powered satellite transmitters worn by individuals breeding in Canada revealed that the birds make the long journey quickly, often migrating at speeds of forty to seventy kilometers (twenty-five to forty-three miles) per hour, and sometimes at speeds in excess of seventy kph. This means that a bird leaving Saskatchewan on September 30, for example, might arrive at its final Venezuelan des- tination around November 21. As the vultures make their way south, more and more birds join the flocks, and by the time they reach the migration bottleneck near Veracruz, Mexico, more than 100,000 turkey vultures sometimes pass overhead each day for weeks; totals for the month of October may number more than two million individuals.

Amazingly, according to Keith, *meridionalis* turkey vultures do not eat during most of their migration; an individual may lose up to 30 percent of its body mass during the trip and arrives on the wintering grounds with quite an appetite. Weighing in at about two kilograms (four and half pounds), *meridionalis* individuals are the largest of all the turkey vulture subspecies, and in order to survive, perhaps they need to be. "The density of turkey vultures in northern Venezuela," Keith explained, "is five times in the winter as it is in the breeding season. Five times. That's amazing. How do you fit five times as many birds into an area? Well, some of those residents move out." Keith calls the phenomenon *reciprocal migration*—when resource availability changes for the resident birds because of the influx of migrants. "Everybody talks about how migrants, whether they're passerines or raptors, tend to go into secondary habitat. You've heard the 'peaceable kingdom' stories. Well, people used to ask me where all these turkey vultures migrating through Veracruz go once they get to South America, and now my snide answer is, 'Anywhere they want.' They push out the local vultures."

Studies from the 1990s showed that migrants arriving in the tropics began gaining weight as resident vultures began losing weight. The migrant *meridionalis* turkey vultures dominate not only the local *ruficollis* turkey vultures, but the local black vultures as well. In North America, the reverse is almost always true; black vultures will dominate turkey vultures at a carcass.

But in South America the "gringo" turkey vultures—"the big bullies," Keith called them—push around the smaller tropical black vultures. "And not only do they usurp those areas and become dominant," Keith continued, "but out of the breeding season they adopt some of the same behavioral patterns as black vultures, foraging in flocks and dominating other birds." A research paper published in the *Wilson Bulletin* in 1991, "Foraging Behavior of a Guild of Neotropical Vultures," determined that in open habitat, a "dominance hierarchy" was established at large carcasses. Although turkey vultures were usually the first birds to find the carcasses, the dominant vulture was the huge Andean condor (*Vultur gryphus*), the world's largest flying land bird; it can weigh up to fifteen kilograms (more than thirty pounds) and sport a ten-and-a-half-foot wingspan. Next in the hierarchy was the colorful king vulture (*Sarcoramphus papa*), followed by the crested caracara (not officially a vulture, but included in this study of avian scavengers anyway), then turkey vultures, and finally resident black vultures.

If the migrants from the north are so successful once they reach the wintering grounds, why not stay there all year? "Well," Keith answered, pointing to southern Canada on a map, "Right now, this is probably a better place to breed. The birds probably have as many thermals here in the summertime as they would down there, and they exist here at lower densities." Some of the Saskatchewan migrants show remarkable site fidelity on both their breeding and wintering grounds. One female bird, named "Leo" for where she nests near the town of Leoville, returns to the same grove of palm trees on a farm in western Venezuela, not far from the Colombian border. She was tagged and fitted with a transmitter in 2007, and as of 2016, she was still sending data revealing her whereabouts—and still returning to the same grove of palms every November.

Many of the tropical *ruficollis* turkey vultures (who I couldn't help feeling a little bit sorry for) leave the areas that North American *meridionalis* birds stream into and head farther south for parts unknown. They don't return and begin breeding until after the migrants leave. In addition to being smaller than *meridionalis*, *ruficollis*'s physical appearance is slightly different, and when in the hand, Keith says it is easy to distinguish between individuals of the two subspecies; a *ruficollis* bird has a large whitish spot on the back of its head and neck, fewer warty protuberances on its face, and darker plumage overall. Heading further south, a *C. a. falklandica* vulture is darker still, with no warty protuberances.

Before Hawk Mountain placed transmitters on Pennsylvania's *C. a. septentrionalis* turkey vultures, some biologists believed that, like broad-winged hawks, the birds filtered from the Appalachians west along Mexico's Gulf Coast to Veracruz, joining the super-flocking *C. a. meridionalis*. But this doesn't seem to be the case. "When people used to ask me something about turkey vulture migration, I thought I knew it all because of the work that was done in Veracruz," Keith admitted. "I thought we weren't seeing the enormous flocks on the East Coast because we weren't drawing from a big enough pool. The reality isn't that at all. They're using a completely different migration strategy. They, the eastern birds that is, are migrating at a fourth the speed, they're feeding all the way through on migration, and some don't migrate at all." The farthest that Pennsylvania turkey vultures appear to travel is Miami, Florida. There, and in other parts of the Sunshine State, the vultures may form loose flocks with dozens to hundreds of others. One famous vulture-gathering place is the historic Dade County Courthouse; photographs taken from across the street by Cliff Shaw of the US Forest Service show swarms of vultures roosting on the tall building's peaks and ledges. According to Keith, vulture populations in Florida swell to three or four times in the winter than what they are in the summer.

Another region of the United States known for its turkey vultures—the American Southwest—is home to the subspecies *Cathartes aura aura*. These somewhat smaller and darker birds breed in Arizona and California and head south for the winter, although not as far south as *meridionalis*. In 2013, biologists from Hawk Mountain and their collaborators placed satellite transmitters on six *C. a. aura* individuals to track their movements. Data from the transmitters revealed that the birds leave the United States in October and follow Mexico's Pacific Coast to southernmost Mexico and the isthmus of Central America. None of the tagged individuals crossed into South America, but they began heading north around the same time as the *C. a. meridionalis* migrants, in mid-March. Whereas *C. a. aura* birds stop in the southwestern desert, *meridionalis* vultures "leapfrog" over them and keep heading north until the last individuals arrive at their breeding territories in Canada's southern boreal forest—quite a change in habitat from the Venezuelan llanos, the Sonoran Desert, the Appalachians, or southern Florida.

Meanwhile, on the opposite end of the hemisphere, where are individuals of the southernmost subspecies—*jota* and *falklandica*—going? Some, like the vultures on the Falkland Islands, are non-migratory and don't go anywhere. But much remains to be learned about the movements of *C. a. jota* in South America's southern cone. Hawk Mountain hasn't placed satellite transmitters on *jota* vultures yet, Keith told me, but they plan to soon. They've done roadside surveys in the region and will return to continue the research in the near future. "In Argentina," Keith said, smiling beneath his mustache, "the word for turkey vulture is *jote*, like the subspecies. But when you cross the Andes into Chile, *jote* is slang for a lounge lizard—

you know, a guy who hangs around bars to pick up girls. We were talking to people at a vineyard in Chile, and they asked what we were doing, and we told them we were studying *jotes*. Everybody looked at us like we'd just said an incredibly bad thing. We went into a long, laborious explanation. We learned they call them *buzzardos*."

While there is still much to discover about the specific migratory patterns for the six turkey vulture subspecies, several things are clear: we know a great deal more about this bird's movements as a result of the efforts of Keith Bildstein and his colleagues at Hawk Mountain Sanctuary and elsewhere. Something else is clear, too, and is true of animal movements in general—migration is an extremely dangerous endeavor.

▼ I often think of migration as a leap of faith; bound by instructions written on their genes, birds suddenly leave their breeding ranges and fly off into the open sky. They may never have made the journey before but answer the call anyway. Some, like tiny songbirds, travel during the dark of night to avoid diurnal predators, many of which are also migrating. They cross forests, prairies, mountains, and sometimes even large bodies of water, such as the Gulf of Mexico. *Migrating Raptors* calls the act of migration "one of the most difficult and dangerous activities birds undertake." In addition to "natural" dangers—storms, predators, fatigue, starvation—migrating birds face a host of other difficulties, both during the act of migration and upon arriving on their wintering grounds. It should come as no surprise that human activity often makes migration more challenging for birds than it already is.

For centuries, birds of prey (including vultures) have been persecuted as killers of game and livestock, and migration provided an opportune time for hunters to slaughter them in large numbers. Historic photographs from Hawk Mountain—before it became "Hawk Mountain Sanctuary" in 1934—show row upon row of dead hawks, eagles, and falcons, migrating birds easily shot from rocky outcrops along the mountain's ridges. According to *Migrating Raptors*, "By 1885 . . . the [Pennsylvania] state legislature placed a 50-cent bounty on the 'heads' of all birds of prey, including owls." Opinion polls at the time showed 90 percent public support for the law, and "over the next two years, 180,000 raptor skins, or 'scalps,' were sent to the state capital in Harrisburg." The law was repealed when rodent and other pest populations skyrocketed, but the state eventually reinstated bounties, and raptors "remained unprotected statewide until 1937 when, except for the three bird- and game-eating accipiters [Cooper's, sharp-shinned, and goshawks] . . . [they] received legal protection." The state extended protection to all hawks in 1969, but it wasn't until the federal Migratory Bird Treaty Act of 1918 was amended in 1972 that *all* raptor species were legally protected from persecution.

In some parts of the world, raptor persecution during migration continues. The Maltese islands are in the Mediterranean Sea, south of Italy's "boot" and north of Africa's Tunisia and Libya, along an important flyway for birds moving between Europe and Africa. According to BirdLife Malta, 389 bird species have been recorded on the islands and more than 170 species "from at least 48 countries (36 in Europe and 12 in Africa) use Malta during migration." Unfortunately for the migratory birds, the islands also have the densest population of human hunters in the European Union. While it is legal and popular to hunt some species of birds, such as turtledoves and quail, poachers illegally kill hundreds—and perhaps thousands—of migrating birds each year, including protected raptors such as the marsh harrier, common kestrel, and honey buzzard, as well as storks, ibis, bitterns, swifts, and more. Reports in the *Guardian* and by the BBC paint horrifying pictures of hunters in easy chairs and on porches shooting into flocks of migrating birds. Hunting harms Malta's breeding bird populations as well; according to BirdLife Malta, it "has the dubious distinction of being the only country in Europe and the Mediterranean with no regularly breeding birds of prey." Peregrine falcons and barn owls are extinct on the islands; "the last breeding pairs are known to have been shot by hunters."

Illegal hunting during migration occurs in other countries as well, including Lebanon. Located between Syria, Israel, and the Mediterranean Sea, Lebanon is another important migratory bottleneck for birds moving between Europe and Africa. Lebanese poachers have been photographed proudly displaying dead (and occasionally still bloody, alive, and suffering) griffon vultures, steppe eagles, spotted eagles, sparrowhawks, cranes, storks, pelicans, and others, including birds wearing leg bands and wing tags. Some of the dead and dying birds are posed with lit cigarettes stuck in their beaks or with ropes around their necks, or draped across the hoods and roofs of vehicles next to the weapons that killed them and even next to smirking children and babies. With a little searching, these disturbing photographs can be found easily on social media. Laws in Lebanon protect many migratory species, but surveys of hunters have revealed that only a fraction can identify the species of birds that they're shooting.

One of the most disheartening recent stories out of Lebanon is the fate of a griffon vulture wearing black wing tags emblazoned with P72. A picture posted on Lebanese social media shows a young bearded man in lace-up boots and blue jeans displaying the dead vulture; the bird's eyes are shut, its legs hang limp, and blood stains the feathers along the left side of its body. The man stretches the vulture's right wing and head, showing the patagial tag bearing P72. I am reminded of my own experiences placing wing tags on vultures—the birds' racing hearts and warm musty smell, the care the biologists take while handling the birds, the way Jesse gently runs his fingers over the birds' wings to make sure the tags are properly placed. According to Europe's Vulture Conservation Foundation, the griffon vulture in the picture "was captured and tagged in Gamla Nature Reserve by the Israel Nature and Parks Authority" in the summer of 2014; the picture of the same bird, dead, appeared on social media in September 2015. While shooting any migrating bird—especially a raptor, especially a vulture—is anathema to me, why would anyone shoot a bird that is very obviously part of a scientific study?

Migrating birds are at risk from other human activities, too, although none as brazen as direct persecution via shooting. Like raptors, humans have discovered how to harness the power of the wind and we place turbines—sometimes hundreds—along mountain ridgelines. Birds that navigate along the same ridges can be injured or killed by the spinning blades of huge windmills. While it is difficult to determine the number of birds killed outright by turbines (some estimates are as low as 10,000 a year and others as high as 600,000, but new studies think the number falls between 140,000 and 328,000), without a doubt they pose a threat to birds on the move.

As of 2016, West Virginia's mountain ridges were home to five wind farms; I frequently drive near two of them—the AES Laurel Mountain Wind Farm, which includes sixty-one turbines along twelve miles of ridges in Preston, Tucker, Randolph, and Barbour Counties, and NedPower Mount Storm, co-owned by Dominion and Shell, which consists of 132 turbines along twelve miles of the Allegheny Front, an important route for migrating birds. Both have been in the news because of the damage they've caused to birds. In early October 2011, lights left on overnight at Laurel Mountain were blamed for causing the deaths of almost 500 migrating birds, half of which were blackpoll warblers. Laurel Mountain made the news again in 2012 when an endangered Indiana bat was killed there. In September 2011, the Mount Storm wind farm reported that fifty-nine birds and two bats had been killed one evening, again after a light had been left on. Biologists believe that the lights on the tall turbines confuse migrating birds that use the stars to guide them at night.

These wind farms are easily viewed from many public roads. US Route 48 offers particularly startling views of the Mount Storm turbines. On a recent trip to Harrisonburg, Virginia, I drove the lonely stretch of Highway 48 that runs below a row of huge turbines, which spun high above me on the ridge. According to Dominion, each windmill stands almost 400 feet high from the ground to the top of the blade tip. I set my cruise control and watched, horrified, as soaring turkey vultures careened right between the spinning blades. Although I'd been alone in my car, I shrieked out loud several times at near misses. Certainly turbines, at least the turbines along this particular stretch of the ridge, injured and killed turkey vultures. I thought about pulling over and scaling the hillside to look for carcasses, and I wondered if anyone had studied the wind turbine–turkey vulture interface.

I asked Todd Katzner if he knew anything about windmills and turkey vultures. "They've been killed by turbines," he answered, nodding. "They're at risk. Nobody is concerned about turkey vultures at a population level—but of course it matters to the individual birds." Much of Todd's research focuses on the development of wind energy and how it affects migrating birds of prey, especially golden eagles. His results have shown that eagles and energy companies both find the same ridges desirable, and his hope is that future wind projects can be sited and managed in ways safe for eagles and other migrating birds. A notoriously dangerous wind farm, located in Altamont Pass,

California, and consisting of more than 5,000 turbines, kills more raptors than any other wind farm in the world, including vultures, hawks, falcons, and eagles. According to BirdLife International, more than 1,000 raptors are killed there annually, including an average of sixty-seven golden eagles. Migrating raptors conserve energy by soaring along windy ridges, but they may pay for it with their lives.

Another high-flyer often uses strong winds to get—and remain—airborne: commercial and military aircraft. A 2011 study, "Vulture Flight Behavior and Implications for Aircraft Safety," reports that "turkey and black vultures have been responsible for more civil aircraft strikes involving human injury than any other bird species except for the Canada goose." A combination of an increasing vulture population, their soaring altitude, and "limited capacity to make evasive flight maneuvers" contributes to "their hazard potential to aircraft." It goes without saying that aircraft pose a significant hazard to vultures as well. According to the study, most vultures were struck by aircraft within 150 meters of the ground; therefore, "low-level flights, including take-off and landing, are most at risk for encountering vultures." A 2005 study estimated that between 1990 and 1998 there were 22,000 bird-aircraft collisions, costing "$400 million annually in aircraft repairs. Further, an estimated 350 people have been killed in bird-aircraft collisions worldwide." The study does not calculate the monetary value of the loss of the birds, of course, and while any loss of human life is tragic, I assume that the birds involved in these collisions are killed nearly 100 percent of the time.

Although several potential solutions are proposed by the studies, including "aggressive harassment coupled with flexible [military] training schedules to avoid times and altitudes of high vulture activity," Keith Bildstein has another idea: "Airports often have sited near them municipal dumps. When you put a dump near an airport, you create a hazardous juxtaposition. The airport in Caracas, Venezuela, is notorious for this, and I always think about it when I'm flying there." I remembered a trip I took to Colombia a few years ago; as our small jet approached the runway in Bucaramanga, I could see soaring black vultures from my window seat. Once I'd deplaned, I realized that *dozens* of black vultures were circling in the sky above the airport. Surely collisions must occur there regularly. Keith nodded. "When I'm traveling internationally in the Western Hemisphere, the first bird I see is at the airport, and it's almost always a black or turkey vulture. Both species are near many airports in Central and South America." Whereas in the Americas most vulture-aircraft collisions occur close to the ground, over Africa's Côte d'Ivoire, a Rüppell's vulture was sucked into a jet engine; the plane was flying at a cruising altitude of 37,000 feet. Thanks to this particular, and unfortunate, individual, this species now holds the record for the world's highest-flying bird.

Despite all the natural and human-made dangers associated with migrating, data from Hawk Mountain's transmitters shows that many birds live to make the trip again and again. Canada's "Leo," a *C. a. meridionalis* tagged in 2007, and "Irma," a *C. a. septentrionalis* tagged in 2004, were all still alive and transmitting their movements in 2016—managing to avoid aircraft, wind turbines, and poachers while grappling with the "usual" challenges of hunger, weather, competition, and loss or change of habitat. It is amazing that *any* birds make it through migration; yet the turkey vulture has, so far, managed not only to succeed but also increase its numbers—not only surviving but thriving as well.

She felt the hunger in her chest and she picked up speed. The skies, which had once belonged only to her, grew crowded. She smelled the salt in the air, and far below she saw the jagged edge where land met ocean. She recognized her kind and joined them, doing her best to stay above the hawks, the ospreys, and the kites.

The landscape beneath her changed again; still familiar, it seemed to increase her hunger, and she swept on. Below, Managua bustled, and then the dense green mountains of Costa Rica, and then the crowded waterway of Panama. She was almost home. South America unfurled and the dense air cleared. She circled Bucaramanga, Colombia, before landing, exhausted and starving, in the sheltering grove of palms between Caracas and the Andean foothills. She breathed. After so much motion, she was finally still.

Virginia Is for Vultures

I often fought the wind while walking to class when I taught English at Virginia Tech. In the winter, horizontal snow would tear at my jacket, and my gale-tossed hair would stick to my face. Sometimes I felt like I'd be swept off the sidewalk. When I'd finally arrive in my warm classroom, my eyes would be streaming because of the cold wind. On these frigid weekday mornings, glancing skyward at southwest Virginia's ubiquitous cruising vultures would remind me that the wind wasn't always an inconvenience; for some, it provided an easier, quicker way to find food and a means to travel great distances without expending too much energy. Perhaps the problem isn't the wind but trying to walk against it.

Blacksburg isn't the only Virginia town with a large number of vultures; the state harbors an abundance of both turkey and black vultures in every season, although their numbers swell in the winter. While the two species are social all year, they tend to congregate in larger groups during the non-breeding season. The turkey vultures in Virginia during the winter could be local birds, or birds from New England or the upper Midwest, and likely a combination. Data from *Cathartes aura septentrionalis* turkey vultures fitted with Hawk Mountain Sanctuary satellite transmitters in Pennsylvania revealed that the northern birds' winter movements vary greatly; however, many end up in Virginia for at least some of the fall and winter months. In 2013, a vulture nicknamed "Black Knight," tagged in Towanda, Pennsylvania, began heading south in October. He traveled through (or above) the Virginia cities of Front Royal, Charlottesville, and Appomattox on his way to Florida, where he spent the rest of the winter. Another turkey vulture, "Mark," tagged near Hawk Mountain in Kempton, Pennsylvania, spent a few autumn days in the lovely Loudoun County town of Leesburg, Virginia, on his way to the Charlottesville area, where he remained for much of November and December; by early January, he was back in Pennsylvania, not far from where he was tagged. Other Pennsylvania vultures, such as "Tesla," pass over Virginia much more quickly on their way to points south; by late October, Tesla was already enjoying the Lakeland, Florida, sunshine.

Whether they're just passing through Virginia or planning to stay for a few months, many birds end up roosting together. These winter roosts may contain dozens to hundreds of both turkey and black vultures, the hunching birds shouldering up to each other on every available branch of a tree. In the case of black vultures, roosting birds may be several generations of the same family. Research suggests that these communal roosts may act as "information centers"—the birds follow each other and learn where to find the best food. This is especially important during the cold winter months, when carrion is less abundant or frozen, and conserving energy could mean the difference between life and death. "The roosts function more as motels than as homes for the birds," Keith Bildstein told me. "You may have a sixty-vulture roost that is relatively constant in number, but the individual birds are different as the weeks pass. There are probably 360 different individuals and they're rotating through different motels. Not as migratory movements, just getting caught up with birds at a carcass or something and following each other."

From November until March, the state of Virginia is blessed (or cursed) with thousands of roosting vultures. If Virginia is for lovers, Virginia is also for vultures, and therefore, for vulture lovers. But not everyone in Virginia loves vultures. Although watching vultures makes me feel peaceful and relaxed, the same isn't true for others living in the vultures' shadows. In the past decade or two, residents of towns and cities throughout the Old Dominion have complained of vulture "problems," from Leesburg in the north to Richmond's central suburbs to the southwest's New River Valley. Even though the large winter roosts are temporary, some residents claim the vultures are messy, scary, a nuisance, and a threat to health and home.

Although many factors determine where vultures roost, sites generally need three important characteristics: a safe, convenient spot to perch; good wind; and an abundance of food. A 1990 paper in the *Journal of Wildlife Management* identifies "Winter Use and Habitat Characteristics of Vulture Communal Roosts." The authors studied roosts in Pennsylvania, Maryland, and Virginia, and found that sites often contained large coniferous trees, such as white pines. While observing vultures roosting in Pennsylvania on a chilly November morning,

Keith explained to me that, for a vulture, a pine tree was akin to "a fleece-lined bed."

The paper further explains that vultures may choose roost sites because of nearby "habitat features that contribute to air currents." The birds use upward air currents and thermals for soaring; the "ruggedness of land surfaces and interfaces of forests and clearings likely created obstruction currents. . . . In addition, roads, buildings, and streams enhance production of thermals during winter." Turkey vultures are again making use of "human subsidies"; as Todd Katzner told me, "Roads are incredibly important. They're a food source and a lift source. Berms on the sides of highways provide lift." Abundant roadkill and enhanced thermals could be the reasons that motorists on Virginia's Interstates 81, 64, and 66 can often view turkey vultures cruising overhead.

Before highways and humans, vultures may have roosted in areas where large groups of wild ungulates gathered; now, roosts may be located near livestock operations (especially where dead cattle are disposed). Some have also suggested that modern vultures roost in or around towns in winter because of "urban heat islands" created by buildings and pavement. Perhaps some of the current Virginia roosts are near traditional, pre-human-settlement roost sites, and the construction of nearby highways and heat islands are an added bonus. *Thanks for building your city near our roost! You've sure made things easier for us!*

▼ The small town of Radford, Virginia, sits along a bend in the New River, a fifteen-minute drive from Blacksburg. Like the Nile, the inaccurately named New is believed to be one of the world's oldest rivers. From its headwaters near Blowing Rock, North Carolina, the New twists north through southwestern Virginia and into West Virginia, where it eventually meets the Gauley River to form the Kanawha. Radford, the "New River City," is home to Radford University, the Radford Army Ammunition Plant, and, especially in the winter, hundreds of black and turkey vultures.

When Jesse and I lived in Blacksburg we often traveled to Radford for an easy hike in Wildwood Park or to visit one of our favorite Italian restaurants. Whenever I could wrest him from his veterinary school studies, Jesse and I would spend afternoons in our old red canoe on the river, often launching from Bisset Park and paddling past Radford University to the Pepper's Ferry Bridge. During our five years living in Blacksburg, we paddled the stretch of the New between the Claytor Lake Dam and Pembroke in sections, most of which is picturesque and gentle, with a few notable exceptions. One rough area is McCoy Falls (class III/IV with a few strong IIs), but the most difficult set of rapids to run in our fat, open canoe was Arsenal Falls, usually categorized as a strong class III. Once, during a particularly dry spell, our canoe got stuck on some rocks in the middle of the falls. We clamored out, wobbled on slick boulders, and rocked the wedged vessel back and forth. We finally leaped back inside when, with the help of the current, we dislodged the canoe. Approaching the falls straight on is not recommended by the guidebooks—most instruct paddlers to head for far river-right, where the current is slower and sandbars make portage possible. But where's the fun in that?

Arsenal Falls gets its name from the Radford Army Ammunition Plant, which occupies the property on one or both sides of the river for much of the eight-mile stretch between the Pepper's Ferry Bridge and Whitethorne. Situated on 4,600 acres, the plant produces propellants and explosives for the military, and it's the largest point source of pollution on the entire stretch of the New River. Because of the topography of the river and of the arsenal's security restrictions, the stretch of

145

the New that flows through army property is wild, lonely, and filled with wildlife. Motorized boats can't make it over the rapids, and the army usually doesn't allow trespassing. The only feasible way to boat through the arsenal is to put in under the Pepper's Ferry Bridge and brave Arsenal Falls. Once through the falls, rivergoers must commit to paddling the entire stretch through the arsenal. The shore is often lined with barbed wire-topped fencing and posted warning signs, and ominous guard towers loom from several points along the river's edge.

An unintended consequence of the army's security measures is abundant wildlife. Northern rough-winged swallows cut and dive overhead, cedar waxwings mob sycamores and silver maples along the shore, and the noses of shy river otters break the water's brown surface. Less shy are the muskrats; the curious rodents approached our canoe on several occasions, sashaying through the current like waterlogged woodchucks, their whiskered muzzles and beady eyes studying us before sinking beneath the surface, only to reemerge further downstream. But the most impressive wildlife display on this stretch of river is the vultures, which we often observed congregating on a stretch of sandy shore. Every tree limb and rock near this strand—which we dubbed "Vulture Beach"—held a black or turkey vulture. Several birds stood on the shore with their wings spread, soaking up the sun. Others ruffled their feathers, dipped their heads, and splashed in the river. And although on one trip we counted more than fifty birds, the gatherings were mostly silent and peaceful. Birds bathed, sunned themselves, and rested—not unlike the ways we enjoyed afternoons on the river.

The number of vultures roosting near the Radford Arsenal increases in the winter, and at one time the arsenal held one of the largest vulture roosts in the United States. A study from the mid-1980s estimated that more than 500 vultures roosted in the arsenal during the winter months. There are also published reports from the 1930s of vultures roosting near Radford, and the birds may have been around even longer than that; journals from the area's early pioneers mention flocks of eagles roosting on the New River. These "eagles" were likely vultures.

The arsenal roost was disrupted in late 2001 when a group of pine trees was cut down; soon thereafter, residents of Radford began to complain about the increasing number of vultures roosting within town limits. A 2003 newspaper article cites Radford's animal control officer's estimate of 1,000 vultures in a wooded area near homes, the Radford Child Care Center, and McHarg Elementary School. People complained about property damage from feces as well as from the vultures tearing up the school's roof and the day care's playground equipment. According to an article in the *Roanoke Times*, the director of the day-care center said, "They were tearing things up, but the main thing was there was poop everywhere." Black vultures have been observed tearing roof shingles, rubber seals on vehicles, and other plastic or rubber items. They don't eat these materials; perhaps the behavior is a result of boredom. Much of the damage probably occurs in the early morning, while the vultures are waiting for the air to warm up and provide ample lift for them to take off for the day.

To try to remedy their vulture "problem," Radford removed several trees from the roost and invested in noisemakers and fireworks to disperse the birds. Eventually, the city enlisted the help of the USDA's Animal and Plant Health Inspection Service (APHIS) Wildlife Services, an agency responsible for addressing problems caused by "nuisance" wildlife. In 2010, APHIS biologists estimated that 200 vultures were roosting in Radford when they began their efforts to disperse them. In addition to pyrotechnics, the USDA hung vulture effigies and carcasses near the roost. This seemed to work, and the number of vultures near the school and day-care center dwindled.

It is unclear why hanging vulture effigies or carcasses discourages roosting vultures. As carrion eaters, it seems that a few dead birds would be a welcome offering. But when faced with a carcass of one of their own, the vultures sometimes abandon the roost site or keep their distance from the carcass. While this at least suggests that vultures recognize members of their own species and do not cannibalize, could it be more than that? Research has shown that black vultures roosting together are often members of an extended family; imagine showing up at Grandma's house for a holiday gathering and seeing Uncle Bob's body hanging on the porch. Who *wouldn't* be deterred? But killing and hanging carcasses in trees—with the intent to intimidate and disperse certain populations—also has troubling historical complications, especially in the South. It seems, at least to me, that this practice should never be normalized, for any species.

Not everyone in Radford dislikes having vultures for neighbors. Resident Lissa Bloomer looked forward to seeing the birds on her drive to work in the morning. "They kind of became friends," she told me. Sometimes, a group of twenty or so vultures would roost in the red oak trees in her backyard. "They always surprised me a little. They were so quiet and watchful. What I found so neat was the sound of their huge flapping wings—they sounded like capes, like thick sheets being shaken out in the wind. And," she added, "I appreciate the fact that they eat dead animals." Another Radfordian, Jenny Lawrence, read about the vulture complaints in the local newspaper, but when she finally noticed the birds in the trees, she thought, "Well, there are those vultures. What's the big deal?"

Dr. Bob Sheehy, professor of biology at Radford University, uses the local vulture population as a way to get his undergraduate students interested in research. "The vultures are easy to observe," Bob told me. "A lot of the research I do is population genetics, which students aren't interested in," he laughed, and added, "Students like to get outside." In addition to a vulture roost webcam, Bob and his students started a "vulture restaurant"; they collected road-killed deer and set up a trail camera so they could study the ways the birds ate and behaved at carcasses. Another student project included an analysis of pellets —clumps of egested indigestible matter, such as bones and fur—collected from the ground beneath the roost.

Bob's office on Radford University's campus is packed with books and photographs of vultures and other birds. A platform bird feeder was built into his office window, and while we talked about Radford's vultures, I was frequently distracted by blue jays swooping into the feeder for a snack. Bob's interest in birds began as a high school student in Oregon, when he worked with a local bird-bander and spent time volunteering at a raptor rehabilitation center. There, he cared for a young turkey vulture that had been stolen from a nest and then confiscated by the police. "I just kind of fell in love with it," Bob said. "I called it 'Puke' because every time you walked in the room it would throw up." Puke was eventually released near a communal roost in southeastern Oregon.

After working closely with this vulture, Bob started to pay more attention to them. "I think nothing flies quite as beautifully as a vulture. I like watching them. But I don't think I would have been as involved with them here if there hadn't been such a stink in the newspapers about how awful they are." I wondered if Bob knew anything about the alleged damage the local vultures had caused. "I asked the city animal control to document damage, and they never did. And when people would complain about there being a lot of poop on their roofs, I'd go over and wouldn't see anything. But there are large groups—400 in a group—and they're pretty impressive, so if you're a little nervous at all, you might overreact. I don't know if there was damage or not. The city certainly didn't document it. I think they should have. If they're going to spend the money to disperse them, they should have. But," he continued, shrugging, "I'm pretty confident that black vultures tore up the roof of McHarg School. They liked to sit on the furnace stack in the morning. The roof was black tar, and I'm told they did quite a bit of damage to that. But it wasn't just the vultures. Kids got up there and threw rocks through the skylight. They replaced the roof."

Besides being blamed for property damage, in Radford, as in other places where vultures roost in the winter, misinformation and panic often outweigh logic and science. Instead of dispelling myths, many media outlets fuel vulture fears by printing the unfounded and sometimes ridiculous concerns of local residents. Articles in the *Roanoke Times* quote people "who worry about their pets and children." One man expressed concern about vultures "creeping into the yard" because his two-year-old child played there. Residents of other Virginia towns where vultures roost make similar complaints; in Staunton, a two-hour drive north of Radford on Interstate 81, a resident described the vultures as disgusting, stinky, and mean. The *Washington Post* told the story of another Staunton resident who encouraged his nine-year-old son to shoot paintballs at the vultures but was then horrified when one of the birds vomited on the boy. "It was so disgusting," the interview reads. "We got it off him. Got his shirt off. And got him to stop screaming." The one who deserved the vomit was the boy's father. Why encourage children to be violent toward an animal whose only defense against aggressors is to throw up on them?

Both turkey and black vultures are afforded protection under the Migratory Bird Treaty Act, which makes harming them a federal offense. But citizens can contact APHIS for help dispersing vultures that have become a "problem." In recent years, the number of farmers and ranchers complaining of vulture predation on newborn livestock has increased in several southern states, including Virginia, and APHIS has been employed in dispersing or removing these birds. But despite frequent complaints from ranchers, there are few documented cases of black vultures killing healthy newborn livestock, and there are *absolutely no* documented cases of turkey vultures doing so, although turkey vultures are sometimes guilty by association, often feeding at a carcass along with black vultures. A 2006 USDA report admits that although "it is widely reported that black vultures prey on newly born livestock, . . . there still is relatively little information on this phenomenon." Another paper by USDA biologists elaborates on the difficulties they face when trying to gather this information: "We do not know what proportion of the total number of depredations is reported. So at best these data might represent the minimal estimates of the extent of the vulture damage problem. Alternatively, these data might overestimate actual vulture-caused mortality because some of the deaths attributed to black vultures could have been due to other factors." Much of the information about vulture damage in Virginia comes from a 1999 report published in *Wildlife Society Bulletin*. The article compiles complaints filed between 1990 and 1996 throughout the state. The complainants accuse black vultures of attacking all sorts of animals—horses, goats, sheep, captive deer, pigs, dogs, cats, and poultry.

The majority of the complaints involve newborn livestock; farmers claimed that flocks of vultures attacked animals as they were being born, and sometimes even killed the animals' mothers. While I don't doubt the sincerity of the livestock owners, these claims are difficult to substantiate. First, and most important, how do ranchers know that the vultures were responsible for killing the livestock? Vultures have been known to hang around breeding operations and feed on placentas. What if a calf was stillborn? Certainly, the vultures would eat it immediately. And if a horse died while foaling, again, the vultures would absolutely eat the carcass. Unless the rancher was present to witness the birth and subsequent attack, how would he know for certain that the vultures were responsible for the death? But, then, if he were present for the birth, why wouldn't he scare the vultures away? As USDA biologists write in a 2004 paper, "In assessing the role of black vultures as livestock predators, it is difficult to obtain objective, unbiased information because direct observations of black vulture attacks on livestock are uncommon. Usually, the investigator arrives at the feeding site after the prey animal is dead and the chain of events leading to the demise of the animal is speculative." Without witnessing a vulture attack firsthand, it is difficult—perhaps impossible—to confirm that the birds killed the animal.

But let's assume that the ranchers' complaints are valid, and that sizeable flocks of black vultures seek out newborn livestock to kill and eat. Doesn't the livestock owner bear responsibility for securing his vulnerable animals? The USDA suggests that "vulture predation can be prevented by isolating lambing, pigging, and calving activities in sheds or buildings, or by using paddocks close to barns or buildings with human activity so that birthing animals can be monitored closely." Some livestock owners have argued that such recommendations aren't feasible. But isn't it worth a try? Perhaps if one does not have the desire or means to secure pregnant, sick, or vulnerable livestock, then one should not own them—and should not blame vultures for doing what they've evolved to do. The USDA points out that "some animals are stillborn and others die for reasons unrelated to black vultures." The birthing process is a dangerous, intense, and vulnerable event for all involved. The USDA concludes, "These birds take the path of least resistance and eat carrion when it is available. Black vultures are opportunists, however, and when the chance arises, they will attack and eat defenseless live animals." It should be the responsibility of the caretaker to protect his or her "defenseless live animals"—not by trying to kill the vultures (which is illegal and probably ineffective as well as being bad for the ecosystem) but by being present for births or by securing pregnant animals away from potential danger.

In addition to the belief that they pose a threat, bad press, their relative abundance, and a "creepy" appearance make vultures easy targets. A quick Internet search for "shooting vultures" turns up more than a few discussions on online forums. On one forum, a poster writes, "I have a half dozen or more turkey vultures that like to hang out and crap on my roof. Looking for ways to discourage them. I guess I could frighten them and then shoot them with my shotgun after they are off the roof." Responses to this inquiry include a variety of suggestions: "Roadkill placed at a pre-selected location next to a pre-dug hole works"; "I think that you could also poison them with varmint poison on some bait"; and "Turkey vultures are not protected. The way I kill them sometimes is I don't use a real gun I use a paintball gun." Another response warns, "These are nasty stinky birds, so they are a mess to deal with if you kill them." If acted upon, all of these suggestions would violate federal law. But that doesn't deter everyone.

A *Washington Post* article from 1994 titled "Virginia Vultures Turn Vicious, Dine on Pets, Terrorize Owners" tells the story of a woman who kept a loaded shotgun by her back door in case she had to defend her home against the birds. She "filmed them circling over children getting off a school bus," and claimed that "her neighbor's cat, Stripe, was grabbed by the tail and carried 25 feet in the air for a distance of 100 yards. A vet stitched up four talon holes in Stripe's body." Despite the fact that vultures rarely attack live prey, both black and turkey vultures lack strong talons—they *cannot* physically pick up a cat, and certainly not with their feet. Even if the cat were unconscious with a vulture standing on top of it, the bird's feet wouldn't leave "talon holes." Vultures sometimes use their toenails to hold carrion in place while they tear chunks with their beaks, but they cannot snatch up and fly away with a cat. Misinformation like this not only fuels public fear of vultures, but it could contribute to unfair roost dispersals and even vulture deaths.

Although the majority of the complaints listed in the 1999 article in *Wildlife Society Bulletin* that summarizes "vulture damage incidents" reported to APHIS in Virginia involve livestock, there are fifteen complaints of vultures either preying on, injuring, harassing, or "threatening" pets. The study defines *threat* as "belief by the pet owner that vultures would attempt to attack." By this logic, if I believe that the squirrels in my yard are going to attack my dog, can I report it to the USDA and demand that they come and remove the squirrels? I wonder if the impossible tale of Stripe's attack is included in the fifteen reported incidences. Whose responsibility is it to refute biologically impossible claims such as this one?

Dr. Bob Sheehy and a group of like-minded others did some mitigation of their own to address Radford's vulture problem—in 2007 they organized the first annual Radford Vulture Festival, which eventually morphed into the Radford Roosting Festival. "We thought that there needed to be some education about vultures. All the misconceptions—you know, people were worried about them attacking their pets, pulling babies out of their blankets. Spreading disease. People just don't know vultures. If they knew them, they'd love them." Bob thinks that the vulture festivals have been effective, at least for children. "I always run into kids who know me as the 'vulture man.' Some are just joyful about seeing a vulture. But I'm not sure how many adults have been swayed."

I attended Radford's inaugural Vulture Festival on a blustery February afternoon. When I arrived at the Radford Recreation Center, I noticed that a small crowd had gathered in the parking lot. I hunched my shoulders against the biting wind and hurried over to see what was so interesting that a dozen or so people would stand out in the cold to witness it. When I reached the group, I saw what held their attention: there was Bob Sheehy with a live turkey vulture standing on his gloved forearm.

The vulture's name was Buttercup, and I learned that a wing injury kept her from returning to the wild. She stood calmly with Bob, turning her head from side to side to size up her audience. Her shoulders were hunched against the wind, too, which ruffled the deep-brown feathers on the back of her neck. While most of her face was naked and red, I noticed that the area around and above her eyes was covered with a layer of black fuzz; it looked like velvet, and I imagined it felt as soft. Buttercup's prominent nostrils—used to help turkey vultures locate carrion by its odor—sat above her bone-colored, delicately hooked bill. She was gorgeous and, Bob promised, "as sweet as a buttercup."

I ducked into the rec center and found an all-purpose room filled with educational vulture displays, constructed by children from Radford's schools. Posters illustrated the differences between turkey and black vultures and enumerated the reasons that vultures were important to local ecosystems. Vulture mobiles hung from the ceiling, and vulture art adorned the tables. The warm room was filled with laughter and excitement as kids in coats and hats pulled their parents to see the posters they'd made. Certainly this—a celebratory, educational, art-filled community gathering—was a more positive, productive way to address the situation than shooting noisemakers, fireworks, paintballs, or bullets at the birds.

I returned to Radford in the winter of 2012 and found a different kind of celebration. Instead of a Vulture Festival, the event had been renamed the Radford Roosting Festival, and it was now a celebration of all the region's birds. It was held in the gymnasium of McHarg Elementary, a former epicenter of the town's vulture problems. Like the first Vulture Festival, the gym buzzed with excitement and children, many of whom worked on dissecting owl pellets or constructing bird feeders. I made my way slowly around the displays, searching for a mention of the town's vultures; other than a few photographs, there were none. Gone were the posters explaining the need for vultures, and no vulture mobiles hung from the ceilings. At one end of the gym, representatives from the Wildlife Center of Virginia conducted a presentation with live birds of prey, but they didn't have any vultures with them, and Bob and Buttercup were conspicuously absent. While I love all birds—not just vultures—I was disappointed that the focus of the festival had changed.

I pulled out of McHarg and drove toward the nearby child-care center. It seemed closed for the day, the parking lot and playground empty. The branches of the leafless trees were also empty, and no vultures soared overhead. Later, I asked Bob what had happened to Radford's vultures, and he said it appeared that APHIS's dispersal efforts had worked, at least for the moment. "I think what finally did it was the effigies," he told me. "They would do some pyrotechnics and noise, and that along with the effigies. . . ." He trailed off and shook his head. "I can't believe people in the neighborhoods think that's better than the vultures."

To an extent, I can understand the concerns of folks living and working near a vulture roost. While I would enjoy it, I'm sure several hundred large birds silently watching children move around a playground is unnerving. Their presence reminds us of our own mortality: life will continue after we die, and some life will continue *because* we die. But without a full-time biologic cleanup crew, our neighborhoods, roads, and fields would get pretty messy. Vultures consume and neutralize dangerous pathogens like anthrax and botulism, and they slow the spread of rabies and distemper by displacing mammalian scavengers. They perform these tasks daily and without fanfare, often out of the public view. But when they return to rest with their families at night, instead of being left peacefully alone, a handful of the people who benefit from their services react violently, with fireworks, lights, or bullets. Some thanks.

On my way out of town that day, I noticed a few turkey vultures sailing high above the Pepper's Ferry Bridge, but it seemed that the hundreds of vultures that had roosted in Radford had, at least for the moment, moved on. But if history were any indication, they'd be back. And I'd return to see them.

She stood on the steer's open abdomen and plunged
her red head into the viscera, tearing and gulping
the smooth, wet organ meat. She lifted her head and
hissed deeply at the crowd that had gathered behind
her; two of the group lowered their heads and stepped
back. She buried her face again and pulled off almost
more than she could swallow, but she got it down.
Sated, she waddled awkwardly away from the steer,
wiped her beak on the ground, and spread her wings.
The meat was heavy in her chest. She watched as
the crowd swarmed the carcass, hissing and nipping
each other, but she'd had her fill. Far across the hill,
she watched the palm fronds tremble. Insects buzzed
as the afternoon heat settled over the landscape.
She flapped her wings once, twice, and again before
folding them over her dark back. She ran her white-
tipped beak down a glossy flight feather and waited.

Battlefield Ghosts

Sing, goddess, the wrath of Achilles Peleus' son,
the ruinous wrath that brought on the Achaians woes
innumerable, and hurled down into Hades many
strong souls of heroes, and gave their bodies to
be a prey to dogs and all winged fowl.
▼ opening of Homer's *The Iliad*, translated by
Andrew Lang

A light snow began to fall over Devil's Den, the Wheat-field, the Peach Orchard, and the rest of the silent battlefield as I crossed South Confederate Avenue to the parking lot at the base of Big Round Top. Mine was the only vehicle. In early July, during the anniversary of the famous battle, Gettysburg, Pennsylvania, would be teeming with tourists, schoolchildren, and Civil War buffs, but on this chilly February morning, I had the nearly 4,000-acre military park to myself—well, to myself, the ghosts, and the more than 1,000 monuments and statues. And the vultures.

I buttoned my coat and started hiking the trail that wound up the wooded hill, wishing I'd worn more appropriate shoes.

My backless clogs threatened to trip me; I walked more slowly and cautiously than usual so I didn't fall onto the cold, frozen ground. I began climbing and the trees thickened. A white-breasted nuthatch *yank-yanked* from a nearby pine, but otherwise, everything was still and silent. I felt eyes watching me, but I seemed to be alone. I exhaled, my breath fogging the air, and I quickened my pace.

In 1863 more than 7,000 Union and Confederate soldiers died here; some 26,000 were wounded and another 10,000 were captured or missing. Historians note that the battle of Gettysburg tallied more casualties than any other battle of the Civil War. Some of the fiercest fighting took place on the fields behind me; the areas between Little Round Top and Devil's Den were known as the Slaughter Pen and the Valley of Death. How could this ground not be haunted? The air seemed to vibrate with strange energy. As I hiked up the hill I imagined broken bodies wedged between the rocks, the echoes of gunfire, the screams of wounded cavalry horses. I shivered and walked even faster, my heartbeat thudding in my ears. I began to regret coming here alone. I tried to push the ghosts from my head and remember why I'd come.

In the 1980s, more than 700 black and turkey vultures regularly roosted in Big Round Top's pine trees during the winter. Reports from the early 2000s, however, claimed the roost had been abandoned, perhaps because of a reduction in the park's white-tailed deer population and an increase in visitors to the park. "Vultures are not as site-tenacious as people think," Keith Bildstein told me when we discussed Gettysburg's vultures, "and roosts are not as stable as people think." Despite this, I wanted to check out this site; so far I'd seen a red-tailed hawk and only two or three turkey vultures overhead. But the landscape around the old battlefield is in many ways favorable to the large birds—hilly and windy, with pines trees for roost-

ing and a reliable supply of food courtesy of livestock operations. Historically, vultures had always been found in this part
of southern Pennsylvania, but according to local legend, their
numbers greatly increased in the aftermath of the 1863 battle.

In addition to the 7,000 men, more than 3,000 horses had
died during the three-day clash. In an interview with wpsu, a
local npr affiliate, park natural resource specialist Hal Greenlee (now retired) stated, "We do know that there were thousands of horses killed here. The experts are sure that the
vultures would have been drawn in by the thousands. . . . They
could not have resisted that offering. . . . They would have come
here from all over the eastern United States. . . . I think there's
a good chance that the population increased from the battle,
and there's probably direct descendants here now from those
birds that fed here in 1863." This statement reminded me of
the "Odyssey" chapter from Aldo Leopold's *A Sand County Almanac*, in which an atom—a nutrient, perhaps calcium—trav-
els from rock to oak, acorn to deer to Indian, bluestem leaf,
mouse, soil, oats, buffalo, soil, spiderwort, rabbit, owl, and
on and on. But in the case of Gettysburg's vultures, the degree of separation is even smaller; if dead Civil War soldiers
and horses did indeed (unintentionally) feed the vultures, certainly the birds in the region today could be kin of those birds
150 years ago, and part of them a part of those who died. In
a way, a physical piece of our nation's history could live on
in the local vulture population, haunting the battlefield where
so many fell. Not unlike the statues and monuments, the vultures are reminders of that battle's losses.

I glanced over my shoulder and tried to imagine what
3,000 dead horses would look and smell like. I have seen dead
horses before; I grew up with horses, and until I was fifteen
or so, I rode my Morgans competitively throughout Pennsylvania and the mid-Atlantic region. When I was twelve years

old, my childhood horse and best friend, J.P., was euthanized after a bout of colic. My parents tried to protect me by confining me to the house, but I insisted on seeing the body. I slid open the heavy wooden barn door and there he was, lying on his side in the aisle, covered by his blue blanket. I couldn't see J.P.'s head or face, but all four of his feet stuck out, and his fat belly swelled beneath the cover. I'd wanted to throw myself against him and hug him and cry, but instead I patted the blanket and retreated to the house. Later, a backhoe came to bury him behind the pasture where we'd spent so many hours together; I stayed inside, staring at the cracks in my bedroom's ceiling.

As I walked up the trail on Big Round Top I thought about my own young child, and I wondered, morbidly, how she would one day learn about death and loss. The world often seems a cruel place. People kill each other, crudely, viciously, for ideas or ideals, for greed or land. Each soldier who died here began like my daughter—a hope, a dream, a blessing, or maybe a regret, maybe resented. Regardless, each one started small, grew up, loved, and was then torn apart by bullet or Minié ball or cannon fire. Or suffered with infection, starvation, gangrene. On the spectrum of ways and places to die, I think a Civil War battlefield would be among the worst. But seen another way—from the perspective of a black or turkey vulture—the aftermath of a Civil War battle could mean easy meals for days or weeks, and therefore, a greater chance for survival and reproductive success.

Vultures seem to have been benefiting from the warlike ways of humans for millennia. One of the world's earliest records of a battle—a limestone monument from ancient Sumer (circa 2450 BC) called the *Stele of the Vultures*—depicts the immediate aftermath of a battle. According to the Louvre, where it's displayed, the stele "commemorates, in text and images, an important victory by Eannatum, king of Lagash, over the neighboring city of Umma." Even though the stele is broken into several pieces, it shows "the triumphant army . . . trampl[ing] the bodies of its enemies, on which a host of vultures has already begun to feed." Another ancient battle scene, this one on a palette from predynastic ancient Egypt, shows a lion, at least two vultures, and five ravens or crows eating dead soldiers. According to the British Museum, "It is assumed that these are enemies fallen in battle, and some have speculated that the lion represents a ruler or king and the palette records a royal victory." The lion is biting the stomach of a limp body, and a vulture seems to be picking at the eye of another. In addition to showing that humans have been fighting with each other (and bragging about their victories) for a very long time, these examples from antiquity also show that vultures have been making use of human subsidies for at least as long.

▼ While some believe that a vulture eating a human body results in spiritual ascendance or translates as a final act of charity on behalf of the deceased, other cultures do not welcome the practice, especially if the body is eaten unintentionally; at times it even produces a visceral response of disgust or anger. For example, in the spring of 2013, a fifty-two-year-old hiker in France "fell to her death off a cliff in the Pyrenees," reports the UK's *Independent*. The region's griffon vultures—the same genus of vultures that make Indian and Tibetan sky burials possible—located the hiker's body and reduced her to "bones, clothes, and shoes" in less than an hour. Although authorities confirmed that she died in the fall, the story made international news. The vultures in this part of France (near the Spanish border) had already angered local farmers, who alleged that the huge birds were too abundant and attacked livestock. After the incident with the hiker, some farmers even sought permission to shoot the protected birds; it is unclear whether their request will be granted.

While reports of turkey or black vultures eating hikers in the United States are rare, the birds have eaten at least one deceased human in Texas. "For more than five weeks," the *Huffington Post* reports, "a woman's body lay undisturbed in a secluded Texas field. Then a frenzied flock of vultures descended on the corpse and reduced it to a skeleton within hours." The woman wasn't "missing"; in fact, researchers working at Texas State University's forensic anthropology research facility, also known as a "body farm," had purposely placed her where she lay. Some of the facility's studies deal with determining time and cause of death in potential homicide victims, and the vulture incident "call[ed] into question many of the benchmarks detectives have long relied on." The event was captured by a motion-sensing camera; footage showed "the vultures jumping up and down on the woman's body, breaking some of her ribs, which investigators could also misinterpret as trauma suffered during a beating." Researchers were surprised that it took the vultures thirty-seven days to begin eating the body, which has implications for homicide investigations, as well; no one is certain why it took the birds so long to find her. Of course, as Keith Bildstein pointed out, the vultures may have "found" her much earlier but didn't eat her because of other available food in the area.

While the flock that descended on the Texas body farm consisted of only black vultures, it is puzzling that local turkey vultures didn't alert other aerial scavengers to the presence of the body much sooner; using their keen sense of smell, turkey vultures will often clue other birds in to the location of carrion. Although now widely accepted, turkey vulture olfaction has long been a topic of debate among ornithologists. After experiments with captive birds, John James Audubon famously declared that vultures did not use smell to find food. But other early ornithologists were not so sure. An 1883 report in the *American Naturalist* describes a group of turkey vultures descending on a New Jersey field where a horse and cow had been buried. The author eloquently writes that "'buzzards' shadowed the farm by scores, seeming to obey from all quarters of the heavens a mysterious summons to convocation. . . . Buzzard after buzzard I traced as they appeared in various portions of the sky with half-folded wings, reminding me of mute, aerial hounds, 'coming down the scent,' their course, as swift, silent, and undeviating as an arrow's." Samuel N. Rhoads, the author, surmised that the birds were attracted to the scent of the deceased horse and cow, whose "pent-up odors" had been released as a result of the field being plowed.

Although Rhoads's 1883 claim may be somewhat dubious, a more recent article (2002) from the *Journal of Raptor Research* documents a turkey vulture exhuming the body of a woodchuck on a Connecticut pumpkin farm. According to the author and two farmworkers, a "vulture descended almost immediately and landed directly on the burial site. . . . It scratched away the soil until the carcass was exposed, and then proceeded to tear off pieces of flesh." Before making this observation, farmworkers had reported that other buried woodchuck carcasses had been dug up and partially eaten in a similar manner, but they'd never witnessed the perpetrator. While the authors of the report admit that they can't "totally discount" that the bird had watched someone bury the woodchuck from afar, they believe "this seems unlikely because turkey vultures normally return to their roost 1–3 hours before sunset, the woodchuck was buried at dusk, and no turkey vulture roost existed" near the field. They surmised that the vulture could smell the dead woodchuck, even beneath several inches of soil.

The truly groundbreaking study on turkey vulture olfaction

came in 1961, "Indication of the Sense of Smell in the Turkey Vulture, *Cathartes aura* (Linnaeus), from Feeding Tests." Published in the *American Midland Naturalist*, the study put two captive turkey vultures from Florida through a series of food trials. In one experiment, the birds were given two pans, one containing dead leaves and one containing horse meat buried underneath the dead leaves. A second experiment also involved two pans with leaves, one with horse meat and one without, although this time the birds had to walk around a wooden screen to reach the pans. A third experiment was similar to the first experiment, except the horse meat was smeared on dead chicks, and there were three pans instead of two. The fourth experiment required the vultures to put their heads through three-inch openings to reach the pans with meat-smeared chicks. The results were conclusive: in experiments 1 and 2, the pans containing food were investigated first 84 percent and 94 percent of the time, respectively; experiments 3 and 4 proved a bit more difficult, although still the birds investigated the meat pans first 64 percent and 57 percent of the time, respectively.

Studies later revealed that the turkey vulture has large and well-developed olfactory bulbs in its brain, capable of detecting "the scent of rotting flesh in concentrations as tiny as a few parts per billion in the air," according to a 2013 article in *Smithsonian Insider*. The article quotes ornithologist Gary Graves, who had recently completed a study on turkey vulture vision and olfaction: "Their sense of smell is so acute that they can even locate hidden food, say something as small as a dead rat under a pile of leaves." Police in Germany hoped to utilize the turkey vulture's excellent sense of smell to help them locate human remains. A captive bird, "Sherlock," was trained for this purpose—sort of like a bloodhound with wings. Vultures could be more effective than canines because police dogs "need to take frequent breaks and can only scout 100 square metres per day, or even less if the terrain is difficult," stated a representative of the Lower Saxony police force, quoted in the *National*. The article also mentioned a "potential disadvantage" of using the birds: "the vultures are likely to start picking at corpses they find." However, as Sherlock's trainer pointed out, "If they take a nibble, what the hell, the victim will be beyond help anyway." The plan was to fit the vultures with transmitters so that police could locate them—and the remains. Unfortunately, the project hit a few snags because of Sherlock's shyness and his apparent preference for walking over flying.

Although the United States does not (yet) train vultures to search for and find dead humans, wild turkey vultures have been known to alert natural-gas workers to the presence of pipeline leaks; an additive to the gas, ethyl mercaptan, smells like rotting flesh, and the birds swoop closer to investigate. Perhaps Gettysburg park specialist Greenlee was correct when he stated that vultures would have been "drawn in" by the odoriferous offering left after the battle.

▼ Few events in the history of the United States have captured our attention as acutely as the battle of Gettysburg. Although it was fought more than 150 years ago, the American Civil War is regularly the subject of books, movies, radio programs, and articles. I grew up and live in a region steeped in Civil War history. My current home in West Virginia is within sight of the Mason-Dixon line, and I lived for five years in southern Virginia, near many Civil War battlefields and historic sites. Our local newspaper there often published letters to the editor arguing Civil War topics, and the Sons of Confederate Veterans marched proudly in parades and reenactments.

When I was a child in Pennsylvania, we took family vacations and school field trips to Gettysburg. My little brother Joe and I sat in the back of my parents' minivan as we crept along the roads through the battlefield, listening to a rented tape recorder explain the troops' movements and strategies. We would pause the tape when the narrator suggested and tumble out of the van to pose for Kodachrome photographs with monuments. Although it was widely dismissed as a myth, I'd heard somewhere that for Gettysburg's equestrian statues, if a stone horse's four feet were on the ground—such as in the famous depiction of General Robert E. Lee on his mount Traveler—the horse's rider survived. If one foot was lifted, the rider had been wounded; a rearing horse meant that the rider had been killed. As a horse-loving child, I'd wondered what happened to the horses of dead soldiers; now I realize that they probably died on the battlefield, too, perhaps becoming food for vultures.

Joe and I always made our parents stop near Devil's Den, the tumble of boulders across the field from Little and Big Round Tops. We pretended to be Confederate sharpshooters, scaling the rocks' rough surfaces and shouldering imaginary rifles. We stood on Cemetery Ridge and stared down the hill, imaging we were part of Hancock's Union forces, fixing our sights on the rebel onslaught during Pickett's Charge. I thought about running up that same hill in the July heat, probably shoeless and hungry, carrying heavy equipment and the weighty certainty that I would die. I imagined the heart-pounding terror. Who runs up a hill toward a bunch of people with cannons and guns? Even as a kid I remember thinking it was a stupid thing to do. Imagining what the area would have looked like in the days and weeks after the battle haunted me. It still haunts me.

Along with mugs, shirts, postcards, maps, and more, the battlefield museum's store sells a wide variety of books. I purchased a copy of Gregory Coco's thorough and disturbing volume, *A Strange and Blighted Land—Gettysburg: The Aftermath of a Battle*. The book compiles news reports, eyewitness letters, photographs, maps, and artist renditions of scenes following the battle. The book's cover photograph, "Scene in the woods at the northwestern base of Big Round Top" by James F. Gibson, caught my attention. In the grainy picture, at least four dead bodies are sprawled among the trees and brush, three in dark uniforms and one in light. As I followed the trail up Big Round Top, I thought of those particular bodies, those four lives lost, their spirits perhaps lingering on this hillside.

As I flipped through Coco's book, another image, this one an illustration from Frank Leslie's *Illustrated History of the Civil War*, shows a family of sightseers staring in horror at a pile of dead soldiers. The sky above them as well as above the distant hills is filled with unmistakable black Vs—clearly the artist's depiction of vultures cruising over the carnage. Because so many journalists, nurses, and curiosity-seekers flocked to Gettysburg after the battle, we have many recorded accounts of its aftermath. Coco frequently quotes from John Howard Wert, who describes "an area of perhaps four acres . . . so thickly covered with the dead that it was scarcely possible to walk anywhere without treading upon them." Wert notices "mangled and shredded" soldiers, piles of bodies, and "festering corpses at every step." A nurse, Sophronia Bucklin, saw "boots, with a foot and leg putrefying within, [lying] beside the pathway, and ghastly heads, too—over the exposed skulls of which insects crawled—while great worms bored through rotting eyeballs. Astride a tree sat a bloody horror, with head and limbs severed by shells, the birds having banqueted on it, while the tattered uniform, stained with gore, fluttered dismally in the summer air."

Interestingly, other witnesses to the aftermath remark about the absence of vultures, and Coco seems to agree with this version. Coco claims that Thomas Duncan Carson "correctly played down the popular notion that buzzards and vultures were everywhere feeding upon the remains of horses and men. In reality, Mr. Carson explained, there were in actuality none of these creatures present, as all had been frightened away by the tremendous noise of hundreds of cannons and thousands of muskets, and by the acrid smell of so much gunpowder." While Coco and Carson may have a point—pyrotechnics and loud noises are used today to disperse roosting vultures, and certainly cannons and gunfire would be loud—it seems as if the local vultures would have returned in the days or weeks following the battle, and from other eyewitness accounts, the birds would have found a feast waiting for them. And, as we now know from the Texas body farm experiments, black vultures do not hesitate to eat a corpse that's been dead for more than a month.

On July 9, almost a week after the battle had ended, a Harrisburg newspaper printed a letter that described what its writer had observed: "Any one anxious about the definition of the word glory will find the answer in the valley in front of Round Top, where numbers of bodies lie bleaching in the sun on the gray granite rocks, in every stage of decomposition, doomed to lie there exposed to the elements in every conceivable position that men killed outright will assume in their fall. Their anxious friends will never know the horrible condition that death left them in." Another account from July 9 describes "over 70 Confederates still scattered around and unburied among the giant granite rocks."

Even if the vultures still hadn't returned a week later, certainly they would have been back within a month or two. Coco summarizes another account, from an Ambrose Emory, who visited the battlefield in mid-August and "commented that there were bodies still on Round Top and Little Round Top, 'lodging in the crevasses,' where they were becoming food for vultures, and their bleached bones a sad spectacle of the ruin and desolation that has been brought upon a once happy country.'" Another witness claimed that "more than a month after the battle in one of these chasms [between piles of rocks at Plum Rum] was presented the hideous spectacle of the remains of five rebels piled upon each other just as they had fallen in a place from which it would have been impossible to extricate the bodies." According to other accounts noted in Coco's book, exposed bones and whole skeletons of soldiers were still being discovered at Gettysburg more than a year later.

While it may be impossible to know for sure whether vultures fed upon dead soldiers and horses after the 1863 battle, it seems clear that many Confederate bodies were left unburied for days, weeks, and even months after they died. Others were "hastily interred," often in shallow graves, and sometimes with hands or feet sticking out of the ground. While many were eventually dug up and reinterred in permanent graves, some soldiers were left in their original shallow plots. And it sounds as if some were never buried at all.

▼ My breath fogged in the cold air as I passed monuments tucked between the trees and brush. Everything was still except for a small mouse rustling in the dry leaves along the trail. I crouched down to watch him. His brownish-gray fur had lost its sheen, and he seemed too exhausted and consumed by the task at hand to worry about me. The mouse seemed desperate. He'd become food for an owl soon, I thought, and straightened, thinking again of Leopold's "Odyssey."

I rounded a bend and soon found myself at the top of the hill. A light snow fell around my shoulders, and before me stretched a panoramic view of valleys and farms. The top of the hill was thinly wooded, but no vultures roosted in the silent trees. It seemed like a logical place for a roost, however, and I tried to imagine hundreds of vultures filling the trees' branches. This battle, this town—Gettysburg—marked the "Confederate High Tide," the northernmost point that rebel forces reached. Most of the Civil War was fought in the South. Historically, the Gettysburg area also marked the high tide of another southerner, the black vulture. Like the rebel forces of the 1860s, in the past black vultures couldn't thrive north of the Mason-Dixon line. While I do not want to compare flocks of black vultures to invading battalions, their range has expanded ever northward. Now, in the summer, black vultures are regularly sighted as far north as New England and parts of maritime Canada.

A chill ran through me, and I decided to begin hiking down the hill to my car, past the silent monuments, between the ghosts. When I noticed a flesh-and-blood human approaching, I was taken by surprise; we nodded solemnly to each other and continued our lonesome hikes. I hunched my shoulders to my chin, channeling a roosting vulture. Not long ago, I stood with Keith Bildstein outside the Bethel Church near Hawk Mountain, about an hour's drive from Gettysburg. We watched a small group of turkey vultures hunching against the cold while roosting in pine trees across a quiet country road from the church and the cemetery next to it. "This roost is perfect," Keith had told me. "They're in exotic evergreens that people have planted. And the graveyard is south-facing. The birds leave the roost in the morning and stand on the gravestones to warm up." I found a photograph showing a mixed group of black and turkey vultures perched on a dozen headstones, wings outstretched, waiting for the sun to do its work. The effect is eerie. Certainly, the birds could not know what lay beneath the ground, and were simply making use of a convenient staging spot—provided, again, by humans, and indirectly by our deaths.

I got to my car and cranked the heat up all the way. I drove slowly through the silent fields, thinking about death—tragic deaths, accidental deaths, deaths that provide life. A red-tailed hawk clung to a tree limb above the road, feathers fluffed. As I left the park and headed for the highway, I saw several turkey vultures slicing through the air like wind-caught kites, and I wondered about their ancestors, and what—who—fueled their families through the decades, centuries, and millennia.

She could feel the change in the air. The days
lengthened, and flocks of warblers began filling
the farm's trees, their buzzy voices tentative in the
early-morning fog. Each evening they disappeared
and were replaced by a new flock, gleaning insects
and bobbing their tails. She grew restless in the palm,
and spent more and more time each day gorging
herself on dead steers and chickens.

Finally, once the sun had cleared the dawn's mist,
she roused, flapped, and stepped into the air. She set
her wings. Fixed her gaze. And didn't look back.

Welcome Back, Buzzards

Through my binoculars I watched a female vermilion fly-catcher eat what appeared to be a small lizard; she'd fluttered to the ground, hovered there a moment, and then returned to a dry, twisted branch with something long and gray in her bill. I lowered my binoculars and caught a flash of red to my right. It was the male, brilliantly crimson in the mid-morning sun, perched on his own dry branch. He lifted into flight, and the contrast of black wings to red body reminded me of a scarlet tanager. But there were no scarlet tanagers here; this was the desert, the Sonoran, and in this rare riparian area—the Nature Conservancy's 770-acre Hassayampa River Preserve—grew towering cottonwoods, willows, and tangled mesquite.

The one-hundred-mile Hassayampa flows mostly underground, except for the area that's now the preserve. The wetlands, stream banks, and surrounding trees and shrubs provide homes for 280 bird species, including rarities like the zone-tailed hawk, white-faced ibis, and the endangered southwestern willow flycatcher. Soon, because of a partnership between the Nature Conservancy and the Maricopa County Parks and Recreation Department, the preserve will become part of the larger (more than 70,000-acre) Vulture Mountains Recreation Area—which bears a lovely name, in my opinion.

Jesse and I had been slowly birding in the preserve all morning—birding as well as we could with a small child in tow. Mostly, Laurel kept herself busy by playing in the sandy soil, picking up sticks, and flipping through our field guide. But by now, more than two hours in, she'd begun to tire, which manifested in whining and refusing to wear her floppy sun hat. Now, she sat on the ground in the middle of the Mesquite Meander trail and tossed tiny fistfuls of dust into the air. It's difficult to wield a pair of binoculars while carrying a baby, so we began to wind our way back to the visitors' center—with its ferocious gangs of black-chinned, Anna's, and Costa's hummingbirds mobbing the nectar feeders and flowers—and the parking lot beyond. Jesse and Laurel moved ahead of me while I paused at an unfamiliar birdsong. I scanned the leafy crown of a tree for the singer, but while I was searching, my eyes turned upward and noticed two high, thin black shapes soaring in the unclouded blue sky. Since arriving in Arizona the day before, these were the first two turkey vultures I'd seen.

In addition to family fun, I had two goals while visiting the desert: to attend the Welcome Back, Buzzards celebration at Boyce Thompson Arboretum State Park near the town of Superior, about an hour southeast of Phoenix, and to locate a turkey vulture nicknamed "Jennie" near Gila Bend. Jennie is one of a dozen Arizona vultures wearing a Hawk Mountain Sanctuary satellite transmitter. In May 2013, Dr. Keith Bildstein and three colleagues, Dr. Jean-François Therrien from Hawk Mountain, Dr. Marc Bechard from Boise State University, and Dr. Jennie Duberstein of the US Fish and Wildlife Service's Sonoran Joint Venture, fitted the first six birds, members of the *Cathartes aura aura* subspecies, with transmitters to monitor their movements. Not much research has focused on the migratory patterns of this subspecies, which is found from the American Southwest throughout Mexico and Central America. I was looking forward to getting to know these southwestern cousins, slightly smaller and darker than our eastern *C. a. septentrionalis* birds. But before we'd begin our search for Jennie the vulture, we'd enjoy the birds here in Hassayampa, and the following morning we'd be up early for the Welcome Back celebration at Boyce Thompson.

I paused again, this time to photograph a large Cooper's hawk perched on a snag, and by the time I caught up with Jesse, Laurel had fallen asleep in his arms. It was only mid-March, but the Arizona sun was fierce, and I gently pulled her floppy hat over her face. We sat on the visitors' center benches amid the swirling hummingbirds and watched the colorful chaos.

▼ Boyce Thompson Arboretum State Park has been celebrating the return of the "buzzards" for more than twenty years. The population of turkey vultures that spends time in the park departs in the fall and returns, very reliably, around the time of the vernal equinox. Traditional wisdom is that these *C. a. aura* vultures migrate to the tropics and return to Arizona to breed in the spring; for the park's vultures, at least, this belief rings true—or at least, the birds leave the park and go *somewhere* in the fall. Hawk Mountain's important migration research is working to answer the question of just where Arizona's *aura* vultures go.

We arrived at the park just before 7:00 a.m. The sun hadn't quite risen all the way, and the air was chilly. We bundled Laurel in a hooded fleece jacket and headed into the park, following the stream of folks wearing binoculars and clutching steaming coffee cups. The park's meticulously landscaped trails wound through a Sonoran exhibit, demonstration garden, Chihuahuan exhibit, cactus and succulent garden, and more. As we passed through the eucalyptus forest, I had the feeling I was being watched; I tipped back my head and saw that I was right. A eucalyptus tree towered above me, and several of its branches contained roosting turkey vultures. One leaned forward and peered down at me, its head cocked to the side. I lifted my binoculars and counted at least ten birds in the tree, although there could have been a few more. Remarkably silent, most perched with folded wings, shoulders slightly hunched. A few buried their beaks in their chest feathers and between tail plumes, preening, and others stretched and flapped their cape-like wings.

Our boots crunched along the dry soil until, just beyond the eucalyptus grove, we joined a crowd of about thirty folks who were listening to a presentation by two park naturalists. Laurel immediately met a jovial yellow Lab, and she and Jesse broke away from the group to play with the dog. I stayed to listen to the presentation. The naturalists told us that the vultures had been back for about a week, that the birds roosted in the eucalyptus trees at night, and in the morning flew across the clearing to the nearby cliffs to warm up before taking off to forage for the day. The reddish-tan cliffs rose at lumpy right angles from the clearing floor, and although they were steep, their walls were not shear. Rounded rocks and boulders made the edges along the cliff face, and spiky agave plants as well as brave clusters of prickly pear, cholla, and saguaro cacti clung to crevices in the rocks.

A few vultures had already moved from the eucalyptus grove to the cliffs; some sat with their wings spread wide and others hunched on the cliff edges, perhaps waiting for the sun. Some perched singly and others in pairs or small groups, and two vultures on one of the highest peaks seemed to politely vie for the pinnacle, jostling each other slightly every few minutes. Occasionally a bird would amble along a rock, wings half open, and then settle again in a sunny spot. As I watched through my binoculars, dark spots along the sides of the cliffs morphed into vultures as more and more of the birds began moving and stretching. I longed to join them, to crouch unnoticed among the agave and cacti, waiting for the sun to warm my joints before spending a day on the wing. Over the next hour or so, one by one the vultures left the roost trees and sailed to the cliffs, and the birds already on the cliffs began stepping off into the air, beating their wings a few times before catching the thermals that lifted them high into the Sonoran sky.

As the crowd increased and the park naturalists began their presentation again for the newcomers, we decided to hike closer to the cliffs to see whether we could get another view of the vultures. *Hiking* is kind of inaccurate; we'd walk a few feet and then we'd stop so Laurel could play in the dirt. Walk a few more feet, then stop so she could pick up a rock. We began to regret not traveling with a stroller. The trail we walked circled behind the vulture cliffs, along shallow Queen Creek. In addition to stopping for Laurel to investigate interesting sticks and lizards, Jesse and I paused frequently to look at the park's non-vultures: lesser goldfinches, Gila woodpeckers, a colorful vermilion flycatcher, abundant verdins, a shy hermit thrush, and a spotted towhee singing from the underbrush.

We crossed the suspension bridge over the creek and began

to climb the High Trail, which ascended the side of a cliff and then turned back to run parallel to the cliffs where the vultures roosted. Not long after crossing the bridge we heard the musical song of a canyon wren; a silky black phainopepla sang from a willow along the creek, its red eyes obvious through my binoculars. While common in this part of Arizona, these birds seemed exotic to us, and we stopped to watch and listen. Eventually, we followed the dusty, sun-filled path up the side of the cliff, and soon we were almost directly across from where the vultures were roosting, on the rocky ledges above the other side of the creek. It seemed that most of the birds were in the process of departing for the day, while a few others still perched with their wings spread.

It struck me that one of the vultures, claiming the highest point between two other birds, reminded me of the famous *Christ the Redeemer* statue that overlooks Rio de Janeiro in Brazil. The iconic statue's arms are open wide, loose sleeves of the robe drooping like flight feathers, head slightly bowed, gazing toward the ground far below, perhaps issuing a blessing. The statue's posture reminds viewers of the shape of a cross; the vulture on the cliff struck a similar pose, its back straight and robe-wings extended, its eyes fixed on all that lay in the valley. As I watched the vultures I thought (perhaps blasphemously) that Rio's *Christ the Redeemer* would make an excellent roost; the winds near that mountain would probably allow for an easy takeoff, and the statue's extended arms could mimic leafless branches or cliff edges. Later, a quick Internet search revealed a photograph of the statue with—sure enough—two large, dark birds soaring above it, their wings fixed in shallow dihedrals.

Jesse and Laurel hiked on, but I sat down on a bench to watch the birds on the opposite cliff and perhaps to receive a blessing of my own from the ministering vulture. I could have sworn that the bird was staring at me from across the chasm that lay between us. I stared back until something buzzed my head; an Anna's hummingbird lighted above me, on the very top of the saguaro next to the bench. He stared down at me, too, and made me wonder what other, unseen beings held me in their eyes at that moment. As I watched the birds watch me, two of the vultures from the cliff suddenly took to the air, soaring and circling high above the creek bed, then directly in front of my seat. I took a few pictures and silently wished them good luck, good health, and good foraging.

▼ Although she was excited when Keith Bildstein contacted her about collaborating on the *C. a. aura* migration project, Dr. Jennie Duberstein admitted that she "wasn't a vulture person beforehand." But working with the birds changed her perspective. "I was unprepared for how beautiful they were up close," she told me. "Their iridescent wings, the colors of their eyes, how the red of their heads changes color." Before, she would see them soaring and think, "Oh, it's just a vulture." Now she appreciates them in a new way.

Jennie is the education and outreach coordinator for the Sonoran Joint Venture (sjv), a binational partnership for bird and habitat conservation in the southwest United States and northwest Mexico. Other regional Joint Ventures—there are twenty-four of them across North America—include the Appalachian Mountains, Atlantic Coast, Prairie Pothole, Rio Grande, and more. Joint Ventures are partnerships that work to conserve habitat for the benefit of birds, other wildlife, and people. In the United States, Joint Venture funding comes through the US Fish and Wildlife Service (usfws), and many jv employees, like Jennie and the rest of the sjv staff, work for the usfws. Other jvs are operated with support from non-profit conservation partners or are standalone ngos. Jennie develops the sJv's website, brochures, and other educational materials, as well as organizes and oversees training—especially in Mexico—for biologists and teachers. Her main role, though, is as a conservation social scientist, understanding the link between social conditions and conservation behavior and then designing outreach and communications efforts to encourage human behavior change. Jennie holds a master's degree and a doctorate in natural resource management and sociology, and she's most interested in the social aspects of wildlife and natural resource issues. "You can count all the birds in the world," she told me, "but if you don't talk to people, it almost doesn't matter." In her capacity as education and outreach coordinator for the sJv, as well as her other work with the American Birding Association, Jennie does just that: she talks to people. Often, she talks to people in both English and Spanish, a vital skill for communicating in the Sonoran Desert region. Along with many other projects, she's conducting research to better understand how those working in conservation in the region communicate and collaborate with each other, helping to support ecotourism in Mexico, and she coleads several camps for young birders, including one in southeast Arizona.

When Keith asked her to help with Hawk Mountain's turkey vulture migration project, Jennie jumped at the chance. A former Hawk Mountain intern, she had worked with other raptor species but not turkey vultures. Keith's plan to trap and place satellite transmitters on *C. a. aura* birds would require local connections and cooperation; Jennie provided that by contacting landowners and ranchers, and by making blind calls to dairy farms in southern Arizona in the hopes that the owners would allow her and the Hawk Mountain team to bait and trap vultures on their properties or donate stillborn calves for the endeavor. Facilitating cooperation and promoting partnerships is an important part of the Sonoran Joint Venture's mission, and Jennie saw the project in part as "a neat way to make new partnerships," especially because turkey vultures often feed on or near livestock operations, again making use of human subsidies—provided there by domestic carcasses. Jennie found a local landowner interested in hosting the team on his family's property near Casa Grande, Arizona, southwest of Phoenix, and the biologists headed there with a simple-sounding goal: trap and place transmitters on six turkey vultures, as well as place wing tags on any black vultures they trapped. Team members arranged several stillborn dairy calves in a location where the landowner had been previously baiting the site; this time, however, monofilament noose traps were set near the carcasses. Keith and his colleagues hid in a nearby blind, waiting to spring into action the moment a vulture became ensnared.

On the first day, they trapped only one young black vulture; the second day, one turkey vulture. The third day proved more fruitful; the team snared and placed transmitters on three more turkey vultures as well as tagging two black vultures. Two additional turkey vultures were trapped and tagged on the fifth day, fulfilling the team's goal of six. Jennie explained that each vulture's satellite transmitter was affixed to a backpack that was custom-made for the individual bird. Once a bird was trapped and in hand, measurements were taken to ensure that the equipment fit perfectly. She described the transmitters and backpack as "handmade works of art" that the team carefully constructed using Teflon ribbon, glue, dental floss, and copper crimps. Once the transmitters were affixed to the backs of the vultures—resting just between the wings, in an area roughly equivalent to between a human's shoulder blades—the birds were released. "It was an honor to be in the field with these three guys," Jennie said, "to see these artists at work."

During the last day of trapping, a few passersby stopped to see what was going on, and, restrained turkey vulture in hand, Jennie gave them an impromptu program in Spanish. "It feels special," she said, "to help people appreciate a bird that's not normally appreciated. A vulture up close makes a big impact —it's a really spectacular bird."

The Arizona *C. a. aura* vultures' transmitters began sending data immediately, and biologists back at Hawk Mountain Sanctuary added the information to their vulture migration website. In October, about five months after being trapped, all six birds began heading south. Although five of the six generally followed the west coast of Mexico to the Central American isthmus, one bird, "Jennie" (named for Dr. Duberstein, of course), did something odd: she flew almost 200 miles into Mexico in October, but then suddenly turned around and flew back to Arizona after only a few days. "And plunked herself down right in the same roost," Keith told me. No one is sure why.

Although Jennie's movements were mysterious, the other birds—named "Linda," "Julie," "Edward Abbey," "T. K. Red River," and "Desert Rat"—migrated more or less as expected, spending the winter months from extreme southwest Mexico through Canal Zone, Panama. Four of those five birds returned to Arizona in mid-March; T. K. Red River, however, did not return. Like the others, he too followed Mexico's Pacific coast south, staying between the coast and a line of mountains. The transmitter stopped moving on October 11 in west-central Mexico, not far from Guadalajara, and has not moved since. While we can never know for certain what happened to poor T. K. Red River, the bird is presumed to have died. Although it is not impossible that the transmitter somehow fell off, it is more likely that the dangerous journey claimed this bird's life. In addition to the "usual" perils of migration, turkey vultures in Mexico may face another potential danger: being hunted for use in traditional medicine.

A 2013 study in the *Journal of Ethnopharmacology* explores the use of the "aqueous extracts" of the turkey vulture to fight certain types of cancer. The article states that the ancient Maya used turkey vulture extract "for the empirical treatment of rabies, wounds and syphilis"; today, it is used "in the Mexican traditional medicine for the empirical treatment of cancer, injuries, infections, and burns." Once the bird is hunted and killed, it's made into a soup and given to an afflicted person (an odd twist on chicken soup). Surprisingly, after extensive laboratory tests the authors of the study determined that turkey vulture extract does in fact "exert immunostimulatory and cytotoxic activities." In other words, it killed cancer cells in laboratory mice. More tests are under way to figure out exactly how it works.

Could T. K. Red River have ended up in someone's soup bowl, his satellite transmitter stripped off his body and left along a roadside? And, somehow, could his meat send a suffering woman's cancer into remission? The idea that our common, underappreciated, overlooked vultures could help us cure cancer seems far-fetched, but it appears to be supported by at least one scientific study. This makes me call other outlandish assumptions into question. Does smoking dried vulture brains *actually* provide clairvoyance? What other odd—by today's standards, at least—traditional treatments might work?

Black vultures have also been used in traditional medicine in other parts of the tropics. A 2012 study published in the *Journal of Ethnobiology and Ethnomedicine* examines the "Use of Black Vulture (*Coragyps atratus*) in Complementary and Alternative Therapies for Cancer in Colombia." Rather than examine the properties of black vulture extract in a laboratory, through interviews the article compiles the "methods of use and the reasons given by patients and caregivers for the use" of black vultures to fight cancer.

The most popular traditional method of use in Colombia is more surprising than cooking a bird's meat in soup; there, a black vulture is captured alive and taken to the home of the afflicted, where its throat is cut. The sick person then drinks the vulture's still-warm blood. Sometimes the blood is drunk "straight," and sometimes it's mixed with wine or juice. One interviewee reported that it costs about thirty-five dollars (US) to pay a person to catch, deliver, and kill a black vulture for this purpose. In order for this treatment to be effective, most interviewees reported that the process had to be repeated over nine consecutive days, requiring nine black vultures. Other methods of administering black vulture in Colombian traditional medicine include cooking the meat in soup, similar to the process used in Mexico; grilling the vulture, then grinding it up and adding the powder to food; or toasting the bones and making them into flour. One interviewee said that after a vulture's blood is extracted, "the vulture is washed in hot water to pluck it, the child is bathed with this water and then wrapped in white sheets so that he sweats, the sweating helps remove the illness."

The article links these practices to pre-Columbian cultures in which "blood possessed a strength so powerful that it could not be touched by anyone other than priests, who offered it to the gods in ritual sacrifices." Because the black vulture is regarded "as an especially hardy animal that can survive adverse conditions," and because it has "the capacity to ingest carrion without being affected," it follows that people could believe that the bird's blood or other organs contained powerful treatments for ailments. And, at least in the case of the turkey vulture in Mexico, they may not be wrong. The mention of pre-Columbian cultures reminded me of other ancient beliefs about vultures—that vultures were "ideal mothers" who self-mutilated to feed their young, that all vultures were female, and that a vulture goddess protected the pharaohs. Something so fascinated people about vultures in ancient Turkey that their likeness was carved in rock at Göbekli Tepe temple. And we are still fascinated by vultures today, millennia removed from the ancient Egyptians and Mayans—although often maligned, they are still revered at festivals from Ohio to Arizona, and some of us still believe that their physical bodies contain the secrets of clairvoyance, healing, and restoration.

▼ Gila Bend, Arizona, seems like a quiet town—at least, it was quiet in the early-morning hours of Monday, March 24, when Jesse, Laurel, and I made the hour or so drive from Phoenix. Hawk Mountain Sanctuary's David Barber sent the GPS locations for Jennie the turkey vulture's most recent whereabouts to my phone, and we were on a mission to find her. Even though locating one particular vulture in the desert seemed a bit like a needle in a haystack, we wanted to give it a try. At the very least, we could observe the habitat utilized by the abundant *C. a. aura* vultures of this region.

Laurel dozed in the backseat while Jesse stood along a barbed-wire fence, searching the distant mountains with his binoculars; according to Jennie's satellite transmitter, she'd spent the previous night roosting in those mountains. The landscape was dry but blooming, the flat earth brown and dusty although densely packed with shrubs and wildflowers. The red-tipped tentacles of ocotillos along the fence reached as high as Jesse's thighs, and mesquite flamed yellow just beyond. The mountains in the distance were brown, too, and, viewed through the binoculars, did not appear to be forested. Perhaps the vultures roosted on cliff edges or in small trees invisible to us at this distance. Next to Jesse was a locked gate

with an ominous sign: DANGER USAF GUNNERY RANGE DO
NOT ENTER. It repeated the warning in Spanish as well.

The land beyond the fence was the Barry M. Goldwater Air
Force Range, where pilots of F-15s, F-16s, A/OA-10S, F/A-18S,
and AV-8BS were trained in aerial gunnery, tactical maneuver-
ing, laser use, and more. Some areas of the range were open
to public use once a permit was secured; getting a permit required a would-be hiker to watch a video about safety and to
sign a release form. The release form was very thorough, asking users to initial that they understood that the range posed
many dangers, including "permanent, painful, disabling and
disfiguring injury or death due to high explosive detonations
from falling objects such as aircraft, aerial targets, live ammunition, missiles, bombs, etc." Other lines warned of venomous
reptiles, extreme temperatures, old mine shafts, unexploded
munitions, undocumented aliens, electromagnetic emissions,
"as well as other natural and/or man-made conditions which
are too numerous to recite herein."

Yes, the Barry M. Goldwater Air Force Range sounded like a
dangerous place to visit. Still, we considered it. We'd planned
for me to get a permit from the Gila Bend Air Force Auxil-
iary, and for Jesse to wait in the town of Gila Bend with Laurel; while I didn't particularly mind venomous reptiles and the
chance for permanent disfiguring injury, the range didn't seem
like a great place to take a baby. But I wanted to find Jennie
the vulture, and the GPS coordinates revealed that she'd been
roosting in those mountains—the Sand Tank Mountains—for
several weeks, not too far from the range's border with the Sonoran Desert Natural Monument.

Unfortunately, my hike in the desert wasn't meant to be;
Jennie's roost was in the middle of the "East Tactical Range,"
which was closed to public use due to active training in the area.
Could I have hopped the barbed-wire fence and made a run for

it? Perhaps, but Jennie's roost was several miles from the road. I imagined sprinting across that dusty, brown expanse, covered with sharp-looking plants, dodging rattlesnakes (the Sonoran Desert is home to eleven species), unexploded bombs, and the yawning mouths of abandoned mines. And I could imagine the headlines: "Military Police Arrest Mother for Trespassing on Active Gunnery Range: Searching for 'Jennie the Vulture,' Woman Claims." I would have to be satisfied searching for the bird after she left the roost for the day. Data from her satellite transmitter said that she foraged in many areas around the town of Gila Bend; we'd eat some breakfast and look for her there.

After cinnamon rolls and coffee (and after seeing two fighter jets scream by overhead), we headed for Gila Bend High School to look for the location where Keith Bildstein had spotted Jennie during a research trip two months earlier in January. It didn't take us long to locate a single turkey vulture roosting in a large tree (we think a eucalyptus, again) in a city park that bordered the school's athletic fields. This had to be the same tree where Keith had seen more than forty roosting vultures, including Jennie. We scrutinized the bird through our binoculars, and the bird seemed to be scrutinizing us, too. It cocked its head and peered down at our car, dark feathers iridescent in the fierce Arizona sun. To our disappointment, the bird didn't seem to be wearing a satellite backpack. But it afforded me good, up-close views of a member of the *aura* subspecies. The vulture's face seemed to have fewer warty protuberances than my West Virginia *septentrionalis* birds; the red of its head looked brighter, and the bird's overall appearance was sleeker, cleaner, and less ruffled and "hunchy" than the birds at home.

Satisfied with our long looks at the roosting vulture, Jesse and I turned Laurel loose to play in the park. It didn't take her long to find a beat-up black feather beneath the eucalyptus tree, and then another nearby. She held a feather in each hand and waved them in front of her face, smiling at the way they made the wind whistle. Both appeared to be molted turkey vulture feathers and provided more evidence that the tree often served as a roost. After carrying them around for a few minutes, Laurel dropped the feathers and investigated the sprinklers that kept the grass green before finally climbing onto a swing—a real, big-kid swing, not the kind with baby seats. Jesse and I took turns gently pushing her while she giggled. Our friend the vulture seemed to be keeping an eye on us. Beyond the fence, the school's grounds crew mowed the grass and raked the baseball diamond's infield. A Say's phoebe hawked insects along the fence line, and white-winged doves cooed *Too soon to tell! Too soon to tell!*

I wondered what the school administrators thought about a vulture roost so close by, and I thought about the potential outreach opportunities here; students could follow the movements of "their" vultures on Hawk Mountain's website, and they could also serve as roost monitors, perhaps scanning the tree during ball games and recesses and reporting any vultures wearing transmitters. They could even count the number of birds using the roost and, if trends became apparent, perhaps publish their observations. I envisioned a pen-pal (or more realistically, an e-mail-pal) program—perhaps even a bilingual pen-pal program—between kids in Gila Bend and kids in southern Mexico where the *C. a. aura* birds spend the winter months. These vultures could be vehicles for cultural exchange, and students in both countries could contribute to the growing body of scientific evidence about this little-studied subspecies.

I was lost in these thoughts when the roosting turkey vulture suddenly departed the tree and was immediately joined by a second vulture. We hadn't seen where this second bird had come from; could it be Jennie? We watched through our binoculars, but we didn't see anything resembling a satellite backpack. The vultures floated further away—and suddenly there were three more. The five birds kettled together for a minute or two, and then all moved off, out of sight. "Jennie!" I called after them.

"Did you see a transmitter?" Jesse asked.

"No," I said, and we both laughed. But even if one of these vultures *wasn't* Jennie, certainly they could've been birds from the same roost. Perhaps Jennie's mate, perhaps one of Jennie's offspring. We rushed to load Laurel into our rental car and took off after the vultures. We passed agricultural fields, stucco homes, and stray dogs. During our drive we spotted a few more single soaring vultures, although it was difficult to tell if any were wearing transmitters. Eventually, Laurel fell asleep again, and we headed north on Route 85 toward Phoenix, saying good-bye to Gila Bend and all the potential Jennies.

I gazed across the sun-drenched Sonoran streaming past the car window and thought about turkey vultures—not just *C. a. aura* birds, but all of them, out there, everywhere. I thought about folks perched on hawk-watch towers in Pennsylvania, Cape May, California, Mexico, and Costa Rica, and all the folks driving North America's interstate highways, and folks on the beaches in Ecuador, or walking a vineyard in Chile, or fishing the Elk River in West Virginia, or working in an office in downtown Miami, or tending cattle in Venezuela, or hiking Canada's boreal forest. Turkey vultures are a common denominator —they unite us, they remind us that our lives are not endless but perhaps our chemical bodies are, and that once we're here, we're a part of it all, this great big world and its natural cycles of birth and death, of rebirth and resurrection. Those brown-black wings, those iridescent sails, can carry us skyward finally, along with everything else that has ever lived, to infinity.

The smell of the first rains of spring hung in the air.
Wind rippled the new grass and caused the prairie
crocuses to tremble; the aspen branch beneath her
feet bobbed in the wind and she flapped her great
black wings, then folded them again. She hunched
her head between them as a few delicate raindrops
wet her back, her face, and the green tag she wore
over her shoulder. It and the white symbols it bore—
T2—seemed like part of her body now.

Rain dribbled onto the roof of the abandoned
farmhouse, into the open attic windows. She turned
her stone-colored eyes to the horizon. Perhaps
watching for something, perhaps waiting.
He'd be back.

Spokesbirds for the Spokesbirds

I sat cross-legged on the pea-gravel floor of the enclosure, as still as stone, half of a dead mouse resting in my outstretched palm. Lew the turkey vulture stood about three feet away and *wuffed* at me. He roused, shaking out his feathers, then stretched both wings back; each flight feather of the right wing was glossy, silken, and impeccably preened. The left wing, however, did not extend well, and several feathers in sheath jutted at odd angles, like porcupine quills. The injury—several fractures near the shoulder joint—had already healed by the time we'd admitted the bird to the ACCA for rehabilitation. We knew he would never fly again. The vulture kept his good eye fixed on me. Like the left wing, the bird's left eye was damaged and not functional.

I swallowed, just a subtle movement, and Lew *wuffed* again. A few weeks earlier we'd received a permit from the US Fish and Wildlife Service to keep this vulture for use in environmental education programs, and I was working to train him. Or perhaps *he* was training *me*. Our goal was for Lew to become an ambassador for turkey vultures everywhere—to allow folks to admire a vulture up close, to give them a chance to *know* a turkey vulture a little bit better. We wanted Lew to be a confident, comfortable bird, which might allow audiences to glimpse a turkey vulture's typical "personality," and not that of a stressed, panicky creature (which is, unfortunately, sometimes the case with wild, non-releasable birds used in programs). We were only using positive reinforcement and operant conditioning with Lew; it could take some time, but we were confident the result would be worth it.

Recently, bird-training experts have begun to recommend that vultures *not* wear anklets or jesses, the leather straps around the legs used to leash hawks, falcons, eagles, and owls. Because vultures excrete liquid droppings on their legs and feet, equipment can wear out or become encrusted, which in turn could harm the bird. Also, a vulture's legs are not as strong as a predatory raptor's, and a vulture jumping (also known as *bating*) while jessed could result in injury. In addition to the potential physical problems with jessing vultures, the International Association of Avian Trainers and Educators explains in a position statement that "there is a gradual movement toward giving birds more power over their environment. The scientific community has shown control is a primary reinforcer for animals. When a bird is empowered with control over its environment it will often perform with more reliable behavior." The position statement further states, "Trainers are now discovering that jesses are often associated with negative reinforcement and positive punishment," which could result in a bird that engages in "escape avoidance behavior, aggression, apathy, phobia or generalized fear of the environment."

I certainly didn't want to punish Lew or cause him to be fearful; I wanted us to be partners. I wanted us to trust each other. Still, I was a bit nervous without jesses. Although I'd given educational programs in the past with un-jessed macaws, cockatoos, and African gray parrots, I'd never worked with an un-jessed hawk, owl, falcon, or vulture. But bird-trainer extraordinaire Erin Katzner and I had worked out a plan for training Lew, and although I remained a bit apprehensive about a truly wild vulture's ability to trust me—and for me to trust him—in public without jesses or a leash, we were willing to give it a try.

Lew lowered his head and took a step toward me. I sat perfectly still. He took another step, and as he drew closer he lowered his whole body, almost slinking as he approached. When his toenails reached the edge of the blue mat—our target, the place he was supposed to learn to stand on to be fed—the vulture began to stretch his neck in my direction. I held my breath. The bone-white hook at the end of his beak was only a few inches from my fingertips. I smelled the musky warmth of his feathers. His good eye, a deeper brown color than the eyes of other vultures I've worked with, rolled in his red head, searching my eyes, my face. He inched his other foot onto the mat, stretched, and deftly nipped the piece of dead mouse from my fingertips. In a flurry, he retreated about three feet away and watched me as he swallowed the morsel. He opened and shut his beak a time or two and kept staring at me, and perhaps relaxed just a bit.

I exhaled. A wild vulture had approached me and eaten from my hand. This was day twelve of our training. The first day, I'd dropped food on the mat, then left the enclosure. After a few days of that, I stood just inside the door. Then I moved a few steps closer, and then I began sitting near the mat, moving a bit closer to it each day until today, when I rested my hand on the mat, food in hand. It took me sitting like a statue for almost twenty minutes, but it worked. Tomorrow, he would be more confident.

A turkey vulture without the ability to fly is tragic. The birds are built to soar, to master the wind. Should we have humanely euthanized this vulture, who now stood just a few feet away from me? That would have been a reasonable decision. Lew's enclosure is equipped with various pieces of furniture to accommodate his handicap. He could only reach his roosting box (complete with a floor heater for chilly winter nights) by climbing a ramp we'd built with "stairs," much like a ramp you'd find in a chicken coop. A series of gently sloping logs, branches, and large rocks allowed Lew to run along them without having to use his wings. From the enclosure's highest perch, he could look out across a field and see the woods beyond. Other vultures often swirled on thermals above the ACCA. Lew would cock his head and watch them.

Perhaps Lew's unfortunate fate could save other turkey vultures. Up close, he is an impressive bird: the bronzed-black contour feathers, interlaid like soft scales; the bone-white hook of his beak; the small, black-pupiled brown eye set in his blood-red face; the delicate black velvet on his wrinkled forehead; the deep, close-mouthed hiss. Even the warm, musty smell is surprising. And when the wings unfurl, you wonder, for a moment, how the bird's been hiding them, how he manages to neatly fold such great capes over his back. The quick turns and bobs of his head show how sensitive he is to his surroundings, and when he fixes his eye on yours, you realize you're in the presence of something trying to figure you out, of something that's thinking.

Perhaps I'm overreaching and anthropomorphizing. Perhaps not. Regardless, this broken bird had a very important job—to be a spokesbird for the spokesbirds, to give folks an up-close-and-personal introduction to the most widespread and numerous scavenging raptor on the planet.

I smiled and reached into my pocket for another piece of mouse.

▼ The best kind of déjà vu: I stood on the overlook at Cooper's Rock State Forest with my daughter beside me. Instead of in a car-seat carrier, however, now Laurel toddled around the rocky outcrop, determined to stay just beyond my reach. A few dozen vulture enthusiasts had gathered, cameras in hand, and listened as Jesse spoke about the importance of vultures to healthy ecosystems. Erin Katzner stood next to him, hugging a once-injured turkey vulture against her chest. A warm breeze swept Erin's blonde hair against her face, and perhaps feeling it too, the bird kicked her legs against Erin's embrace and attempted (unsuccessfully) to loose her wings.

This vulture still held three shotgun pellets embedded deep in her soft tissue; removing them would cause more harm than good, Jesse determined, so the pellets remained. But this bird's real challenge was mental; she was the vulture who'd begun to mutilate herself shortly after arriving at the ACCA. We'd worried that she'd irreparably damaged the broad muscles of her chest necessary for flight. After several months— and a variety of toys to keep her busy as well as relocating her to a large, private enclosure—she stopped the self-mutilation, and it seemed that "Esmeralda" (as Erin had named her) was ready for flight conditioning on a creance. A wild light seemed to return to her eyes. And then, muscles stretched and exercised, we decided it was time to return her to the sky. As a parting gift, the day before Erin had given Esmeralda the head of a road-killed white-tailed deer, which the bird tore into with gusto.

On the overlook, Jesse finished his presentation. Erin positioned herself at the back corner of the outcrop, and the crowd stilled. Cameras raised. I crouched on the rock and pulled Laurel onto my lap despite her protests. After a count of three, Erin tossed the vulture toward the clouds. The bird spun, twirled, and instead of soaring into the heavens, she landed, somewhat heavily, on the overlook's thick, wooden railing. The crowd gasped, cameras clicked. With her back to the crowd, she looked over her shoulder at us, and if a vulture could look bemused, she did.

From this angle, the folks on the outcrop had an excellent view of the most special thing about this vulture's release; between her shoulders sat a small rectangular object. The object —a transmitter, of course—was attached to a custom-fitted backpack that Esmeralda wore around her body. The transmitter, the same design that Todd Katzner used on golden eagles and California condors, would send signals to cellular towers and allow us to monitor the vulture's movements. To our knowledge, Esmeralda would be the first wild turkey vulture from West Virginia to wear a transmitter. Would she go to Disney World or the Jersey shore, like some of Hawk Mountain's Pennsylvania vultures? Or somewhere else? This gunshot, self-destructive bird could help us answer questions about turkey vulture migration—and she would become a spokesbird for her species in the process.

After a few moments on the railing, Esmeralda suddenly launched, and after a few strong wing beats, she soared, joining a few other vultures buoyed by warm mountain air. For

Esmeralda's fans on the ground, now the fun would begin. Supporters of the ACCA sent messages: *Where is she now? Is she still alive?* Data from the transmitter started rolling in immediately. The vulture stayed in the area of Cooper's Rock and Morgantown, West Virginia, until November, when she started heading almost due south. She crossed the rugged mountains on the West Virginia–Virginia border, and in early December she haunted the skies above Blacksburg, Virginia, perhaps cruising over Virginia Tech's campus, where I, too, once hunched into the winter wind. From there, Esmeralda crossed into North Carolina and headed for Winston-Salem. Did she spend a few nights roosting in the trees near Wake Forest University before heading farther south? She crossed into South Carolina and flew over the Carolina Sandhills National Wildlife Refuge, home to rare red-cockaded woodpeckers and longleaf pine trees. Finally, just beyond Augusta, Georgia, Esmeralda stopped. She remained there until March, when something—instinct, photoperiod, hormones, temperature—told her to head back home.

Shotgun pellets and all, the once down-and-out turkey vulture swept quickly above Columbia, Charlotte, Winston-Salem, Lynchburg, Staunton, and Harrisonburg before arriving back in Tucker County, West Virginia, where she'd originally been found injured. She remained there for the duration of the spring and summer. Perhaps—we hoped—raising babies of her own, new birds to add their dark shapes to the eastern sky.

▼ "There's a buzzard," the woman said, sighing, "by our dumpster. I can't find anybody to come take care of it. Been here for days."

Jesse, Laurel, and I parked along the curb across the street from Maverick's, a small bar in Morgantown's Sabraton neighborhood. I lugged myself heavily from the Jeep and waddled into the bar's parking lot. I was more than eight months pregnant, and every part of my body felt swollen. I peered into the dark corners behind the dumpster and into the overgrown weeds behind a nearby home. Jesse and Laurel prowled around the other side of the small lot. We could hear the sound of a televised Saturday-afternoon college football game floating through an open window, and traffic crawled on Route 7 below us. But no "buzzard." We drove around the nearby side streets, but the injured bird was nowhere to be found.

On the next day—a most beautiful day, a day of high, sunny skies and gentle September breezes—my second daughter was born. Propped in the hospital bed while our new baby slept in a bassinet, I made a list of potential names; Jesse sat in the rocking chair beside me with his phone and searched the Internet for their meanings. I'd already crossed out Willow, Lily, Jane, and Rose. We liked Ivy, Suzanna, and Hazel. But none seemed to fit. When my phone vibrated on the tray next to the bed, I assumed it would be congratulations from a friend or family member. Instead, the text from one of the ACCA's volunteers read, "We caught the vulture." They'd snagged the bird from the same area we'd checked the day before; it was a black vulture, emaciated, with a drooping wing.

Jesse kissed us and quietly snuck out of the hospital room; he headed to the veterinary clinic to exam our new admission, and I curled on my side to watch our sleeping baby. She wore an owl-print hat and a thin white shirt, and was swaddled tightly in a gauzy blanket. I must have fallen asleep while watching her because I awoke with a jolt when my phone vibrated again.

"I might euthanize this vulture," Jesse said. "Old shoulder injury, already healed. It's not going to fly."

I stared at our baby, who stirred slightly and sighed. I thought of the way the injured black vulture had begun its life,

tucked in a cave or an attic, warmed and fed by devoted parents. Helpless at first, squirming, then growing stronger and
stronger until finally taking flight, then perhaps raising chicks
of its own, before finally being bumped by a car: in pain, helpless again, and grounded. Suddenly I was crying. "Not today,"
I said. "Can you not do it today?"

Jesse paused. "OK, you're right. I'll treat him and be back
in a few minutes."

We hung up, and I wiped away my tears. Hormones, I
thought, and took a deep breath. I began thinking about the
black vulture again, *Coragyps atratus*, scared but safe, rehydrated, medicated, and fed. *Coragyps*. I whispered the name,
turned it over in my head.

I pulled out our list of baby names and added one: Cora.

▼ Nearly every seat in the classroom was full. Late-afternoon
sun beamed through the windows along the wall as I paced
back and forth on a small stage, gesticulating as I've been
known to do when speaking in public. Behind me, a screen
displayed natural-history facts and photographs of vultures,
and as I clicked through my slides, I grew more and more
nervous. I had given presentations with Lew from inside his
enclosure at the ACCA, but this would be his first off-site program, at a nearby state park. The audience—mostly older folks
with a few kids mixed in—smiled and laughed easily, patiently
waiting for the star of the show to make his appearance.

And then it was time. I took a deep breath. "So, the rest of
this presentation will probably be different from the kinds of
presentations you're used to. Lew the vulture won't be tethered or attached to a leash." The audience murmured and nodded. "He will have some control over his environment. We've
conditioned certain behaviors, but if he doesn't want to come
out, he doesn't have to. But I think he will."

Lew's travel carrier sat at one end of a collapsible table, and his blue mat sat near the other end, closer to me. I swung open the carrier door and moved away to the other end of the table, just beyond the mat. Lew stood on the green turf inside the carrier and looked at me, *wuffing* softly. I reached into the food bag attached to the waistband of my pants and placed a small piece of mouse onto the mat. Lew stepped one foot out of the carrier, noticed the audience, and rapidly stepped back inside. I placed a second piece of mouse and began talking again to the audience, continuing my presentation about vultures. I watched Lew out of the corner of my eye.

He peeked around the side of the carrier, then pulled his head back in. Then he peeked again, and back inside. Then he looked at the mouse. Slowly, cautiously, he stepped out of the carrier. He paused and stared at the audience, who gasped and stared back. Then he snapped up the bits of mouse from the mat. I reached out with my hand, and he leaned forward and took a piece of mouse from my fingers. My spirit soared. It was working! Lew turned to get a better look at the audience, and in a horrifying instant, stepped one foot off the mat onto the slippery table, lost traction, and fell off the table, onto the stage.

He landed on his feet and stood there, perhaps not sure what to do next. My heart pounded, but I tried to remain calm. "Well," I told the audience, "I'm just going to keep talking. We'll help get Lew back on the table and into his carrier when we're finished." I hoped I'd hidden my horror at this unexpected turn of events. As I kept talking—enumerating the many fascinating adaptions of vultures—Lew took a stroll across the stage, pausing every few steps to turn his good eye to the audience. Near the end of the stage was an old trunk; Lew stopped in front of it and hunkered a bit. "Buddy, you're not going to able to make that jump," I said. But jump he did

—and he made it. The audience laughed. Lew got his footing on the trunk's lid, then surveyed the audience calmly, roused, loosing a small cloud of feather dust and down, and began to preen. Once satisfied, he yawned, revealing his wide gape. The audience, all smiles, began snapping pictures of handsome Lew on the trunk.

Unstressed and unperturbed, Lew perched there for the remaining half hour of the program, alternately watching, yawning, preening, and rousing. At the end of the presentation, members of the audience filtered past him, pausing to smile and take more pictures. I beamed. Here was an ambassador, and I couldn't have been prouder. (Well, I wished he hadn't slipped off the table, but that was my fault—next time, I'd bring a yoga mat to roll out over slick surfaces for him.) I was pleased that folks saw a calm, if cautious, bird strutting around the stage on his own terms. Instead of vomiting in fear or trying to bite me, Lew delicately snipped a piece of mouse from my fingers, hopped up on a reasonable perch, and relaxed.

After the program, our host, park ranger Caroline Blizzard, commented that Lew "won over all the people there." I remembered what Dr. Bob Sheehy had told me in Virginia: *People just don't know vultures. If they knew them, they'd love them.* Lew and I had a mission: to spread the word, to allow more folks to get to know vultures, to raise awareness and appreciation for this humble, overlooked, often misunderstood, perfect creature.

They stood side by side on the peaked roof, preening, sated, sunshine warming their backs. She could feel the eggs swelling within her, the heaviness of shells and embryos. Her children. Like the spring before, and the spring before that, and the spring before that, they would enter the world in the Saskatchewan farmhouse, warm on the dusty floor, warm beneath her feathers. She knew the seasons in her bones. She felt the length of days, the sun's movements, the changes in the winds. Knew the smells of mud, gasoline, fish, rot. Knew palms, aspens, oceans, deserts. All were reborn in her, all connected. She held the whole world in her eyes.

What You Can Do

Although populations of North America's turkey and black vultures are stable or increasing, worldwide, vultures are in trouble. Studying a common species may lack the urgency of working to save an endangered species, but it is still vitally important. As Keith Bildstein explained to me, "Understanding how a species works while it is still common provides us with important ammunition for protecting the species. It's important scientific evidence that allows us to explain to people why vultures elsewhere are not doing quite as well." Because of the vital role they play in healthy ecosystems, conserving both stable and declining species of vultures is necessary. A few suggestions for protecting—and maintaining—populations of vultures follow.

SWITCH TO NON-LEAD AMMUNITION. The leftovers from human hunter-killed game can be a huge benefit to avian scavengers; indeed, cleaning up after the kill of a large predator is what vultures have evolved to do. If lead bullet fragments remain in the offal, however, the feast can be deadly. Switching from lead ammunition to copper or copper-alloy ammunition will benefit all birds that scavenge—California condors, bald and golden eagles, turkey vultures, black vultures, common ravens, American crows, red-tailed hawks, red-shouldered hawks, and others. Human health, too, could be affected by meat contaminated with lead. Letters in support of stronger regulations against lead ammunition can be directed to your state and federal elected officials as well as the Environmental Protection Agency and state wildlife resources divisions. The Institute for Wildlife Studies provides a wealth of resources for finding and using non-lead ammunition on its website: http://www.huntingwithnonlead.org.

DO NOT PURCHASE PRODUCTS MADE OF IVORY. When African elephants are killed for their tusks, other members of the ecosystem suffer, including vultures, which are often poisoned so their flight does not alert authorities to the locations of poached carcasses. Reducing the demand for ivory will result in its value decreasing. In early 2014, the United States made the commercial importation of African elephant ivory illegal, but other countries, especially in Asia, still participate in its trade. There is a direct link between ivory and vulture persecution in Africa.

SUPPORT SENSIBLE REGULATION OF THE VETERINARY USE OF DICLOFENAC. The non-steroidal anti-inflammatory drug responsible for Southeast Asia's vulture crisis is still available in many parts of the world, including, as of late 2015, the European Union. Continued or increased use of diclofenac to treat livestock could affect vulture populations (and perhaps populations of other species of scavenging birds) in Europe, Africa, and other parts of Asia. Vulture conservationists fear that the continued use of this drug could run counter to important conservation work under way in parts of Europe.

SUPPORT NONLETHAL ALTERNATIVES TO DISPERSING VULTURE ROOSTS. Shooting vultures and hanging vulture carcasses—while perhaps effective in temporarily dispersing roosting vultures—is barbaric and sends the wrong message, especially to children, about how to live with and among native wildlife. Remind your neighbors that vulture roosts are temporary, swelling in the winter but petering out on their own by early spring. If a roost absolutely must be dispersed, suggest that officials try visual and auditory disruptions instead of lethal ones. It may be possible to lure vultures away from a roost by providing food (road-killed deer or stillborn livestock) near an alternative site that provides somewhere to perch, good wind, and warmth, such as a grove of evergreen trees.

TRAVEL TO SEE WINTER VULTURE ROOSTS, AND TELL PEOPLE YOU'VE COME TO SEE THEIR VULTURES. While some people may find a group of dozens (or hundreds) of vultures terrifying, most would agree that a vulture roost is an impressive sight. Many easily accessible eastern cities may harbor roosting vultures in the winter months, including Leesburg, Staunton, Radford, Front Royal, Dutch Gap, Fredericksburg, Lynchburg, Vinton, and Charlottesville, all in Virginia. Other winter vulture roosts may be found in Maryland, North and South Carolina, Tennessee, Georgia, and Florida. Birding and nature groups will likely know the specific locations where the vultures roost; the birds typically arrive before sunset and leave sometime after sunrise, depending on the weather. When you're not out looking for vultures, you no doubt will eat in local restaurants, visit local museums and other attractions, and shop. Even vultures can be good for business! The Loudoun Wildlife Conservancy in Leesburg, Virginia (http://www.loudounwildlife.org) can provide resources for viewing vultures near their town.

ATTEND A VULTURE FESTIVAL. In addition to supporting local economies, strong attendance at vulture festivals illustrates that the birds have a lot of fans despite their negative reputation and "scary" appearance. Check local information about specific dates and locations for the following vulture festivals: Return of the Buzzards, Hinckley, Ohio (March); Welcome Back, Buzzards (March) and Bye-Bye, Buzzards (September), Superior, Arizona; East Coast Vulture Festival, New Jersey (March); Coralville Lake Turkey Vulture Festival, Iowa (June); Vulture Fest, Makanda, Illinois (October); and Kern Valley Autumn Nature and Vulture Festival, Weldon, California (September). The Mullet Festival in Goodland, Florida, holds an annual "Buzzard Lope Queen" dance competition in late January. In addition, many zoos and nature centers around the world hold International Vulture Awareness Day celebrations on the first Saturday in September.

CHALLENGE NEGATIVE PUBLIC OPINION AND MISCONCEPTIONS ABOUT VULTURES. This may be the most difficult task of all. I often encounter unpleasant resistance when I insist that turkey vultures *do not kill* their food; even some self-proclaimed bird experts believe that they kill—and carry off—their prey. I usually challenge these folks, nicely, to document this behavior, write it up, and submit it to the *Journal of Raptor Research* or another scholarly publication because it would be groundbreaking. Defending black vultures can be even more difficult because of their reputation as killers of livestock. While this accusation may be true, there are ways to counter this behavior besides killing the vultures, such as securing newborn, heavily pregnant, or vulnerable livestock.

SUPPORT THE WORK OF HAWK MOUNTAIN SANCTUARY. Hawk Mountain is on the cutting edge of turkey vulture migration research. Your support will help fund these efforts.

Hawk Mountain Sanctuary
1700 Hawk Mountain Road
Kempton, PA 19529
(610) 756-6961
www.hawkmountain.org

SUPPORT THE WORK OF THE AVIAN CONSERVATION CENTER OF APPALACHIA AND OTHER CONSERVATION-MINDED ORGANIZATIONS. Supporting the ACCA and other organizations will help conserve vultures (and other birds) through rehabilitation, education, and research efforts. The following list is not exhaustive; many organizations, both in the United States and abroad, care about vulture conservation.

Avian Conservation Center of Appalachia
(turkey and black vultures)
286 Fairchance Road
Morgantown, WV 26508
www.accawv.org

International Association of Avian Trainers and Educators
(supports conservation of vultures and other birds
through their grants program)
www.iaate.org

The Peregrine Fund and World Center for Birds of Prey
(California condor, Andean condor,
Asian vultures, African vultures)
5668 West Flying Hawk Lane
Boise, ID 83709
www.peregrinefund.org

Ventana Wildlife Society
(California condors)
19045 Portola Drive, Suite F-1
Salinas, CA 93908
www.ventanaws.org

Vulture Conservation Foundation
(Europe; bearded, cinereous,
griffon, and Egyptian vultures)
Wuhrstrasse 12
CH-8003 Zürich
Switzerland
www.4vultures.org

Vulture Conservation Programme (VulPro)
(Southern Africa; Cape vultures
and other species)
www.vulpro.com

Vulture Programme
(Asian vultures)
Royal Society for the Protection of Birds
The Lodge, Sandy, Bedfordshire, SG19 2DL, UK
www.vulturerescue.org
www.save-vultures.org

NOTICE VULTURES. Throughout the United States and most Central and South American countries, turkey vultures can be viewed easily during several months of the year. Once you start looking for them, you will see them everywhere—floating high over an interstate, standing in a hayfield with wings spread, hunching together at dusk in a ragged pine tree.

ACKNOWLEDGMENTS

This book would not exist without the generosity and kindness of others. Like a mountain updraft or a warm thermal, Hawk Mountain's Keith Bildstein guided me along as I completed this book. He patiently talked me through his turkey vulture migration research, and he shared his enthusiasm for these remarkable birds. He also read and edited drafts of these chapters, gently correcting my mistakes and offering helpful suggestions. I encourage all readers to visit Pennsylvania's Hawk Mountain Sanctuary, especially during late September, to witness the raptor spectacle overhead. Thank you, Keith.

Thank you to Todd Katzner and Erin Estell Katzner for contributing much to this book. I am grateful for their expertise and their passion for vulture conservation, but most of all I am grateful for their friendship.

Thanks to David Scofield at the Meadowcroft Rockshelter and Doug Knox in Claysville, Pennsylvania, for sharing their vultures with biologists and students. Thank you to Jennie Duberstein for speaking with me about her work as well as about her experiences trapping and tagging vultures in Arizona. Thank you to Bob Sheehy for talking with me about the vulture situation in Radford, Virginia, and for advocating for them there. Thank you to Ellessa Clay High for telling me about Grandfather Buzzard and the Cherokee creation story. Thank you to Julie Mallon for sharing her experiences conducting research on vultures, and to Macy Sheehan, future avian veterinarian, for dedicating many hours to restoring injured vultures to health.

Thank you to the volunteers at the Avian Conservation Center of Appalachia for donating blood, sweat, and tears to help conserve wild birds. Thanks, too, to the veterinarians and veterinary technicians at Cheat Lake Animal Hospital, especially owners Jean Meade and Al Munson, for unwavering support. Grandma Jean and Grandpa "Owl" are mentors and friends, and we love them both.

Thank you to fellow vulture-phile and writer David Gessner for inspiration, guidance, and friendship. Thanks to Matt Haas, Kevin Oderman, and Manisha Sharma for reading sections of this book and making them

ACKNOWLEDGMENTS

better. Thanks to the Hot Shots and to Natalie Seabolt Dobson for reading very early versions of essays that would eventually become parts of this book. Thank you to Jeff Mann and John Ross for defending vultures in Pulaski, Virginia.

Thanks to my agent Russ Galen for his sage advice and support, and for sharing my fascination with vultures. Thank you to Stephen Hull, my editor at the University Press of New England, for working with me on this project, along with Amanda Dupuis, Anne Rogers, and the staff at UPNE.

Thank you to the literary journals *River Teeth*, *Terrain*, the *minnesota review*, and *Pine Mountain Sand and Gravel*, and to the Vulture Chronicles, the website of Hawk Mountain Sanctuary's vulture research, where some of these chapters appeared in different forms.

Thank you to my family: Joe and Emily Sallitt, Joey Sallitt, Dennis and Linda Fallon, Dennis Fallon and Bandy Killion, and Liz Fallon; to Mr. Bones, Liza Jane, and Sally Ann; and to Laurel and Cora for expanding my capacity for love. Thank you most of all to Jesse.

Finally, thank you to the vultures, past and present, that I've had the pleasure to work with—both the non-releasable vultures I've known intimately (especially Lew, Maverick, Boris, and Vader), and the wild vultures in rehabilitation and in the field. May your roosts be warm, your thermals strong, and your carrion only slightly spoiled.

BIBLIOGRAPHY

INTRODUCTION

Banks, Richard C., R. Terry Chesser, Carla Cicero, Jon L. Dunn, Andrew W. Kratter, Irby J. Lovette, Pamela C. Rasmussen, J. V. Remsen Jr., James D. Rising, and Douglas F. Stotz. "Forty-Eighth Supplement to the American Ornithologists' Union *Checklist of North American Birds.*" *Auk* 124, no. 3 (July 2007): 1109–1115.

Bildstein, Keith L. *Migrating Raptors of the World: Their Ecology and Conservation.* Ithaca, NY: Cornell University Press, 2006.

Callaway, Ewen. "Microbes Help Vultures Eat Rotting Meat." *Nature News,* November 26, 2014. http://nature.com.

Chesser, R. Terry, Richard C. Banks, F. Keith Barker, Carla Cicero, Jon L. Dunn, Andrew W. Kratter, Irby J. Lovette, Pamela C. Rasmussen, J. V. Remsen Jr., James D. Rising, Douglas F. Stotz, and Kevin Winker. "Fifty-First Supplement to the to the American Ornithologists' Union *Checklist of North American Birds.*" *Auk* 127, no. 3 (July 2010): 726–744.

"Convergent Evolution." *ScienceDaily.* Accessed April 20, 2016. https://www.sciencedaily.com/terms/convergent_evolution.htm.

"IUCN Red List." *Birdlife International.* Accessed September 10, 2015. http://birdlife.org.

1 . VULTURE CULTURE

Batuman, Elif. "The Sanctuary." *New Yorker,* December 19 and 26, 2011.

Carter, Howard. *The Tomb of Tut-Ankh-Amen.* New York: Cooper Square, 1963.

Conrad, Nicholas J., Maria Malina, and Susanne C. Münzel. "New Flutes Document the Earliest Musical Tradition in Southwestern Germany." *Nature* 460 (August 6, 2009): 737–740.

"Hinckley Hunt." Ohio History Central. Accessed February 20, 2012. http://www.ohiohistorycentral.org/w/Hinckley_Hunt.

Hotz, Robert Lee. "Magic Flute: Primal Find Sings of Music's Mystery." *Wall Street Journal,* July 3, 2009.

Mann, Charles T. "The Birth of Religion." *National Geographic*, June 2011.

Mooney, James. *Myths of the Cherokee*. New York: Dover, 1995.

Owen, James. "Bone Flute Is Oldest Instrument, Study Says." *National Geographic News*, June 24, 2009. http://news.nationalgeographic .com/.

te Velde, Herman. "The Goddess Mut and the Vulture." In *Servant of Mut: Studies in Honor of Richard A. Fazzini*, edited by Sue H. D'Auria, 242–245. The Netherlands: Koninklijke Brill NV, 2007.

———. "Mut and Other Ancient Egyptian Goddesses." In *Ancient Egypt, the Aegean, and the Near East: Studies in Honour of Martha Rhoads Bell*, vol. 1, edited by Jacke Phillips, 455–462. San Antonio, TX: Van Siclen Books, 1998.

Wakin, Daniel J. "Pondering Prehistoric Melodies." *New York Times*, June 28, 2009.

Wilford, John Noble. "Flutes Offer Clues to Stone Age Music." *New York Times*, June 25, 2009.

———. "Full-Figured Statuette, 35,000 Years Old, Provides New Clues to How Art Evolved." *New York Times*, May 14, 2009.

2. THE PRIVATE LIVES OF PUBLIC BIRDS

Bildstein, Keith L. *Migrating Raptors of the World: Their Ecology and Conservation*. Ithaca, NY: Cornell University Press, 2006.

———. "My Love for the TV." *Hawk Mountain News* 118 (Spring 2013): 12–15.

———. "The Turkey Vulture Migration Project." Hawk Mountain Sanctuary. Accessed November 10, 2014. http://www .vulturemovements.org.

Houston, C. Stuart, Phillip D. McLoughlin, James T. Mandel, Marc J. Bechard, Marten J. Stoffel, David R. Barber, and Keith L. Bildstein. "Breeding Home Ranges of Migratory Turkey Vultures Near Their Northern Limit." *Wilson Journal of Ornithology* 123, no. 3 (September 2011): 472–478.

Rollack, Chloe E., Karen Wiebe, and Marten J. Stoffel. "Turkey Vulture Breeding Behavior Studied with Trail Cameras." *Journal of Raptor Research* 47, no. 2 (June 2013): 153–160.

Adovasio, J. M. *The First Americans: In Pursuit of Archaeology's Greatest Mystery*. New York: Modern Library, 2003.

Adovasio, J. M., J. D. Gunn, J. Donahue, and R. Stuckenrath. "Excavations at Meadowcroft Rock Shelter, 1973–1974: A Progress Report." *Pennsylvania Archaeologist* 45, no. 3 (1975): 1–30.

Behmke, Shannon, Jesse Fallon, Adam E. Duerr, Andreas Lehner, John Buchweitz, and Todd Katzner. "Chronic Lead Exposure Is Epidemic in Obligate Scavenger Populations in Eastern North America" *Environment International* 79 (June 2015): 51–55.

Campbell, Kenneth E. "The World's Largest Flying Bird." *Terra: The Natural History Magazine of the West* 19, no. 2 (Fall 1980): 20–23.

Campbell, Kenneth E., Jr., and Eduardo P. Tonni. "Size and Locomotion in Teratorns (Aves: Teratornithidae)." *Auk* 100 (April 1983): 390–403.

Carpenter, James W., Oliver H. Pattee, Steven H. Fritts, Barnett A. Rattner, Stanley N. Wiemeyer, J. Andrew Royle, and Milton R. Smith. "Experimental Lead Poisoning in Turkey Vultures (*Cathartes aura*)." *Journal of Wildlife Diseases* 39, no. 1 (2003): 96–104.

Chatterjee, Sankar, R. Jack Templin, and Kenneth E. Campbell. "The Aerodynamics of *Argentavis*, the World's Largest Flying Bird from the Miocene of Argentina." *Proceedings of the National Academy of Sciences* 104, no. 30 (July 24, 2007): 12398–12403.

Doddridge, Joseph. *Notes on the Settlement and Indian Wars*. Wellsburgh, VA: Office of the Gazette, 1824.

"Hunt for Truth." National Rifle Association. Accessed March 1, 2015. http://www.huntfortruth.org.

"Hunting." West Virginia Division of Natural Resources. Accessed May 15, 2015. http://www.wvdnr.gov/Hunting/.

Hunt, W. Grainger, William Burnham, Chris N. Parish, Kurt K. Burnham, Brian Mutch, and J. Lindsay Oaks. "Bullet Fragments in Deer Remains: Implications for Lead Exposure in Avian Scavengers." *Wildlife Society Bulletin* 34, no. 1 (2006): 167–170.

"Lead." United States Environmental Protection Agency. Accessed November 10, 2013. http://www2.epa.gov/lead.

MonsterQuest. "Birdzilla." Produced by Whitewolf Entertainment. Distributed by A&E Television Networks. November 21, 2007. Television show.

"Pennsylvania White-Tailed Deer." Pennsylvania Game Commission. Accessed May 15, 2015. http://www.portal.state.pa.us/portal/server .pt/community/deer/11949.

Watson, Richard T., and Dominique Avery. "Hunters and Anglers at Risk of Lead Exposure in the United States." In *Ingestion of Lead from Spent Ammunition: Implications for Wildlife and Humans*, edited by R. T. Watson, M. Fuller, M. Pokras, and W. G. Hunt, 169–173. Boise, ID: Peregrine Fund, 2009.

4. WINGS AND PRAYERS

Abbey, Edward. *Desert Solitaire*. New York: Ballantine Books, 1968.

"California Condor Recovery." Arizona Game and Fish Department. Accessed January 24, 2015. https://azgfdportal.az.gov.

Church, Molly E., Roberto Gwiazda, Robert W. Risebrough, Kelly Sorenson, C. Page Chamberlain, Sean Farry, William Heinrich, Bruce A. Rideout, and Donald R. Smith. "Ammunition Is the Principal Source of Lead Accumulated by California Condors Re-Introduced to the Wild." *Environmental Science and Technology* 40, no. 19 (2006): 6143–6150.

Collins, Paul W., Noel F. R. Snyder, Steven D. Emslie. "Faunal Remains in California Condor Nest Caves." *Condor* 102 (2000): 222–227.

Emslie, Steven D. "Age and Diet of Fossil California Condors in Grand Canyon, Arizona." *Science* 237 (August 14, 1987): 768–770.

Fox-Dobbs, Kena, Thomas A. Stidham, Gabriel J. Bowen, and Steven D. Emslie. "Dietary Controls on Extinction versus Survival among Avian Megafauna in the Late Pleistocene." *Geology* 34, no. 8 (August 2006): 685–688.

Hunt, W. Grainger, Christopher N. Parish, Kathy Orr, and Roberto F. Aguilar. "Lead Poisoning and the Reintroduction of the California Condor in Northern Arizona." *Journal of Avian Medicine and Surgery* 23, no. 2 (2009): 145–150.

Rideout, Bruce A., Ilse Stalis, Rebecca Papendick, Allan Pessier, Birgit Puschner, Myra E. Finkelstein, Donald R. Smith, Matthew Johnson, Michael Mace, Richard Stroud, Joseph Brandt, Joe Burnett, Chris Parish, Jim Petterson, Carmel Witte, Cynthia Stringfield, Kathy Orr, Jeff Zuba, Mike Wallace, and Jesse Grantham. "Patterns of Mortality in Free-Ranging California Condors (*Gymnogyps californianus*)." *Journal of Wildlife Diseases* 48, no. 1 (2012): 95–112.

Snyder, Noel F. R., and Helen A. Snyder. *Introduction to the California Condor*. Berkeley: University of California Press, 2005.

Walters, Jeffrey R., Scott R. Derrickson, D. Michael Fry, Susan M. Haig, John M. Marzluff, and Joseph M. Wunderle Jr. "Status of the California Condor (*Gymnogyps californianus*) and Efforts to Achieve Its Recovery." *Auk* 127, no. 4 (2010): 969–1001.

5. REBIRTH

Jeffers, Robinson. "Hurt Hawks." *The Selected Poetry of Robinson Jeffers*, edited by Tim Hunt, 165–166. Palo Alto, CA: Stanford University Press, 2001.

6. HILL OF THE SACRED EAGLES

Abbey, Edward. *Desert Solitaire*. New York: Ballantine Books, 1968.

Bildstein, Keith. "Faunal Collapse." *Hawk Mountain News* 117 (Fall 2012): 8–11.

Cuthbert, R., R. E. Green, S. Ranade, S. Saravanan, D. J. Pain, V. Prakash, and A. A. Cunningham. "Rapid Population Declines of Egyptian Vulture (*Neophron percnopterus*) and Red-Headed Vulture (*Sarcogyps calvus*) in India." *Animal Conservation* 9 (2006): 349–354.

Denyer, Simon. "India Advances in Battle to Eradicate Polio." *Washington Post*, January 12, 2012.

"Eagles Enhance the Sanctity." *Hindu*, August 2, 2002. http://www.thehindu.com.

Green, Rhys E., Ian Newton, Susanne Shultz, Andrew A. Cunningham, Martin Gilbert, Deborah J. Pain, and Vibhu Prakash. "Diclofenac Poisoning as a Cause of Vulture Population Declines across the India Subcontinent." *Journal of Applied Ecology* 41 (2004): 793–800.

Human Planet. "Mountains—Life in Thin Air." BBC, 2011. Television show.

International Conservation Caucus Foundation. http://internationalconservation.org/hq/iccf. "IUCN Red List." Accessed April 20, 2016. http://iucnredlist.org.

Jeffers, Robinson. "Vulture." *Selected Poems*. New York: Vintage, 1965.

Markandya, Anil, Tim Taylor, Alberto Longo, M. N. Murty, S. Murty, and K. Dhavala. "Counting the Cost of Vulture Decline—An Appraisal of the Human Health and Other Benefits of Vultures in India." *Ecological Economics* 67 (2008): 194–204.

National Geographic Special. "Cave People of the Himalaya." National Geographic Television, February, 2012. Television show.

Oaks, J. Lindsay, Martin Gilbert, Munir Z. Virani, Richard T. Watson, Carol U. Meteyer, Bruce A. Rideout, H. L. Shivaprasad, Shakeel Ahmed, Muhammad Jamshed Iqbal Chaudhry, Muhammad Arshad, Shahid Mahmood, Ahmad Ali, and Aleem Ahmed Khan. "Diclofenac Residues as the Cause of Vulture Population Decline in Pakistan." *Nature* 427 (2004): 630–633.

Offices of the South Indian Railway Company. *Illustrated Guide to the South Indian Railway.* Higginbotham, 1926.

Oganda, Darcy, Phil Shaw, Rene L. Beyers, Ralph Buij, Campbell Murn, Jean Marc Thiollay, Colin M. Beale, Ricardo M. Holdo, Derek Pomeroy, Neil Baker, Sonja C. Kruger, Andre Botha, Munir Z. Virani, Ara Monadjem, and Anthony R. E. Sinclair (the Peregrine Fund). "Another Continental Vulture Crisis: Africa's Vultures Collapsing toward Extinction." *Conservation Letters* (2015): 1–9.

Pfeiffer, Morgan, Andre Botha, Jan Venter, and Colleen Downs. "Silent Slaughter of Africa's Vultures." *Wildlife Professional* 8, no. 1 (Spring 2014): 24–26.

Rattner, Barnett A., Maria A. Whitehead, Grace Gasper, Carol U. Meteyer, William A. Link, Mark A. Taggart, Andrew A. Meharg, Oliver H. Pattee, and Deborah J. Pain. "Apparent Tolerance of Turkey Vultures (*Cathartes aura*) to the Non-Steroidal Anti-Inflammatory Drug Diclofenac." *Environmental Toxicology and Chemistry* 27, no. 11 (2008): 2341–2345.

"Vulture Programme." Bombay Natural History Society. Accessed June 12, 2015. http://bnhs.org.

Welch, Lew. "Song of the Turkey Buzzard." *Ring of Bone: Collected Poems of Lew Welch.* San Francisco: City Lights, 2012.

7. ON THE MOVE

Avery, Michael L., John S. Humphrey, Trey S. Daughtery, Justin W. Fischer, Michael P. Milleson, Eric A. Tillman, William E. Bruce, W. David Walter. "Vulture Flight Behavior and Implications for Aircraft Safety" *Journal of Wildlife Management* 75, no. 7 (2011): 1581–1587.

Bildstein, Keith L. *Migrating Raptors of the World: Their Ecology and Conservation.* Ithaca, NY: Cornell University Press, 2006.

————. "New Tools." *Hawk Mountain News* 119 (Fall 2013): 12–15.

Curry, Andrew. "Will Fewer Wind Turbines Mean Fewer Bird Deaths?" *National Geographic*, April 28, 2014. http://news.nationalgeographic .com.

DeVault, Travis L., Bradley D. Reinhart, I. Lehr Brisbin Jr., and Olin E. Rhodes Jr. "Flight Behavior of Black and Turkey Vultures: Implications for Reducing Bird-Aircraft Collisions." *Journal of Wildlife Management* 69, no. 2 (2005): 601–608.

Geinzer, Jay. "AES Laurel Mountain Overview." West Virginia Department of Commerce. Last modified 2012. http://www.wvcommerce.org/.

Hedlin, Erik M., C. Stuart Houston, Philip D. McLoughlin, Marc J. Bechard, Marten J. Stoffel, David R. Barber, and Keith L. Bildstein. "Winter Ranges of Migratory Turkey Vulture in Venezuela." *Journal of Raptor Research* 47, no. 2 (2013): 145–152.

Houston, Stuart C., Philip D. McLoughlin, James T. Mandel, Marc J. Bechard, Marten J. Stoffel, David R. Barber, and Keith L. Bildstein. "Breeding Home Ranges of Migratory Turkey Vultures Near Their Northern Limit." *Wilson Journal of Ornithology* 123, no. 3 (2011): 472–478.

"Illegal Bird Hunting Drives Rare Species toward Extinction." *Daily Star Lebanon*. December 18, 2008.

"Illegal Hunting." BirdLife Malta. Last modified March 23, 2011. http:// www.birdlifemalta.org.

"Largest Wind Farm in the World Impacts Birds of Prey in California, USA." BirdLife International. Accessed October 21, 2015. http://www .birdlife.org.

Lemon, William C. "Foraging Behavior of a Guild of Neotropical Vultures." *Wilson Bulletin* 103, no. 4 (December 1991): 698–702.

Mooney, James. *Myths of the Cherokee*. New York: Dover, 1995.

"NedPower Mount Storm." Shell Wind Energy. Accessed July 6, 2015. http://www.shell.us/energy-and-innovation/shell-windenergy.html.

"One More Griffon Vulture Shot in Lebanon—The Middle East Continues to Be a Sink for Vultures and Other Soaring Birds." Vulture Conservation Foundation. Last modified September 13, 2015. http://www.4vultures.org.

Steelhammer, Rick. "Hundreds of Migrating Birds Die at Laurel Mountain Wind Farm." *Charleston (WV) Gazette-Mail*, October 29, 2011.

Zakrajsek, Edward J., and John A. Bissonette. "Ranking the Risk of Wildlife Species Hazardous to Military Aircraft." *Wildlife Society Bulletin* 33, no. 1 (2005): 258–264.

8. VIRGINIA IS FOR VULTURES

Avery, M. L., and J. L. Cummings (USDA). "Livestock Depredations by Black Vultures and Golden Eagles." *Sheep and Research Journal* 19 (2004): 58–63.

Avery, Michael L., John S. Humphrey, Eric A. Tillman, and Michael P. Milleson. "Responses of Black Vultures to Roost Dispersal in Radford, Virginia." In *Proceedings of Twenty-Second Vertebrate Pest Conference*, edited by R. M. Timm and J. M. O'Brien. University of California, Davis, 2006.

Barrel Point. Online forum. Accessed April 22, 2016. http://barrelpoint .com.

Fears, Darryl. "Vultures Are Wintering Locally, to the Disgust of Residents." *Washington Post*, January 15, 2011.

Ingram, Bruce. *The New River Guide.* Corvallis, OR: Ecopress, 2002.

Lowney, Martin S. "Damage by Black and Turkey Vultures in Virginia, 1990–1996." *Wildlife Society Bulletin* 27, no. 3 (Autumn 1999): 715–719.

Matzke-Fawcett, Amy. "Vulture Fight Splits Radford Community." *Roanoke (VA) Times*, September 21, 2010.

Nickens, T. Edward. "There Goes the Neighborhood." *Audubon* (November–December 2008): 77–82.

Rabenold, Patricia Parker. "Family Associations in Communally Roosting Black Vultures." *Auk* 103 (January 1986): 32–41.

Sweeney, Thomas M., and James D. Fraser. "Vulture Roost Dynamics and Monitoring Techniques in Southwest Virginia." *Wildlife Society Bulletin* 14, no. 1 (Spring 1986): 49–54.

Thompson, William L., Richard H. Yahner, and Gerald L. Storm. "Winter Use and Habitat Characteristics of Vulture Communal Roosts." *Journal of Wildlife Management* 54, no. 1 (January 1990): 77–83.

Tousignant, Marylou. "Virginia Vultures Turn Vicious, Dine on Pets, Terrorize Owners." *Washington Post*, February 19, 1994.

"Vultures Roosting in Radford Despite Efforts to Dispel Them." *Roanoke (VA) Times*, November 16, 2003.

Barrat, John. "Study Shows Turkey Vulture Is Doubly Blessed with Acute Vision and Sense of Smell." *Smithsonian Insider*. November 14, 2013. http://insider.si.edu/?s=study+shows+turkey+vulture+is+doubly+blessed.

The Battlefield Palette. The British Museum. Accessed September 18, 2015. http://britishmuseum.org.

Byman, David H. "Behaviors of Turkey and Black Vultures at a Winter Day Perch." *Northeastern Naturalist* 7, no. 3 (2000): 297–308.

Coco, Gregory A. *A Strange and Blighted Land—Gettysburg: The Aftermath of a Battle*. Gettysburg, PA: Thomas, 1995.

Coleman, John S., and James D. Fraser. "Food Habits of Black and Turkey Vultures in Pennsylvania and Maryland." *Journal of Wildlife Management* 51, no. 4 (1987): 733–739.

Colimore, Edward. "Vultures Prosper on Battlefield at Gettysburg—Then and Now." *Houston Chronicle*, February 27, 1985.

Crossland, David. "Police Train Vultures to Find Human Remains." *National*, January 8, 2010. http://www.thenational.ae/news/world/europe/police-train-vultures-to-find-human-remains.

Graczyk, Michael. "Texas Body Farms Study Vultures Feasting on Human Remains." *Huffington Post*, August 3, 2012. http://www.huffingtonpost.com.

Legge, James. "Vulture Eat the Remains of 52-Year-Old Woman Who Fell to Her Death in France." *Independent* (UK), May 6, 2013.

Leopold, Aldo. *A Sand County Almanac*. New York: Oxford University Press, 1949.

Outdoor Odyssey: Civil War Vultures. WPSU, NPR. September 4, 2007. http://live.psu.edu/vod.

Owre, Oscar T., and Page O. Northington. "Indication of the Sense of Smell in the Turkey Vulture, *Cathartes aura* (Linnaeus), from Feeding Tests." *American Midland Naturalist* 66, no. 1 (July 1961): 200–205.

Pouysségur, Patrick. *Stele of the Vultures*. The Louvre. Accessed September 18, 2015. http://www.louvre.fr.

Rhoads, Samuel N. "The Power of Scent in the Turkey Vulture." *American Naturalist* 17, no. 8 (August 1883): 829–833.

Roen, Keely T., and Richard H. Yahner. "Vulture Winter Roost Abandonment and Reestablishment." *Journal of Raptor Research* 38, no. 3 (2004): 288–289.

Smith, Harvey R., Richard M. DeGraaf, and Richard S. Miller.
  "Exhumation of Food by Turkey Vulture." *Journal of Raptor Research*
  36, no. 2 (2002): 144–145.
Yahner, Richard H., Gerald L. Storm, and Anthony L. Wright. "Winter
  Diets of Vultures in Southcentral Pennsylvania." *Wilson Bulletin* 98,
  no. 1 (1986): 157–160.

10. WELCOME BACK, BUZZARDS

"Arizona: Hassayampa River Preserve." The Nature Conservancy.
  Accessed March 10, 2013. http://www.nature.org.
"Barry M. Goldwater Range." Global Security. Accessed March 20, 2013.
  http://www.globalsecurity.org/military/facility/goldwater.htm.
Jacobo-Salcedo, Maria del Rosario, Maria del Carmen Juarez-Vazquez,
  Luis Angel Gonzalez-Espindola, Sandra Patricia Maciel-Torres,
  Alejandro Garcia-Carranca, and Angel Josabad Alonso-Castro.
  "Biological Effects of Aqueous Extract from Turkey Vulture *Cathartes
  aura (Cathartidae)* Meat." *Journal of Ethnopharmacology* 145 (2013):
  663–666.
Sanchez-Pedraza, Ricardo, Magda R. Gamba-Rincon, and Andres
  L. Gonzalez-Rangel. "Use of Black Vulture (*Coragyps atratus*) in
  Complementary and Alternative Therapies for Cancer in Colombia:
  A Qualitative Study." *Journal of Ethnobiology and Ethnomedicine* 8,
  no. 20 (2012). http://www/ethnobiomed.com/content/8/1/20.
"Visiting the Barry M. Goldwater Range." Luke Air Force Base. Accessed
  March 20, 2013. http://www.luke.af.mil/library/factsheets/.

EPILOGUE

"Position Statement: Tethering and the Use of Jesses." International
  Association of Avian Trainers and Educators. Last updated July
  2014. http://www.iaate.org.

Abbey, Edward, *Desert Solitaire*, 70-73, 77, 79, 83, 86, 117

Adovasio, James, 53

Africa, vultures in, 109-13. *See also specific types*

aircraft collisions, 138-39

American Bird Conservancy, 61

American Birding Association, 182

American Ornithologists Union (AOU), 11-12

Andean condor (*Vultur gryphus*), 11, 13, 130

Animal and Plant Health Inspection Service (APHIS), USDA, 9-10, 147-48, 151, 152, 154

Argentavis magnificens, 56-58

Arizona Game and Fish Department, 70, 73, 74

Association of Avian Veterinarians, 61

Audubon, John James, 164-65

Avian Conservation Center of Appalachia (ACCA), 4-5, 9, 10-11, 45, 60, 88-103, 193, 197, 199, 208

Bambenek, Greg, 57-58

Barber, David, 187

Barry M. Goldwater Air Force Range, AZ, 188-89

battlefields and vultures, 159-73; ancient battle scenes, 162-63;

deceased humans, vultures consuming, 163-64; Gettysburg, 159-62, 167-73; horses in battle, 160-62, 165, 166, 168, 170, 171; turkey vulture olfaction and, 164-67

bearded vulture (lammergeier, ossifrage; *Gypaetus barbatus*), 13, 116

Bechard, Marc, 177

Bildstein, Keith: *C. a. aura* migration project, 177, 181, 182, 189; on California condors, 83; on distinguishing subspecies, 131; Hawk Mountain Sanctuary and, 34, 35-37, 40, 43; on human bodies consumed by vultures, 164; on increasing turkey vulture population, 7-8; *Migrating Raptors of the World*, 35, 127, 128, 133, 134; on migration, 18-19, 126-33; on Old World vultures, 110-11, 112, 113; on roosting, 143, 144, 160, 172; on siting airports near dumps, 138-39; on studying common species, 205; on threats to vultures, 6

BirdLife International, 6, 138

BirdLife Malta, 134-35

"Birdzilla" episode, *MonsterQuest* (TV series), 57

"Black Knight," 142
black vultures (*Coragyps atratus*): abundance and rising population of, 6, 8, 205; Caracas airport sited near dump attracting, 139; dominance at carcass, 129–30; in Ecuador, 42, 43; human bodies consumed by, 164, 170; injured bird captured at birth of author's second daughter, 200–201; livestock predation claims, 151–53, 207; photos, *photos*; range expansion, 172; social nature and roosting behavior, 13, 89, 147, 148, 150, *photos*; taxonomic classification of, 11–12; in traditional medicine, 185–86; Western black vulture (extinct), 76; white feathers on wings, 46
Blacksburg, VA, 123, 124, 142, 144–45, 199
Blizzard, Caroline, 203
Bloomer, Lissa, 148
body farm, Texas State University, 164, 170
bounties on raptors, 34–35, 133–34
Boyce Thompson Arboretum State Park, AZ, 176, 177–81, 207, *photos*
breeding. *See* pairing, breeding, and reproduction
Bright Angel Trail, 84
Bucklin, Sophronia, 169
Buddhist "sky burials," 115–16
"Buttercup," 155, 156

buzzards, turkey vultures known as, 2
Bwabwata National Park, Namibia, 111

California condors (*Gymnogyps californianus*), 69–86; appearance of, 72; Big Sur and Baja California release sites, 74; critically endangered status, 7; decline and recovery of, 73–75; food finding and feeding, 73; human subsidies, reliance on, 79–82, 86; inappropriate items consumed by, 80, 83; lead toxicity in, 60, 81–83, 85–86; mortality, causes of, 80–81; as obligate scavengers, 75; Pleistocene extinction of magafauna, survival of, 75–77; Vermilion Cliffs release site, 70, 74; viewing and photographing, 71–72, 77–79, 83–86; wing tags and transmitters fixed to, 11, 74–75, 198
Cape vulture (*Gyps coprotheres*), 110, 209
carbofuran, 111
carcasses of vultures used as dispersal method, 148, 156–57, 206
Carson, Thomas Duncan, 169–70
Carter, Howard, 23–25
cartoon depictions of vultures, 27–28
Cathartes aura aura, 3, 126, 132, 177–78, 181–84, 187–91

Cathartes aura falklandica, 3, 126, 131, 132

Cathartes aura jota, 3, 126, 132–33

Cathartes aura meridionalis, 3, 126, 128–29, 131, 132, 139

Cathartes aura ruficollis, 3, 126, 129, 131

Cathartes aura septentrionalis, 3, 18–19, 125, 126, 131–32, 139, 142, 177

Cathartidae, 12

cemeteries, as vulture roosts, 172

Cherokee culture, vultures in, 2, 125–26

Christ the Redeemer, Rio de Janeiro, 180

climate change, 8, 172

Coco, Gregory, *A Strange and Blighted Land*, 168–71

Coggswell, William, 19

condors. *See* Andean condor; California condors

convergent evolution, 12

culture. *See* human culture, vultures in

deer hunting and lead ammunition, 59–62, 81–83, 85–86

deer population and vulture numbers, 7

"Desert Rat," 184

diclofenac, 108, 119–20, 206

disease spread and vulture activity, 8, 9, 109, 157

Doddridge, Joseph, 58

Duberstein, Jennie, 177, 181–84, 187–91

dumps, vultures attracted by, 138–39

Eagle Temple (Vedagiriswarar), India, 105–7, 113–15, 117–20

eagles, turkey vultures compared to, 2, 11–12, 41–42

ecosystem, role of carrion eaters in, 1, 2, 9, 10, 107–8, 113, 157, 205

Edge, Rosalie, 35

educational "spokesbirds." *See* spokesbirds

"Edward Abbey," 184

Egyptian culture, ancient, vultures in, 22–25, 163, 187

Egyptian vultures (*Neophron percnopterus*), 13, 105–8, 113–15, 120

Emory, Ambrose, 170–71

Emslie, Steve, 79

endangered status of Old World vultures, 6–7, 37, 107–13, 119–20, 205

enrichment, 97–98, 197

Environmental Protection Agency, 59, 61

"Esmerelda" (self-mutilator, later released), 96–98, 197–99, *photos*

euthanization, 9, 10, 92–93, 196, 200–201

Fallon, Cora (daughter of author), 199–200

Fallon, Jesse (husband of author): ACCA, founding of, 4; at bird release, 197, 198; on California condors trip, 70, 71–72, 77–78, 83–86; Hawk Mountain Sanctuary, working with, 40–41, 43–49; at Hinckley, OH, Buzzard Sunday, 20–21, 31; in India, 105; injured birds, working with, 10–11, 45–49, 90, 92–93, 98, 100, 101, 102, 199–201; at Meadowcroft Rockshelter, 58, 60, 63–64, 65–66; photo, *photos*; in Radford, VA, 145; on Sonoran Desert trip, 176–80, 187, 188, 189–90; veterinary training and specialization, 46

Fallon, Laurel (daughter of author), 21–23, 28, 94, 96, 99, 100, 162, 176–80, 187–91, 197, 198

fledglings and pre-fledgling chicks, 45–49, 68–69, 88–89, 90, 91, *photos*

flight behavior, 1–2, 36–37, 41–43, 144, *photos*

flute, prehistoric, from vulture wing bone, 29

food and feeding: California condors, 73, 79–82; eyesight, food finding by, 12; inappropriate items, 80, 83; infant birds, 51, 64; migration, birds not eating during, 129; photos, *photos*; rocks, use of, 13; smell, food finding by, 13, 73, 164–67; spokesbirds, 195–96, 202; strategies for finding food, 12–13, 15, 42, 43, 73; water, turkey vultures drinking, 101–2

food chain, role of carrion eaters in, 1, 2, 9, 10, 107–8, 113, 157, 205

funerary practices involving vultures, 115–17, 163

Gates, Gibson, 19

Gettysburg, battle of, 159–62, 167–73

Gibson, James F., 169

Gila Bend, AZ, 176, 187–91, *photos*

Göbekli Tepe carvings, 30–31, 187

Grand Canyon National Park, 69, 78–79, 83–84

Graves, Gary, 166

Greenlee, Hal, 161, 167

griffon vulture (*Gyps fulvus*), 22, 29, 116, 135–36, 163

Hanging Rock Raptor Observatory, WV, 123–26

Hassayampa River Preserve, AZ, 175–77

Hawk Mountain Sanctuary, PA, 7, 34–39, 42, 124–26, 132–34, 142, 177, 182, 184, 187, 190, 208

Hinckley, OH, Buzzard Sunday, 18–22, 25–26, 28, 31, *photos*

Hindu culture, vultures in, 28, 106, 107, 113–14

Homer, *Iliad*, 159

hooded vulture (*Neocrosyrtes monachus*), 36, 110

human culture, vultures in, 17–31; ancient Egyptians, 22–25, 163, 187; cartoon depictions, 27–28; flute, prehistoric, fashioned from wing bone of vulture, 29; funerary practices involving vultures, 115-17, 163; Göbekli Tepe carvings, 30-31, 187; Hinckley, OH, Buzzard Sunday in, 18-22, 25-26, 28, 31, 207, *photos*; Hindu culture, 28, 106, 107, 113-14; motherhood, vultures associated with, 21-23, 187; Native Americans, 2, 19, 57, 125-26; negative popular impressions and persecution, 6, 8-10, 17, 26-27, 143, 147-55, 157, 207; traditional medicine, 112-13, 185-87

"human subsidies," birds using, 7, 59-62, 79-82, 81-83, 85-86, 107-8, 110-11, 183, *photos*

hunting and lead ammunition, 59-62, 81-83, 85-86, 205

hunting migratory birds, 133-36

imping, 93-94

India, vultures in, 7, 107, 108, 113-15, 117-20. *See also specific types*

Indian vulture (*Gyps indicus*), 7, 107, 108

injured turkey vultures, treating, 88-103; ACCA specialization in, 3-5; author's first experience of, 5-6; back broken by vehicle collision, 91-94; bird's experience of, 47, 48; Claysville vulture with broken wing, 45-49, 88-89, 91; euthanization, 9, 10, 92-93, 196, 200-201; eyes, covering, 45; imping (grafting feathers), 93-94; for lead toxicity, 62, 98-99; nonreleasable animals, 11, 13-14, 100-103, 193, *photos*; releasing rehabilitated birds, 88-89, 99-100, *photos*; self-mutilation, 96-98, 197-98; soft-tissue injuries, adult with, 90-91; sunken eye and older injuries, bird with ("Lew"), 10-11, 13-14, 101-3, *photos*; tail guards, 93; trap, bird caught in, 94-96, 99-100; types of injuries, 4, 89-90; water exposure or lung infection, pre-fledgling with, 90

Institute for Wildlife Studies, 205

International Association of Avian Trainers and Education, 5, 208

International Conservation Caucus Foundation (ICCF), 111

International Union for the Conservation of Nature (IUCN), 107, 108, 109, 113

International Vulture Awareness Day, 99

"Irma," 139

ivory demand and vulture persecution in Africa, 111-12, 206

Jeffers, Robinson: "Hurt Hawks," 93; "Vulture," 116

"Jennie," 176-77, 184, 187-91

jesses, 194-95

"Julie," 184

The Jungle Book (Disney animated movie), 27-28

Katzner, Erin, 4, 5, 195, 197–98
Katzner, Todd, 4, 5, 39–41, 43–44,
  58, 60, 65, 74–75, 137, 144, 198
king vulture (*Sarcoramphus papa*),
  11, 13, 43, 130
Knox, Doug, 40, 88–89

La Brea tar pits, 56, 76
Lang, Andrew, 159
lappet-faced vulture (*Torgos
  tracheliotos*), 110
Lawrence, Jenny, 148
lead toxicity, 4, 7, 59–62, 64,
  81–83, 85–86, 98–99, 205
Lebanon, hunting migratory birds
  in, 135–36
Lee, Robert E., 168
Leesburg, VA, roosting in, 9, 142,
  143, 206, 207
leg banding, 39–40, 135
"Leo," 130, 139
Leopold, Aldo, *A Sand County
  Almanac*, 161, 171
Leslie, Frank, *Illustrated History of
  the Civil War*, 169
"Lew" (nonreleasable bird with
  old injuries), 10–11, 13–14,
  101–3, 193–94, 201–3, *photos*
life span of turkey vultures, 13
"Linda," 184
livestock and pet predation claims,
  8–9, 13, 151–54, 163, 207

Macy (ACCA volunteer), 88–89
Mallon, Julie, 41–45, 48, 62–63,
  64
Maltese Islands, hunting migratory birds in, 134–35

"Mark," 142
mates. *See* pairing, breeding, and
  reproduction
"Maverick," *photos*
Meadowcroft Rockshelter, 52–66;
  conducting research on turkey
  vultures at, 55–56, 58–59,
  62–66; dead body of chick,
  63–64; lead toxicity in birds
  and, 59–62, 64; as nesting cave
  for turkey vultures, 55–56, 58,
  64, *photos*; prehistoric use of,
  52–55, 56–57, 64–65; teratorns,
  ancestral memory of, 56–58
migration, 122–39; aircraft, birds
  harmed by, 138–39; *C. a. aura*
  migration project, 177–78,
  181–84, 187–91; defined, 127;
  evolution of, 127–28; flyways,
  123–24; Hanging Rock Raptor
  Observatory, watching migrations at, 122–26; reciprocal
  migration (displacement of
  local birds), 129–31; research
  on, 126, 130, 132–33, 137–39,
  177–78, 181–84, 187–91;
  shooting of migrating raptors,
  133–36; site fidelity, 38, 130;
  subspecies patterns, 126,
  128–33; vignettes, 87, 104,
  121, 140; wind turbines, birds
  harmed by, 136–38
Migratory Bird Treaty Act, 8, 134,
  151
Miller, Albert, 52–53, 58
Miller, Trish, 58, 64
motherhood, vultures associated
  with, 21–23, 187

National Rifle Association (NRA), 61, 62

Native Americans, 2, 19, 52–55, 56–57, 125–26

Nekhbet (Egyptian vulture goddess), 22–25

Oaks, Lindsay, 108

Old World vultures, 105–20. *See also specific types*; in Africa, 109–13; funerary practices, Parsi and Buddhist, 115–17, 163; global conservation concerns, 6–7, 37, 107–13, 119–20, 205; in India, 7, 107, 108, 113–15, 117–20

Oriental white-backed vulture (*Gyps bengalensis*), 107

pairing, breeding, and reproduction: age of first reproduction, 39; feeding infant birds, 51, 64; helper adults, 39; meeting up of mates, 15–16, 192; monogamous pairing, 38; research on, 38–39; slow reproduction and long life span, 13, 113; vignettes, 32, 51, 68–69, 192, 204

palm nut vulture, 13

Parsi funerary practices, 115

Pennsylvania Game Commission, 34, 59

Peregrine Fund, 73, 111, 208

poachers in Africa, vultures killed by, 111–12, 206

police use of vultures, 166–67

pregnancies, of author, 21–23, 28, 199–200

Project Gutpile, 61

"Puke," 149

Radford, VA, roosting in, 144–50, 156–57, 206

Radford Vulture/Roosting Festival, 154–56

Ramayana, vultures in, 28

reciprocal migration, 129–31

red-headed vulture (*Sarcogyps calvus*), 107, 108

reproduction. *See* pairing, breeding, and reproduction

research on turkey vultures, 33–49. *See also* Hawk Mountain Sanctuary; Meadowcroft Rockshelter; bird's experience of, 44, 63; breeding biology and behavior, 38–39; capture and examination of young birds, 33–34, 41, 44, *photos*; flight behavior, 36–37, 41–43; food finding strategies, 42, 43; importance of, 205; leg banding, 39–40, 135; migration, 126, 130, 132–33, 137–39, 177–78, 181–84, 187–91; olfaction, 165–67; roosting, 142–44, 149; transmitters, 37–38, 74–75, 126, 130, 132, 139, 142, 177, 183–84, 198, *photos*; wing tagging, 39–40, 44, 45, 55, 74, 89, 135–36, 183, *photos*

Rhoads, Samuel N., 165

roadkill, 7, 144, 149, 153, 206

roosting, 141–57; cemeteries, in or near, 172; damage caused by roosting birds, 147, 149–50;

dispersal of roosts, 9–10, 147–48, 156–57, 206; Gettysburg, PA, 160–61; in Gila Bend, AZ, 189–91, *photos*; human responses to, 9–10, 143, 147–55, 157; in Leesburg, VA, 9, 142, 143, 206, 207; photos of, *photos*; predation behavior claims, 151–53; purpose of, 143; in Radford, VA, 144–50, 156–57, 206; Radford Vulture/Roosting Festival, 154–56; release of rehabilitated birds near roost site, 89; research on, 142–44, 149; site selection, 144; as social behavior, 10, 13; as tourist attraction, 206–7; Virginia, as popular roosting site, 141–44; as winter/nonbreeding season behavior, 142–43

Rüppell's vulture (*Gyps rueppellii*), 110, 139

Sallitt, Joe (brother of author), 167–68

San Diego Wild Animal Park, 73

Sangu Theertham, India, 119

Scofield, David, 58

self-mutilation, 96–98, 197–98

sexing turkey vultures, 96

Sheehy, Bob, 149–50, 154–55, 156

"Sherlock," 166–67

shooting turkey vultures, 4, 8, 10, 34–35, 80, 96, 133–36, 153–54, 164

silver undersides of turkey vulture wings, 45–46, *photos*

Sinclair, Upton, 82

site fidelity, 38, 130, 160

"sky burials," 115–17, 163

slender-billed vulture (*Gyps tenuirostrisis*), 7, 107, 108

Snyder, Noel and Helen, *Introduction to the California Condor*, 73, 76–77

social nature of vultures, 10, 13, *photos*. See also roosting

Sonoran Desert, AZ, 175–91; Boyce Thompson Arboretum State Park, AZ, Welcome Back, Buzzards festival, 176, 177–81, *photos*; *C. a. aura* migration project, 177–78, 181–84, 187–91; Hassayampa River Preserve, 175–77

Sonoran Joint Venture (SJV), 177, 181–82, 183

specialized diets, 13

spokesbirds, 193–203; "Buttercup," 155, 156; feeding, 195–96, 202; "Lew," 10–11, 13–14, 101–3, 193–96, 201–3, *photos*; presentation of, 201–3; released rehabilitated bird with transmitter, 197–99; training, 194–96

Stele of the Vultures (ancient Sumer), 162–63

"T. K. Red River," 184, 185

tail guards, 93

te Velde, Herman, 22–23

Teratornithidae and *Teratornis merriami*, 56-58, 76

"Tesla," 142

thermoregulation, 178-79, *photos*

Therrien, Jean-François, 177

Thirudalukundram, Eagle Temple (Vedagiriswarar), India, 105-7, 113-15, 117-20

thunderbird, in Native American culture, 57

traditional medicine, vulture body parts used in, 112-13, 185-87

transmitters, 37-38, 74-75, 126, 130, 132, 139, 142, 177, 183-84, 198, *photos*

traps, vultures caught in, 9, 94-96

turkey vultures, 1-14. *See also* battlefields and vultures; human culture, vultures in; injured turkey vultures, treating; migration; research on turkey vultures; spokesbirds; abundance and rising population of, 6-8, 37, 205; beauty and overall appearance of, 2, 43, *photos*; disease spread and activity of, 8, 9, 109, 157; distribution and species, 2-3; flight of, 1-2, 36-37, 41-43, *photos*; food chain and ecosystem role of, 1, 2, 9, 10, 107-8, 113, 157, 205; intelligence of, 13, 91, 96; livestock and pet predation claims, 8-9, 13, 151-54, 163, 207; names for, 2; protecting and maintaining, 205-9;

sexing, 96; taxonomic classification, convergent evolution, and diversity of, 11-13; tropical origins of, 127-28; viewing, 209

Tutankhamen (pharaoh), 23-25

urohydrosis, 39-40

US Fish and Wildlife Service (USFWS), 73, 177, 181, 194

Vedagiriswarar (Eagle Temple), India, 105-7, 113-15, 117-20

vehicle collisions, 7, 9, 91-92, 98, 101

Ventana Wildlife Society, 73, 208

Vermilion Cliffs National Monument, 69-70, 74, 79, *photos*

vignettes: food and feeding, 15, 50, 158; meeting up of mates, 15-16, 192; migration north and arrival in spring, x, 15-16, 174, 192; migration south in autumn, 87, 104, 121, 140; nesting and fledglings, 32, 51, 68-69, 204

vomiting, as defensive response, 33-34, 48-49, 91, 92, 149, 150

VulPro, 209

Vulture Conservation Foundation, 136, 209

vulture festivals, 207; Boyce Thompson Arboretum State Park, AZ, 176, 177-81, 207, *photos*; Hinckley, OH, Buzzard Sunday in, 18-22, 25-26, 28, 31, 207, *photos*; Radford

Vulture/Roosting Festival, 154–56

Vulture Mountains Recreation Area, 176

Vulture Programme, Royal Society for the Protection of Birds, 209

vultures. *See* turkey vultures, *and other specific types*

water, turkey vultures drinking, 101–2

Welch, Lew, "Song of the Turkey Buzzard," 101, 116–17

West, John Howard, 169

Western black vulture (*Coragyps occidentalis*), 76

white-backed vulture (*Gyps africanus*), 20, 107, 110

white-headed vulture (*Trigonoceps occipitalis*), 110

white-rumped vulture, 7, 107, 108, 109, 110, 113

Wildlife Center of Virginia, 156

Wildlife Professional, 111

wind turbines, migrating birds harmed by, 136–38

wing tagging, 39–40, 44, 45, 55, 74, 89, 135–36, 183, *photos*

women, in wildlife biology and prehistory, 64–65

Wyandot culture, vultures in, 19

yellow-headed vulture, 11, 13, 43